Dearest Brother

Published in the UK in 2021 by Tricorner Press

Paperback   ISBN 978-1-8383315-0-4
.epub eBook   ISBN 978-1-8383315-1-1
.mobi eBook   ISBN 978-1-8383315-2-8

Cover design and typeset by SpiffingCovers

Dearest Brother

A MEMOIR OF SUICIDE
AND SIBLING RIVALRY

Andrew Bethell

ANDREW BETHELL

After a year teaching at a Canadian boarding school, Andrew spent the next seventeen in Inner London comprehensives, where he helped pioneer media studies as a curriculum subject, wrote and edited a series of play-scripts and media studies textbooks. In 1987 he set up Double Exposure, a television production company which went on to make a wide range of documentaries and educational series, many of which won awards and large audiences in the UK and US. In 1997 he won the BAFTA for best documentary series for The House, a six-part series that went behind the scenes at the Royal Opera House to much acclaim and controversy. He was the CEO and Creative Director of Teachers TV, a television channel for teachers and parents and in 2011 he went to San Francisco to set up Teaching Channel, which runs to this day. He lives in Hackney with his partner of forty years, has three children and four grandchildren. He paints portraits in his East London studio.

CONTENTS

Through many countries, over many seas I've come
in sadness, brother, to perform this parting rite,
to honour you in death with these, my final gifts,
and pay my vain addresses to your silent ash.
Since Fate has snatched your very self from me – alas,
poor brother, stolen from my sight unworthily –
accept, at least, these offerings my tears have washed,
these tokens of my grief, my taking leave, bequeathed
by ancient custom of our family. And take
this greeting, brother, and, for ever, fare you well.

Gaius Valerius Catullus
Translated by John Richmond

Dearest Brother,

I am on my way to Perth. Would you believe I am flying non-stop? Sixteen hours without refueling. You can do that now. There's a new plane and it's called the Dreamliner. Apparently they have made it lighter. They can only get to Perth though. It's closer, although it didn't feel closer when you were there in the early 70s. It felt like an outpost: on the other side of the world.

I've decided to use these sixteen hours to write to you: to explain myself. I am writing a book and it's about you. It's a selfish endeavour. I could pretend that I am doing it because I want others to remember you. That is part of the reason, and I'm thinking especially of your two sons (you would be so proud of them, Oliver is 42 and Alun is 39, and both have so many of your qualities as well as a whole lot more from their mother). I do want them to know their father, to have a picture of the boy and the man you were: because you were a star. You may not have thought so at the time, but let me tell you, writing this book, investigating you, reading your letters, meeting your friends has been an inspiration. Those friends are all in their late sixties now but they remember you. Vividly. So yes, I do want to spread the word. Make sure that all the people that

1

matter do not just remember the sadness and the loss, but can celebrate the person you were. But really it is for me. I want, no I need, to get you back. To put you back into the story of my life. And to be honest, it's about time.

I ought to warn you that the process of gathering the material that makes up this version of your story took many years. It started with my first trip to Perth in 2013. That is when I tracked down some of the key witnesses. Then, over the next few years the evidence and testimony kept building through emails and Skype calls (neither means of communication will mean a damn thing to you). Now it is 2019 and I am heading back on the Dreamliner to consolidate my findings: re-engage with my friends from that first trip and meet up with my more recent discoveries. I am juggling both the story and the discovery of the story. I will do my best not to confuse you.

I have a Kindle (don't ask!) and to save money I agreed to let them send me recommendations on the home page, and as I put it away to start writing this, the book that came up on the screen was Where Memories Lie. It is a nicely turned double meaning that suits my purposes. As you will find, in setting out to rebuild you and your history, I have had to rely on memories; mine and those of the people who knew you. I discovered that the memories I do have are so often based on a lie. Not deliberate falsehoods, but *misguided distortions. I fear the same may be true for what other people remember about you, but I tend to respect their narratives rather more than my own. That's probably a mistake. At the same time, this whole business has caused me to work out where the memories lie and why they have remained hidden for so long. It's a tortuous business. The worst part is that the memories I have the most trouble with are memories of you. I want to confess that up front, so you are under no illusions. What follows is dug up with difficulty, and reflects badly on my loyalty and my love.*

It is a harsh truth, but I need to get it off my chest at the start: from the moment you died, I was bloody furious with you and spent the next thirty years denying everything about you. I will try to explain why I think this happened. I know you will be sceptical, if not downright dismissive. But stick with me please, because I think I work it out, at least in part.

I am going to start by going back to June 1980 and a memory that required no digging. It was there in all its awful detail. Clear as yesterday. I am confident it is no lie. It goes some way to explaining why I turned into the resentful one, because you left me the task of telling our dear mum that you had killed yourself. That's where I am going to start this story.

1. A Death in the Family

The suicide does not go alone. He takes everyone with him.
William Maxwell

When I was fourteen I was a gangly youth with an underdeveloped body: very tall with little strength to match my height. My public school was devoted to physical prowess: sport was almost everything. For several years it caused me much torment. One of the worst activities took place in the gym: circuit training, gymnastics and the dreaded medicine ball. A large leather ball, a yard in diameter, heavy and rough to the touch was thrown from boy to boy, hard. It had to be caught, in the midriff, absorbed and held, even as the stomach was compressed and the breath expelled in a humiliating gasp. The whole class watched as you wrestled and did your best to disguise the pain and the humiliation. Then you had to summon up the strength to throw it on, passing all that misery to the next poor sucker.

Memories of the impact of that medicine ball came back to me some twenty years later when my partner Claire, who was eight months pregnant with our first child, handed over the phone for me to hear my brother's father-in-law tell me that Robin was dead. My response was wholly physical. The breath rushed out of me, my gut collapsed and I staggered. I had been hit by something far, far more destructive and debilitating than any medicine ball.

I have little recollection of the conversation. I recall a powerful sense of the man's own distress and a vague recollection of the toxic logistics. Robin had gone out on his own, with a carefully prepared rope made into a tidy noose, to a tree on the edge of a small park, which no doubt he had previously identified, and hanged himself. That was enough to be going on with. (Recalling it all now in tranquillity, I discover that it is in fact the first lie. A total distortion. I made it up. I had conjured up a reconstruction. It was to be many years before I found out the precise details of his self-destruction.)

After the physical assault came the shock. The blood seemed to drain away from the brain. There was a different tightness in the chest: the medicine ball gasps faded, and instead I felt a simultaneous desire to both collapse and to spring into action. To curl up in a foetal ball and to unleash like a coiled spring. I needed to move purposefully and yet there was, as yet, no purpose. My body was not yet responding to the demands of the moment.

As my heart rate returned to what would pass as normal for the foreseeable future, I found my purpose. I was the person in command of the dreadful news. I had a task.

I remembered one further detail from the jumbled memory of that phone call. I had told this bearer of bad news that I did not want him phoning my mother. The father-in-law was a virtual stranger and my mother was alone. I knew that this was my job.

My parents lived in a small cottage on the edge of the busy A25 in the village of Nutfield, between Redhill and Godstone. It had cost £1000 in 1946 and had been a wedding present from my mother's father. My own father, her husband, had been a general in the British army but had been retired from his high-level post a lot earlier than he would have liked. He was assuaging his boredom and lack of status by sailing his small yacht to distant parts, single-handed. I had no idea where he was, but knew he was not at home.

I could not phone my mother and be on the end of the line whilst she reeled and recoiled from the news that would surely shatter her already fragile peace of mind. My brother's growing number of psychotic incidents over the previous few years had already destabilised her. This news was going to be devastating. So there was only one thing to do. I had to drive across London and find her and tell her, in person. I could not see an alternative although I had a powerful hallucinatory feeling that if I just curled up into that ball and closed the shutters and my mother never found out, perhaps her precious son would not be dead.

There are laws about alcohol and impaired vision that should keep you away from the wheel of a car. But as far as I know there are no laws to stop you driving through one of the busiest cities in the world under the influence of a raw and primal grief. I did not, in the current parlance, 'do crying'. I could count on one hand the number of times I had been moved to tears as an adult. Ten years in English boarding schools had taught me that 'blubbing' was a sign of weakness. As a result, in highly charged emotional situations where they would have offered a welcome release, I was denied the catharsis of tears. But on that drive I broke the instincts of a lifetime. The tears seriously impaired my vision and my roadworthiness was jeopardised by the wracking sobs.

Throughout that awful journey, across Blackfriars Bridge, up Brixton Hill, through Streatham and onto the Brighton Road, behind those tears I was writing: rehearsing and rejecting my script for this frightful encounter. I had tried my hand at writing plays with modest success, but this piece of dialogue was way beyond my limited skills.

'Mum, I have the most dreadful news...'

'Mum, I have to tell you about Robin...'

'Mum, you know we have talked about Robin's illness, well...'

'Mum, we knew Robin was getting worse, and in our hearts we suspected there was only one way this could end, well...'

Croydon, Purley, Coulsden. Merstham. The route was hard-wired, which was just as well. This was no time to be poring over maps. After an hour and half I was parked outside Rose Cottage and the eponymous roses were still out and the sun was shining. I knew the back door would be open and I let myself into the empty kitchen. It is a tiny cottage, two up and two down, and the ground floor was eerily quiet. I did not want to call out. I did not trust my voice. Two o'clock. I prayed to a God I had little faith in that she was not out with friends or shopping. I could not bear the thought of careering around the village from one possibility to the next. So I went upstairs and called out, 'Mum.'

She was on her bed. An afternoon nap. My call had reached her and as I entered she was just starting to emerge from sleep. I recognised that moment of transition from a daytime nap when you are at peace but a little disorientated. Then she saw me standing in the doorway and she smiled.

'Darling,' is all she said. Then the smile faded and the rest of the script was written on her face. ' You shouldn't be here. If you are here there is a powerful reason. And that is not a good reason. This is not good news. This is bad news. It must be very bad news if you are standing in my bedroom when you should be in London waiting for the birth of my third grandchild.'

And all I could come up with was 'Mum!', although I feared the rest of the script was written on my face.

'Darling, what is it?'

At that moment the full force of my predicament hit me. I was now the only son. I was her boy. Her man. My father had dropped out of the equation: he was absent with leave. Suddenly the thirty-year-old dynamic of the leader and the led had been reversed. I had become the person who was going to be in charge of managing both the emotional earthquake and the interminable aftershocks. The one who was going to have to stand up when others were breaking down. I could no longer let the tears flow. I had to absorb her raging grief and provide some sort of crazy justification.

I sat down on the bed, took her hand and kept it simple:

'Mum, I have just heard. Robin is dead. I am afraid he committed suicide.'

There was an awful silence as her eyes widened and her hand reversed the hold and gripped mine with a desperate ferocity. She had nothing to say. She shook her head slowly. I could not let the silence linger. The garbled version of that carefully prepared script tumbled out.

'He was so unhappy... It was a choice he made for us... It was a selfless act. He was tormented and he knew that he was tormenting us... He was so ill... This was inevitable... He is happier now...'

'But what about the children?' she wailed. Rather too quickly for my liking, my mother had fixated on his two sons. 'What will become of them? We will be responsible for them, for their future.'

I find it very hard to write the script of the next few hours. Much of it has disappeared: expunged from my creaky memory. I recall holding her (we were not a family who hugged much). I also remember the way we both kept returning to the same formulations. A spiral of repeated re-workings of the same few comforting tropes. Punctuated by a litany of 'What ifs?' and 'What nows?'.

What I do remember was that once we had settled into a quieter mode, drinking tea and staring into the middle distance, she began to articulate the first flutterings of her own guilt and sense of failure. 'What did we do wrong? Am I to blame?' These fledgling queries would, as time went on, turn into fully fledged vultures that would circle over her for many years to come and never fully leave her. I was yet to be a parent, so was ill equipped to appreciate quite how elemental this self-inflicted guilt must be. Now, having children of my own, I know differently.

It took us three days to find my father and get him to a phone in a Spanish fishing village (coincidentally, not many miles from the place where he would die seven years later, suddenly of a heart attack, whilst on holiday with my mother). This time, on a poor telephone line, in my new role, I was the one who had to break it to him. At the best of times, we had never been great at communicating and he was not a man who found it easy to articulate emotion. The way he dealt with shock and grief was to shift into administrative mode. It was all about flights and funerals and money. Just like my mother, he transferred his own feelings of loss onto my brother's wife and his two sons. There was talk of looking after their future, of trusts and school fees. That was his way and I suppose, I have to recognise, it was my way too. When it comes to matters emotional, as with much else, we inherit more than we transform. I like to think there has been some transformation over the intervening years, but back then I was still my father's son. Now I was comfortable talking logistics if it helped avoid the gaping maw of our collective grief.

My father returned, and I can only imagine how he coexisted with my mother. He made lists, drafted letters to lawyers and to my brother's wife, laying out his plans for her future in a manner that could only offend. The cremation was arranged but my mother could not face the public agony and stayed away. (I know she regretted that decision, a terrible error in retrospect. However awful the prospect, there is a vital long-term benefit from even the most basic of funereal rites.)

I felt like I was absorbing and assuaging everyone's grief and trying to meet the impossible demands of our wounded family. I could find little time for tears, but allowed myself to sit and write a poem. I am no great poet, but I do understand that through compressing and trying to capture a raw emotional truth, you can find some easing of the pain. I had not planned it, but I read it out at his cremation, and managed to get through to the end without those pesky tears. It ended:

'We did not see your final simple step
All we know is,
(and this was the purest form of love and bravery)
It was up not down.'

That poem marked a turning point. It was the last time I allowed myself to feel the love for and the loss of my brother. Convention demands that if your brother hangs himself you take on the mantle of a slowly dissipating grief and wear it with dignity, and to most of those around me that is exactly what I did. I played the part of a grieving brother and a caring son. But it was a sham. Just beneath the surface there was a pulse of fury, fed by a grinding sense of guilt. In the immediate aftermath and for many years to come this toxic brew poisoned my memories of him and wiped out any vestige of brotherly love.

Dear Robin,

Now we are flying over the Middle East. I seem to be taking you on a tour of locations that prove the world has not got any better since you left us. In fact, many of the premonitions that you had, which we dismissed as just a little 'mad,' have turned out to be remarkably prescient. If you were still around, you would be tempted to say 'I told you so.' I have no trouble imagining how you would be reacting to Brexit, Trump (yes, you heard me right, Donald Trump, in your day a grubby, loud-mouthed New York property developer, currently president of the US of A) and Climate Change. Your letters, which will come into their own later in the book, include some terrific rants about the state of the world in 1970. You would certainly have ammunition for some ranting in 2020. (As I write that date I realise it really must sound like we are in a sci-fi movie; I mean, you didn't even get to see 1984!)

This next chapter is, frankly, a bit of special pleading. It is an attempt to explain just why I have found this whole thing so very difficult. You could say I am trying to blame my own failure to remember you and celebrate you and generally behave like a decent brother, in external conditions over which I claim to

15

have little control. But you will see through it, I am sure. The truth is: I wiped you. So, you may well ask: 'Why me and why now?' I will try to explain.

2. Ghost Child

Denial is not forgetting. Trauma fragments memory, but I want to believe that the splinters we collect between us can be reassembled.

Richard Beard, *The Day That Went Missing*

The next few years were full of quiet despair and noisy re-alignment. I found myself holding the ring between my mother's roiling grief and my father's urgent sense that plans must be put in place. And then there was Carole. Five years before his death, during the time when he was fighting off the sporadic but debilitating impact of mental disturbance, his life was enriched by his last love. Carole was in her early twenties when they met and fell in love. By the time Robin died they had two very young children. Whilst my parents and I were grappling with the shock of losing a son and a brother, Carole was faced with the far more pressing matter of abandonment. She was on her own, and however much we felt we could help her, the day-to-day reality demanded a loyalty and courage far beyond what was required of us. In the following years her dedication to bringing up my parents' grandchildren was fierce and devoted. That they flourished was a testimony to her resilience. But it was not easy.

Carole had to find the balance between seeking support from our parents and retaining her independence. It was tricky course to steer. Those boys were my mother's only physical link to her son and her desire for engagement must have been overpowering. And although I took on the mantle of 'he who makes things better', I failed to successfully act as mediator. This failure compounded a guilt that had turned into the anger that would close down my loyalty to Robin.

This closure was caused, in part at least, by the fact that up to his suicide and beyond, through the years of anger and denial, the trajectory of my own life was in stark counterpoint to that of my brother. As we will see, his life as a student in Australia was full of promise. His many qualities seemed to out-shine my own, or at least appeared to when seen through the prism of my sibling envy. But once he returned to England, his life direction took a downward turn just as mine seemed to take off. I was no high flier, but I was successful in my own professional sphere and was lucky enough to quickly settle into a fulfilling domestic life.

At a time when many university graduates were still aligned with the radical ideology of the 'liberated sixties', I was a socialist and started a career in education. By the time Robin came back into my life I was a dynamic and passionate teacher working in a challenging inner-city comprehensive. I taught English and Media and was an active participant in a dedicated group of radical teachers doing our best not only to make education more relevant to our working-class pupils but also to change the political structures of the time. They were heady days and my participation in that world seemed to play to my skills. I quickly took on senior responsibility in school and developed a name for myself in the wider educational scene. And, whilst in full flight as a creative and engaged teacher, I met my partner, herself a teacher working in the same school. By the early eighties we not only had two children but owned a large run-down Victorian house in an unfashionable part of town. We were the baby boomers whose good fortune has continued right through to our comfortable retirement with that Victorian house in a now desirable part of London and worth a small fortune.

At the age of forty, some seven years after Robin's death, and now with a third child to consider, I took a huge gamble with my own future and that of my family. I left teaching to found a television production company. I believed that although I was a late starter, the skills I had developed as a teacher easily transferred into the world of film and television production. It was a time when Channel Four was encouraging anyone with a story to tell to do so for the newly established television station whose mission was to let a thousand flowers bloom. It was an audacious leap from the certainties of a career in education, but I was right about the transferable skills and my fledgling company slowly established itself as a serious player in the industry. We had a number of mainstream successes but the most fulfilling was a BBC 2 series The House, that went behind the scenes at the Royal Opera House and won awards around the world. From independent production I went on to help found and run Teachers TV, a television channel funded by the government. It was aimed at teachers and parents and it too flourished until its untimely demise at the hands of Conservative Secretary of State, enraged by a New Labour success. Meanwhile, my three children grew up and built futures for themselves. I was and am an affront to my brother's fate. I made it through and he didn't.

This stark contrast between my own fortunes and those of my brother seems to have exacerbated my denial and the subsequent guilt that sustained my refusal to engage with his memory. I suffered from a kind of 'survivor's guilt', made worse because I not only survived but flourished. And, as we will see, I flourished in exactly the way he aspired to in those days before his mental instability ground him down. This journey has taught me that he did indeed have all the qualities that could so easily have caused him to succeed in the world of theatre, film or literature. I still believe he was more talented than me, and so my success was partially soured by the bitter memories of his failure to survive and succeed.

I also need to acknowledge that whilst my mother was an enthusiastic devotee to my every success and advancement, that devotion was compromised, blunted by her grief. She too was haunted by what might have been for her younger son, and this diminished the satisfaction she could feel in my solo success. I was alive to pursue my ambitions and enjoy a growing family, whilst Robin was not. His children were growing up like mine, but without a father. That appeared to diminish her appreciation and perhaps possibly even her love for me and my family. I resented that and, without fully realising it, blamed my brother.

* * * * * *

While my mother was alive I had to keep my anger hidden. I had to tolerate the symptoms of her grief and guilt. I had to accommodate her natural inclination to privilege the lives of my brother's children over an interest in and concern for my own children.

Then my mother died and everything changed. Remarkably, I found that my anger began to dissipate once I no longer had to protect myself from her raw and all-encompassing grief.

And as my anger faded I began to realise that there was a gaping Robin-shaped hole in my world. I had allowed him to fade from my consciousness: pushed any memory of him into the darkest recesses of my personal history. The truth was that, for me, he had ceased to exist. I spoke about him, it is true, and I went through the motions of acknowledging the tragedy of his death, but I was paying lip service to a person with whom I had lost all touch. For me he was a ghost, only dimly discerned.

I find it hard to explain this lacuna. It disturbs me that when I am motivated to conjure up memories, indeed even desperate to do so, Robin is eerily absent. We were at school together and yet I cannot see him amongst the hazy memories I have of classrooms, dormitories and playing fields. We spent time with my parents in various exotic locations around the world and yet I cannot picture him. He lived in my flat for months and yet I cannot recall him sitting on my sofa or eating at my kitchen table. Why could that be?

As I grow older I have become more preoccupied with the fragile nature of memory. I have reached a stage in my life where I often find it hard to remember why I have gone up the stairs, but still harbour a misguided trust in those longer-term recollections upon which I have built my own autobiography. Addressing the absent memory of my brother has caused me to question the foundations of the whole edifice. Facts may be provable but the underlying meanings and the longer-term emotional impact of those facts seem particularly untrustworthy.

There is now extensive research, which confirms my recently acquired uncertainties.

'Our memory of events is not a verbatim playback of what happened. Rather, it's a reconstruction based on the retrieval of some stored remnants of the original experience that may have persisted in memory, along with our conceptual framework for other similar previous experiences, that serves to make the memory coherent.'[1]

That is all well and good and clearly you would be a fool not to be deeply suspicious of your own memories. But what does it mean if you are having trouble with the retrieval? How can you come to terms with the past if certain memories simply will not lend themselves to reconstruction? The paltry quality of my memory is a matter of some unease. I feel diminished whenever I hear someone talk about his or her inspiring or problematic relationship with a sibling. They appear to be able to conjure up rich and vivid accounts of childhood antics, of deprivations, tensions and triumphs, all of which contributed to a deeply felt affection or, in some cases, a palpable mistrust. I on

---

1   *Memory Distortion: an Adaptive Perspective,*
Daniel L. Schacter, Scott A. Guerin and Peggy L. St. Jacques, 2012

the other hand must either pretend or dissemble. But why?

There must be a reason. I can only assume that there are more powerful forces at work that deny me access to so many of the incidents and occasions that should be available and from which I could build a clear picture of my brother and our relationship.

One of those forces must concern the dislocation of our family. From the start our family was itinerant. My father was in the army; he and my mother travelled the world from posting to posting. We were both sent to boarding school. From the age of eight, Robin and I spent only two months of the year in the company of our parents. We were separated from our parents by geography, which in turn put emotional distance between us. We would have said that we were a happy family because there were occasions when we conformed to that convention. Then, at a critical time of our lives, education forced as apart, first to boarding school and then to university, when we both elected to cross oceans and continents to put even more distance between us and our parents. In my case I travelled to Canada and for Robin it was to be even further.

We were a family that put physical distances between us, and then seemed surprised when we found it difficult to 'pick up where we left off'. It is not a surprise that those distances made it all the more difficult to connect the shards of memory so as to create a reassuring and heart-warming narrative. It is likely that this physical distance, while not the cause of an obvious dysfunction, must have contributed to a loss of connection and, in the words of the research, an absence of 'the conceptual framework' that could help me reconstruct a set of happy childhood memories.

You can blame emotional distance on physical distance, but there are plenty of families just as separated that retain a strong sense of familial connection and the memories that go with it. In our case you need to look at an unfortunate inheritance in the form of a residual emotional restraint. We did not, as a family (or, it has to be said, as a class) 'do' emotional transparency and we inherited that from our grandparents and presumably their grandparents. Some families managed to overcome the 'stiff upper lip' that was presumed to have sustained them through the last war. My family not so much. In many ways it was a corollary of the separation we imposed on ourselves. Saying good-bye, which we seemed to do an awful lot, is so much harder if you let emotions get in the way. Too many tears would certainly have made it a lot harder to say goodbye to our mother as she put us on the plane taking us back to the UK and boarding school at the start of another six-month separation. Which is not to say that she did not feel that pain, she surely did, as did we. It was just that in our family we did not want to burden each other with the impact of a publicly tearful farewell.

It is my hypothosis that this inherited (and of course conditioned) propensity for emotional concealment led to my paucity of unobstructed memories. As we have seen already, the clear memories I do have are linked to moments of emotional intensity. I recall with startling clarity the day, sixty-six years ago, when Robin crashed though a plate-glass window. My memory is in fine fettle when it comes to recalling some of the worst of his psychotic episodes in the last few years of his life. But such scenes are infrequent. I believe that this historical emotional deficit is a likely driver of my struggling memory and an indirect cause of the many black holes that obscure my past in general and my relationship with my brother in particular.

* * * * * *

Families shape their own narratives to accommodate their tragedies. Ours was that Robin had started to take drugs in his last two years at the University of Western Australia, which had propelled him onto the slippery slope, which resulted in mental illness and death. My mother found comfort in a version of events that shifted the blame away from her. In part at least.

The problem with that particular mythology was that it offered very little comfort to those of us who did not share in her parental guilt. It was this narrative of despair, combined with those other emotional avoidance strategies, that had closed down any chance I had of constructing a vibrant picture of my brother and, far more disturbingly, it had left his two sons with little to admire in their father.

So when my mother died, the sadness at her loss seemed to liberate my long-smothered grief for my brother. Suddenly, I could weep for both mother and brother. I could start to confront my past failures. I could make amends.

To do that I needed to go back and find the boy I had grown up with and the man whose life had once glowed with promise. Above all I wanted to find an answer to the question that my mother howled as she absorbed the news of Robin's suicide: WHY? How did her son and my brother, whose life started with so much promise, who seemed to have sparkled and shone as a young man, have taken his own life? Where are the clues that might make some sense of his eventual misfortune and the mental turmoil that engulfed him?

There are, of course, no easy answers: mental illness stalks the world we live in and can take any of us down at any time. All too often we are denied the satisfying correlation between cause and effect. Indeed, many suicides seem to defy logic. It is why they are so much harder to bear than a car crash or a fatal illness. And yet there is some comfort to be gained from piecing together the clues. Tracing the story and filling in the gaps. Cold-case investigation can be therapeutic, and even an unresolved understanding helps survivors to find some reconciliation with the past. It took me a long time to decide that I and those around me could benefit from just such a reconciliation.

But eventually I did get onto the case. After a slow start I found I was not a bad detective. I dug up a host of revealing details and incident. I brought him – or at least a coherent manifestation of the boy and the man – back to life. I discovered that had I got going sooner, I would have had a reassuring story to tell my mother. Far too late for her, of course, but not for the rest of us survivors.

Once I had given myself permission to start looking for answers, I realised I had to go back to the beginning.

Dear Robin,

Before we start on your story, I want to go back and consider our father and our inheritance. What role did he and his family play in all of this? In fact, we need to go back one more generation, to his father. Did you know he had committed suicide? Could that have given you ideas? I don't think so. However, since I am on the lookout for clues and explanations, it seems right to at least consider the possibility that there might be a genetic throwback on the Bethell side of the family tree. I'll be frank and say that I think it is bound to be tenuous at best. But then, I do think you would have been fascinated to know more about our grandfather. He, like you, seems to have been someone to be proud of. He killed himself when his two sons were in their teens. I am proud to have found out about the late Donald Leslie Bethell, Treasurer of the British Protectorate of Gibraltar. His suicide appeared to come out of the blue. Finding out what he had achieved in his life felt very much like exploring your achievements, especially in that golden four years in Perth. Still 7145 miles away.

3. Inheritance

Yes, truly, for look you, the sins of the father are to be laid upon the children. Therefore I promise ye I fear you. I was always plain with you, and so now I speak my agitation of the matter. Therefore be o' good cheer, for truly I think you are damned.

William Shakespeare, The Merchant of Venice

In his infamous poem 'This Be The Verse', best known for its first line, 'They fuck you up, your mum and dad', Philip Larkin also writes:

'Man hands on misery to man.
It deepens like a coastal shelf.'

Robin certainly ended his life in misery and in looking for reasons why, it is worth tracking back along our family's coastal shelf. Larkin also writes about the impact of previous generations: '...fools in old-style hats and coats', and he asks us to focus on the men, which in my male-dominated family is probably appropriate. My father had a brother just a year and a half younger than him and their relationship to each other and to their own families was certainly conditioned by the untimely fate of their own father. How much of his misery was passed on down the line to us?

There had always been a powerful sense of omertà in our family when it came to the death of my grandfather. My father never, to my knowledge, made any reference to his own father's life, let alone to his death. I cannot remember quite when I became aware that Donald Leslie Bethell had committed suicide. It hovered in the background of my consciousness, but for fifty years I made no effort to find out about this dark moment in our family's history. It is possible that my mother made mention of it long after my father died, as she explained the reasons behind the toxic relationship she had had with her mother-in-law Kay Bethell, Donald's widow. What I do know is that no one in my immediate family seems to have made any connection between Robin's suicide and that of his grandfather. It was time to put that right.

There was remarkably little to go on. Diligent online searches revealed some dates but no details. I did know that he had died in Gibraltar and that my father was a teenager at the time. Then, just as I was starting to despair of ever filling in any details, I came across a short entry in, of all publications, the Dundee Evening Telegraph for 1936: it read as follows:

FOUND SHOT IN OFFICE
Gibralter Treasurer's Death

A verdict of suicide whilst of unsound mind was returned at the inquest on Mr Donald Leslie Bethell, treasurer and collector of Gibralter, who was found shot in his office.

It was stated that all the Government's cash books were in order.

Mr Bethell was born in 1895 and leaves a wife and three sons. He was educated at King Edward VI School Stourbridge and Cambridge University.

During the war he was wounded several times and afterwards was assistant treasurer at Berbera, Somaliland and Tanganyka.

These were rich pickings: full of resonant detail. This man, my grandfather, who had been virtually invisible to me for fifty years, suddenly came into focus. The story of his life and death could be dug out of those three short paragraphs. Born at the turn of the century he would have been in his very early twenties when he enlisted and found himself on the Western Front where he was wounded 'several times'. Then he joined the Colonial Service where he served in the tougher outposts of the British Empire.

At the age of 40 he had shot himself. Not in his home or out in the open air, but in his office. It was the coroner's view that he was of unsound mind. And yet, no doubt to everyone's relief, the cash books were in order. He had upheld the traditions and protocols of the Colonial Service right to the end.

Despite my collusion in the eighty-year news blackout, I needed to find out more. Partly, of course, because I was looking for any clues to my brother's suicide, but also because it matters to me. I have children and I am part of the genetic stream that flows through generations of Bethells. If there is a suicide gene, could it be lurking in my bloodline? Through this investigation I find that I am claiming that I have a dispassionate interest in finding the truth about Robin. When in fact he is no longer here to care. But I am. At each stage of the journey I am brushing against my own insecurities and suppressed anxieties. Tracking down my grandfather is just as much about understanding my father and his impact on me, as it is about explaining Robin's decline and death.

I contacted the Gibraltar National Archives and asked them to look out anything that might help. Some two months later, three 1935 newspaper cuttings dropped into my inbox. The first was a far more detailed description of that coroner's report, the second an obituary and the third an account of his funeral. These were remarkable documents, not least because I am absolutely certain that no one else in my family, with perhaps the exception of Donald's widow, had ever set eyes on them. The man was as absent from his immediate family as Robin has been absent from mine. If you commit suicide, whether in 1936 or in 1980 it seems, it makes no odds; you disappear from the narrative.

The Coroner's report was a cool account of a strangely subdued demise. It appears that my grandfather had turned up for work as usual and the Clerk to the Treasury reported that *'he had spoken to Mr Bethell several times during the morning and he appeared to be just the same as on other days.'*

At around 11.20, the Clerk reported that he had *'heard a bang, followed by another sounding like a door banging but did not suspect that anything was wrong. With the windows and doors open all kinds of noises could be heard in the Treasury.'* He assumed the first bang was a car backfiring. Shortly afterwards, he went next door with a query and found the Treasurer's office empty, *'although his hat was on the desk.'* I found that detail strangely affecting. I have since found a couple of very blurred photos of him, and in both he is sporting a fetching light fedora. It looks rather dapper and I can clearly imagine it sitting on his desk: a style statement about the man he had been.

Shortly afterwards, a visitor arrived in the Clerk's office asking for the Treasurer. A call was put through but there was no answer. *'...after waiting some time the caller had to leave for another appointment.'* A little later, the Assistant Treasurer, Mr Bacarisas, went next door to investigate. His boss was nowhere to be found. He then tried the door of the private lavatory that he and the Treasurer shared. The door was locked. After knocking and calling, the door was broken down and there was the body of my grandfather.

The Acting Colonial Surgeon found:

'...the deceased lying on the floor with a bullet wound in the right side of the head, life being extinct. The bullet that had inflicted the injury was fired from an automatic pistol in which there were two other cartridges of similar type.'

As a medical man, he was not going to jump to conclusions and ended his testimony: *'The wound could have been self inflicted or caused by another person holding the revolver to his head.'*

A further witness, Mr Frederick Hird, the office messenger, said he had noticed 'the deceased looked rather drawn that morning and had not greeted witness with his usual smile'. The Coroner was not deflected by the Surgeon's introduction of possible foul play and recorded a verdict of 'suicide whilst of unsound mind'.

The account of his funeral was another eye-opener. I rather imagined that the suicide of a colonial officer would be treated as an ignominious end, liable to bring the service into disrepute. I would have expected a quiet and private funeral with little exposure to the public. But in the case of my grandfather, the very opposite was true.

'*The funeral of the Hon D.L. Bethell took place on Saturday morning from his residence in Europa Road. The coffin was covered with the Union Jack and was borne on a gun carriage. There were many magnificent wreaths including one from the Governor General Sir Charles Harington-Harington. In the procession were detachments of the Civil Police and Revenue Officers and numerous friends of the deceased. All premises in main Street were closed and route was lined with sympathetic onlookers.*'

My grandfather was clearly a big man on the Rock, and his self-destruction was not going to be held against him.

All in all, the man that emerged from those clippings could hardly be described as a tortured soul with suicidal tendencies. Yet we know from so many accounts that all too often relatives and close friends can find no rhyme nor reason, nor premonition of a loved one's suicide. This suicide, like that of his grandson, was a cool affair: carefully planned. A pistol prepared, the lavatory identified as a place of privacy and a couple of spare bullets just in case something had gone wrong. And yet, from the evidence we have, it seems to have been treated as an act of God rather than a humiliating surrender.

There is one clue as to a possible motive and I found it in his obituary. It describes how he was an '*enthusiastic race-goer*' and '*almost invariably present at meetings of the Jockey Club.'* This triggers for me a half-recalled suggestion from my uncle Denis, my father's second brother, who was thirteen years younger than his elder siblings and my only real source of family history. I think he told me that his father had killed himself to escape from his gambling debts. I really cannot remember how definite an assertion this was and, like all the main witnesses, Denis too died far too early from cancer aged 44. So I can only surmise. But if my grandfather was a regular race-goer he would almost certainly have liked a flutter, and it is no stretch to imagine that modest outlay turning into a crushing debt, the revelation of which could only have brought humiliation and disgrace to the family. The Coroner and those who worked with him were keen to make it clear that the government finances were all in order. He was not fiddling the books. However, if you are the Chief Treasurer and are found to have personal debts that are unsustainable and threaten your family's wellbeing, then suicide may well have been the honorable way out.

There is one other piece of evidence, which could point to financial meltdown. Donald's wife, my grandmother Kay, and by default my father and his brother, were by all accounts left in penury. She had to return to England immediately and to rely on the generosity of family and friends for free accommodation, and try to maintain some semblance of her place in society, of which she had an acute awareness, on a paltry stipend from the Colonial Office. Donald had no savings and even if he had organised life insurance, it would almost certainly have been annulled by his suicide. If you were the Colonial Treasurer and you were found to have unsustainable debts then you would have been dishonoured and probably ostracised from Gibraltar's high society, in which he and my grandmother were so clearly active participants.

What is clear from the widespread and fulsome appreciation of Donald's many qualities and achievements was that his contemporaries took a far more benevolent view of his demise. None of the hundreds who turned out for his funeral and listened to the eulogy in the Cathedral of the Holy Trinity appear to have questioned his motives. The Honourable Donald Bethell had taken his life *'whilst of unsound mind'* and that was a perfectly acceptable way to go.

However, it seems plausible that his gambling problem had run through the family funds and he could see no way out of the consequences. My problem with this supposition is that it makes him out to be merely selfish; he could not face the opprobrium and so he would escape the scene, leaving his wife to pick up the pieces. This may be the case, but it is an uncomfortable conclusion, especially since, when I come to consider the motives of his grandson, I will very much want to believe that his motives were far from selfish. I like to think that, in the words of my poem, his last step was 'up not down'.

In looking for alternative causes I was drawn to the fact that he had been wounded 'several times' in the Great War. Could he have been suffering from what we now call post-traumatic stress? We know that the effects of PTSD can linger long in the life of those it afflicts, even after lying dormant for many years.

Could Donald have been affected by a traumatic wartime experience? I needed to find out about his service and those wounds. At first, all I could find was a name, a date of accession and a regimental number, but nothing about his service nor his wounds. I could see that he joined up in January 1915 aged 19, but little else. One record did make it clear that he had actually joined up with a Canadian regiment, so I tried the Canadian World War archive. To my astonishment, with one search and one click, forty facsimile pages filled my screen. In an instant I was in touch with my invisible grandfather: a register of his service, his medical checks, his pay and his leave. Best of all, a detailed description of his wounds, received six weeks before the end of the war.

On September 27th 1918 his battalion was ordered to take Bourlon Wood, as part of General Hague's big push to end the war. Accounts suggest it was a fierce battle (an unprecedented twelve Victoria Crosses were awarded). My grandfather was wounded during that first day's battle, but he seemed to have been very lucky. It was a flesh wound. A doctor eventually saw him four days later and wrote in his notes:

'Bullet T&T wound in left thigh

Entrance wound almost healed. Exit healing well.

No damage to bone.

Xray reveals a piece of shrapnel in his little finger (right). Wound healed'

'T&T' meant *'Through and through.'* It was a flesh wound and he seemed to heal well. Within three weeks they write: *This officer is ready for transfer to Matlock.* Where his assessment read: *No appreciable disabilities from wounds.* Canadian officers were sent to Matlock in Derbyshire, where the Royal Hotel had been commandeered as a convalescence centre. It appears that the hotel retained its luxury status and there were reports that the men were *'very happy and hosted regular parties to which the local women were invited'.* It certainly does not sound like a place where the shell-shock victims were sent.

Donald was discharged from the army in April 1919 and I notice that on the discharge checklist, in answer to the question: *'Has this officer ever or does he now suffer from an affection to…?'* the following categories were included:

'1) The Nervous System; NO.

4) Disturbance of Mentality: NO.'

Obviously, a discharge review in 1919 when there was a reluctance to openly identify the insidious effects of post-traumatic stress or even 'shell shock', as it was then described, a declaration that there was no sign of 'disturbance of mentality' is not conclusive proof of anything. However, a rapidly healing flesh wound and smooth transfer to a luxurious convalescence centre seem to suggest that he emerged from the war reasonably unscathed in both mind and body. He joined the Colonial Service in 1920 and within thirteen years he was appointed to the post of Colonial Treasurer and Collector of Gibraltar, aged just 36.

This appears to be a man who was not wracked by mental illness. Even allowing for the rose-tinted spectacles of an obituary, there are enough clues to indicate that Donald Bethell was fully functioning, highly competent and stable. He was much respected and, more importantly, much liked: 'Gibraltar has lost an officer who by his amiable character, his tact and pleasing manner, had made himself popular with all sections of the community.'

There is plenty of research on the 'totally unexpected' suicide. Not surprisingly, it turns out that however 'unexpected' or 'inexplicable' a suicide appears to be, there are always underlying symptoms that have merely been kept well hidden from family and friends. A recent Harvard Medical School study led by Dr Michael Miller concludes with the following assertion:

'The paradox is that the people who are most intent on committing suicide know that they have to keep their plans to themselves if they are to carry out the act. Thus, the people most in need of help may be the toughest to save.'

It would appear that Donald Bethell conformed to that paradigm. If he was showing signs of mental instability then the combination of his own defensive strategies, and the passing of over eighty years and all the key witnesses, mean that there will be no definitive answers. I will never know to what extent his *'unsound mind'* had been an ongoing condition, or whether it was a momentary lapse caused by some personal crisis. That, however, does not stop me from speculating as to whether there is any chance that an 'unsound mind' and a propensity to suicide could be an inherited trait and jump a generation.

There is research that claims to have identified a 'suicide gene': it is called BDNF Met allele and it does seem to be present in the DNA of a significant number of suicide victims. However, even those scientists who believe that this gene could have a significant impact acknowledge that in nearly every case it is a complex mixture of hereditary and environmental influences. There was one paragraph in an overview of the subject that did strike me as potentially important in untangling the causes of Robin's suicide:

'*Complicating matters further, a process called epigenetics also comes into play when considering the effect of genes on suicide. This process controls when certain genes are turned on or off as a person grows and develops, and it can be influenced by what happens in a person's environment.*

For example, if someone goes through a difficult event as a child, that experience could have an impact on how or when a gene is activated within that person's brain. Researchers speculate that negative experiences influencing epigenetics in a person who has a family history of suicide could further compound that person's suicide risk.'

This concept of a hereditary gene being activated by a traumatic event could possibly provide one explanation for Robin's condition and his eventual fate.

As I am struggling with the voluminous and often contradictory research into the genetic component of suicide, I receive an email from my cousin Rafe. He is my father's brother Tony's eldest son and lives in San Francisco. I had told him about my research into our grandfather's death and asked him whether he had any photographs from that time which could shed some light on those days. He has sent me a photo collage put together by our grandmother: twenty or so photos of my father and his father between the ages of two and twenty. They were undated and seemingly random but they did include just three photos of Donald Bethell, faded and blurred but nonetheless revelatory. Wearing his fedora in the Gibraltar sunshine, it was impossible to look into his shaded eyes, and yet his physical presence was unmistakably Bethell. A certain off-kilter muscularity that reminded me forcefully of my father, my own sons and, of course, myself.

But the photo that caught my eye did not include the head of the household. He was away at the office or the race track. Instead it featured my father aged 14 and his brother Tony aged 13. They were born just fourteen months apart. They are standing on the terrace of what looks like a substantial, well-appointed house with business-like shutters on the window. Behind them are railings and the suggestion of a vista and since this is in Gibraltar and they lived on Europa Road, high up on the Rock where the affluent class had made their homes, it would have been a view of the sea. The two brothers are both dressed in white shirts with rolled-up sleeves and soft grey flannel trousers. Between them totters their younger brother Denis. He is about fourteen months old and his two brothers are each holding a hand. Denis was born in March 1934. It is almost certain that the photo was taken during the summer of 1935. It would be the summer holidays and they would have come by ship from their public school: the same Sherborne School that Robin and I would endure. (My father and his class had no qualms about visiting on their own offspring the same bracing privations that had made them the men they were.) In June of that year, possibly only a matter of days after that photograph was taken, their father and my grandfather shot himself.

They are smiling into the camera, and it caused me to wonder how they were going to deal with the explosion that was about to rip their family apart: the telephone call from the Assistant Treasurer Mr Bacarisas, informing Mrs Bethell that her husband had shot himself in his private lavatory, and would she please come down to the morgue to identify his body.

As we have seen, I have had some experience of the devastating impact of a phone call like that, but I find it hard to imagine quite what happened on that day. In the collage there are also photos of my grandmother. She was an attractive, sturdy woman. She survived for many more years after her husband's demise, and I knew her well. Even in her seventies and eighties she was someone who cared disproportionately about what others were thinking of her. I rather imagine she would have quickly switched from shocked incapacity to dogged stoicism. Like the men in her family, she would have been trained to keep a tight hold on her feelings and would have been determined to maintain her dignity above all else.

But what of her sons? Where were they when Mr Bacarisas made his fateful call? I look back at the picture of them smiling in their shirtsleeves holding their baby brother's hand. I try to imagine their faces as their mother breaks the news. Does she tell them the truth or does she deflect from the brutal reality: a sudden, unexplained death, 'his heart, you know'? They had both been at boarding school since turning seven. They would have been well versed in the emotional survival strategies expected of them: the expectation that actively discouraged any show of untoward emotion, anything that might embarrass the other 'chaps'. They would have been expected to 'take it like a man'.

I go back to the description of the funeral to see if there is any sign that they had been there, doing a 'William and Harry' behind the gun carriage. But we are told that 'the principal mourners were Mrs Bethell and Mrs Wilson Smith, who were accompanied by Mrs Brooks and Lady Robinson'. No mention of the late Treasurer's sons; perhaps they we were back in the house on Europa Road looking after their baby brother.

The medical literature is clear that the suicide of a parent has the potential for serious consequences:

'A consideration of how surviving a suicide might affect a child should involve the following outcome variables: mental health (e.g., mood disorders, anxiety disorders, suicidal behavior, post-traumatic stress disorder, traumatic grief); emotions (e.g., sadness, anger and guilt); functional problems (e.g., social problems, academic difficulties), and physical health (e.g., onset or exacerbation of disease, physiological changes).' [2]

And yet these two boys seem to have 'got over it' remarkably well. The Sherborne School archive shows me that on the surface at least both my father Drew and his brother Tony suffered from none of the more obviously debilitating symptoms. The archives tell a story of consistent achievement. There is a team photo of the school swimming team posed around the diving board. My father front and centre. It caused me to remember that he once told me that in metalwork he had made a diving helmet, which he had tried out

---

2   *The Impact of Suicide on the Family*, Julie Cerel, John R. Jordan and Paul R. Duberstein

in that same swimming pool. A couple of years later my uncle is seen sitting proudly in the front row of the successful First XV team. He was clearly a star and a little later went on to play for Blackheath and the Barbarians.

They too were boarding school survivors and true to its primary raison d'être, the preparation of men to run the Empire and lead the armed forces, Sherborne had equipped them both with the emotional resilience required to flourish during the war. Both enlisted at nineteen. My father went into the army in 1939 when he was posted to the British Expeditionary Force in France, which promptly withdrew to the beaches of Dunkirk. There he was, sitting in the front of a lorry waiting to be evacuated, when a Stuka dropped a bomb into the back. He was concussed and lost all his teeth. He spent a further five days on the beach waiting for eventual rescue. Two years later, he was captured at Tobruk and imprisoned in a POW camp in Italy from where he escaped, walked five hundred miles down to the Allied lines and spent the rest of war in action. This was not a man who had been incapacitated by his father's suicide.

His brother took a little longer to get into the action, but only because when he joined the RAF he was assigned to fly Mustangs and spent his first six months training in Alabama. Then at the end of December 1942 he was shot down over Holland and captured. He ended up at Stalag Luft III, where he escaped with seventy-five others in what is now known as the Great Escape. Once recaptured he ended up in the Gestapo fortress of Gorlitz where he and his fellow escapees, almost all recaptured, were subject to torture and vicious treatment. Then fifty of his fellows were driven away and shot. He never really understood why he survived and admitted to a longstanding sense of *'survivors' guilt.'* He saw out the war back at Stalag III and, with the end of hostilities in sight, he was force-marched some four hundred miles to Lübeck in one of the worst winters on record. The record suggests that he was marching in conditions that killed several of his fellows. He, however, seems to have recovered and, given his enthusiastic re-entry into London social life, appears to have survived unscathed. At least on the surface.

These extraordinary traumatic wartime experiences laid on top of the suicide of their father ought to have caused some lasting mental damage. And yet, like many of that generation, both men appeared to have survived double trials with remarkable resilience. By that I mean they swiftly embarked on successful careers and then relationships and eventually produced their own children. Like so many others, they applied the same omertà to their wartime experience as they had to their father's suicide. Neither spoke about it until they were well into their sixties. And yet it was not as simple as that. It never is. The demands of a harsh public-school regime, an appallingly disruptive and traumatic war, laid on top of the total denial of their father's suicide caused them both to rigidly control their emotional vulnerability. This is turn caused them to be starkly deficient when faced by the demands of familial turbulence. In the case of Tony, it was the mental illness of his first wife, and in the case of my father it was the suicide of his son.

* * * * * *

My father didn't change even after Robin's death, and breaching his emotional defences never got any easier. He had always been a largely absent father, so the opportunities to scale those fortified walls were few and far between. We sometimes talked politics, but never explored our feelings. Seven years after my brother's death I forced us into the closest association we had ever had, when I arranged to make a film about that escape from the Italian POW camp and his 500-mile walk down the spine of Italy to rejoin his regiment. We shared a hotel room for three weeks and he allowed us both to delve into his fractured memories of that extraordinary time.

Emboldened by this unique level of intimacy as well as by several glasses of Chianti, and with the camera rolling, I suggested that we had never spent so long in each other's company before and that I felt I was getting to know him better than I ever had. 'Are you getting to know me better?' I asked. There was a long pause. Everything in his demeanor suggested that indeed we had crossed an emotional Rubicon. Then he took a drag on his cigarette, hesitated and shrugged: 'Not really.' The old bastard couldn't even look me in the eye. But despite the closing of the door, despite the denial, this was a golden moment in our relationship because he went on: 'I suppose you could say that one was brought up not to talk about oneself.'

A moment of the purest clarity. A self-evident truth that spoke for his generation. A generation that found it difficult to use the first person. So much safer to refer to 'oneself' rather than 'myself'. The disconnected third person was a place of safety for men – and I believe it was a male affectation – who had been brought up to avoid raw emotion. It was a defence against the emotional vulnerabilities that might otherwise spill out. I, on the other hand, believed that I came from that post-war generation that felt at ease with the first person. As I sat at that table breaking with the habits of a lifetime and challenging my father with my feelings, I would have been confident that I and my kind had freed ourselves from the constraints of the third person. We were the sixties generation that could talk freely about our feelings. We had reversed Larkin's generational slope. We believed that the misery handed down from father to son does not deepen, but was dissipated as we got in touch with our feelings and felt comfortable to share them.

Yet, as I look back at that scene some twenty-five years later I start to doubt my assumptions of superiority. It is too easy to chuckle at my father's cautious reticence. As I take on the role of emotional archeologist in my brother's name, I have to acknowledge that maybe I inherited more of my father's protective strategies than I care to admit. It is dawning on me that despite my baby-boomer certainties, I am a lot less able to 'talk about one's self' than I like to imagine. As I embark on this journey I need to acknowledge that I too have been brought up not to talk about myself, and although I shall be doing my best to understand Robin and explain his fatal trajectory, I shall need to guard against hiding my story behind his.

On the other hand, my investigations into our inheritance suggest that, regardless of any subsequent genetic transmission, the inevitable suppression of the turmoil of his father's suicide left my father totally incapacitated when faced with his own son's suicide. Now I have to reconcile myself to the discovery that I might have inherited more of that emotional incapacity than I would like to acknowledge.

DISTANCE TO DESTINATION IS 6543 MILES. TIME TO
DESTINATION 14 HOURS 23 MINUTES.

Dear Robin,

*It's starting to get dark. We are flying into the sunset.
Things are quietening down in the economy cabin,
which is a relief. The eight-month-old baby in the next
aisle is now sleeping peacefully; I have no right to
complain. 'He's a good 'un,' as the Aussie father assures
me and I see no need to argue. Thank the Lord I have a
seat by the emergency exit and room to stretch out my
legs. You know how bloody tall I was, well I've not got
any shorter.*

*We are travelling back to our childhood. Well, I
say 'our' because I have done my very best to include
you in what is essentially my version of events. But the
truth is, you are still pretty absent. You see, I have so
little to go on. The primary witnesses are dead. Dad
died ridiculously early at 67 while mum lasted another
twenty years, but she has been gone ten years now. Of
course, I should have talked to her about it. But that's
what all my friends say: we wish we had respected
our parents enough to properly debrief them about
their past and ours. It is still shameful that in so many
of these memories I really cannot see you. And yet
you were there and during these early days we must
have done stuff together. Played, argued, shared and,*

yes, I fear, competed. This will be a running theme, certainly until you get back home after Australia; I was competitive. I may have been older but I believed you were the favoured one. I really don't think you believed that or in any way made me feel inferior. I just knew that you were the one mum really loved.

This chapter tells about the time when we lived like a family, and I hope it will bring back happy memories. As you will see, I know that those two years in Canada were the happiest of my young life. And you must have played your part, so I hope you felt the same.

Because of the lack of witness testimony, I have had to rely on two things: the Visitors' Book and family photos. You will have read John Berger's Ways of Seeing; in fact I have a dim memory of even discussing it with you. You understood how photographic images can have multiple and layered meanings. I have used these photos to reinforce my narrative. I have constructed my meanings where I am pretty sure you would construct alternative readings. For example, I use a picture of you in your bathing costume by the side of the Gatineau river with an anxious look on your face; it fed nicely into my memory of your accident. But a long time after I had written it up, lo and behold, I find another photo, at exactly the same time and place, in which you are larking about without a care in the world. I had to put that one aside; it didn't match my narrative. I wish you were still around for me to ask you which represents your version of our story. Neither is true of course. I have given up chasing the truth. It is long gone.

4. Childhood

But Midhat was only half listening, because he was thinking about the way his own character might be told after he was dead, when he no longer held the reins on his memories, and they galloped off into the motley thoughts and imaginations of others.

Isabella Hammed, The Parisian

My mother died at the age of 86 of a sudden and comprehensive heart attack after a brief stay in hospital. It was a good death after a full life. There was shock and sadness but the consensus was she would have wanted it that way. I set about writing her eulogy. Some of it was easy, but when it came to the early years I was short of evidence. We had never been a family of archivists and the details of her long life were hard to find. My own memory was certainly not going to come to the rescue. But there was one document that served me well as I tried to piece together her chronology: the family Visitors' Book. In the army you changed jobs every two years and sometimes more often. My mother had lived at 23 different addresses before settling in her Dorset village for the last twenty years of her life, after my father died. Without the Visitors' Book, I could never have constructed her chronology and, by default, ordered my own early years.

I flip to September 1st 1950, the day my brother was born. Their family home was that tiny cottage in Nuffield. They lived there when my father worked in the War Office in London and that was where Robin was born. I am inclined to a jealous whinge that he was lucky enough to be born at home, in contrast to my no doubt highly medicalised birth in hospital almost three years earlier, in 1947.

So, and I have never considered this before, Robin was born in the very bedroom where some thirty years later I had to wake his mother with news of her son's precipitous death. As I grow older I have become a little obsessed with the circularity of life: how significant moments long separated in time and thought, suddenly come full circle and re-assert the significance of the original. A virtual loop in our chronology. In this case it is the primal circle of existence. That room saw both birth and death: joy and deep despair.

The Visitors' Book gave me the chronology of our early childhood but there was little to wake my dormant memory or help me reconstruct those early days. Those memories were unlocked a few weeks later when I was clearing out my mother's garage.

It is always a disturbing experience, dismantling your parents' life, but for me it was not so demanding, as mother's 23 house moves had stripped away much of the usual detritus of a long life. She travelled light and knew how to make a home with the minimum of family heirlooms, and certainly she could not cart around the accumulated archives that have proved so demanding and rewarding for my friends in a similar position.

I found a rusty metal trunk in the corner of the unused garage, under a pile of dismantled garden furniture. It had my father's initials roughly painted on the lid: D.A.D.J.B. His was a time when each additional name seemed to add status. Although unlocked, it was not easy to open, like my father. It had seen hard service in foreign parts. Eventually I did get it open and as I gazed down at the dusty and uncared-for bundles and folders, I realised that I had indeed found the family archive. Such as it was!

Once the trunk was out on the lawn I had the evidence that was going to further my quest to understand my brother and to unfurl another layer of my own dim and foggy memory: two boxes of family photographs. The first contained pictures of Edwardian shooting parties on the Welsh estate where my mother grew up. Our own family snaps had been stashed away randomly in the second, a battered cardboard box with barely a clue as to who, what or when.

The random heap now scattered at my feet defied any chronology but immediately began to prod and probe at my sludgy memories. A few were resonant with significance. Pictures that caused the memory synapses to sing. These were the photos that would kick-start my investigation into my brother and the search for the clues that might reveal something about the causes of his eventual fate.

* * * * * *

When we were bringing our own children into the world it was fashionable to read Penelope Leach, and we all learnt a lot from her day-by-day advice for the new parent. When she came to the arrival of your second child she used an image that has stayed with me. She wrote that if you want to understand the emotional impact on the first-born of a new sibling's arrival, you should imagine how you would feel if your lover announced that after several years of devoted love and attachment, she plans to bring another lover into the home. She will love this interloper, whilst reassuring you that she will still love you as she always has. It struck home then, but it came back to me forcibly as I uncovered one particular photo of my brother and me.

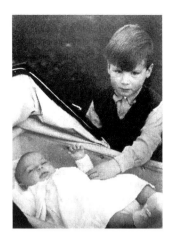

Robin is lying in a pram. He is probably about six months old. I am standing next to the pram with my hand holding his arm in an awkward pose that feels very much as if I had been instructed to do so. He is looking chubby and content. I, aged three, am dressed in a dark sleeveless jumper and Viyella shirt firmly buttoned under my chin. I am looking at the camera and my expression seems to say: 'I know you want me to love my brother but actually he is taking up far too much of your time and I am feeling left out and I don't much like him.' It hardly needs saying that such a projection is loaded with pre-conceptions, but I have a very similar photo taken some thirty years later of my three-year-old daughter gazing at her younger brother in his pram. She has assured me that her feelings were much the same as those I am projecting onto my younger self.

There are numerous studies that confirm that this early alienation is very common and does not necessarily lead to long-term sibling antipathy. As the baby turns into a companion, then the foundations of a fulfilling relationship can be built. But I find this photo hard to look at. It seems to touch a hidden vulnerability. I have some evidence that Robin grew to be my companion in childhood, and that I did indeed find some common fellowship with him. But as I continue through this journey of reconstruction, I am finding it hard to convince myself that I was not carrying that same resentment through much of his life. We shall see.

The next photo to demand my attention and re-kindle the dead embers of reminiscence is taken at Christmas time in 1952. I was five and Robin was three.

We are in the British garrison town of Hildesheim, on the North German plain. We are standing with our nanny, Heidi, and her husband Ulli, who is dressed in a fine Weinachstmankostum.

My father had signed up as a regular officer after his distinguished and action-packed war. I never asked him, but I suspect that was always the plan, rather than a loss of nerve when the alternative was a leap into what must have seemed like an alarming civilian world. In 1951 his regiment was in the front line defending Germany's Eastern border against a new enemy, the Warsaw Pact.

The Visitors' Book tells me that we were living at 19 MozartStraße at the time of that photo. My first clear memories come from that house. It was a large rambling building that had been commandeered from a disgraced Nazi gauleiter. Because of the size of the house my brother and I had separate bedrooms. He was two and half years old and I suspect, like me, would have found comfort in the company of his brother, but it was not to be. I do remember he cried a lot and that the sound of his crying was muffled and thereby all the more distressing. My father had a robust approach to sleep therapy. He once announced without an apparent shred of regret that when my brother cried too much, he would put him in the cellar, so as not to disturb the grown-ups enjoying their duty-free gin and tonics in the drawing room. As with much of their child rearing, looked at from the end of a sixty-year-old telescope, it seems inhumane and deeply damaging, but my mother would be quick to remind me that things were different then: much more Truby King than Penelope Leach.

The harsher memories of my father's sleep therapy are balanced by my own memories of Heidi. Although my mother did not work, Heidi was employed full time to look after us and I have nothing but the fondest memories of her. In fact, I have more early memories of my nanny than I have of my mother. This may be unfair, but it presages the fact that for much of my life both my brother and I were separated from my parents. If not nannies, then boarding school. For these two years though, there was another element of separation: Heidi spoke only German. We learnt German and responded to her in German. I was bilingual but Robin was not. Heidi took over when he was still developing his language, and his first fluent language was German.

I have no idea whether that was a good thing or a bad thing. Many parents crave bilingualism at an early age. But as I looked at the photograph and Robin's look of wary anxiety, I could not help but wonder whether his early separate linguistic identity combined with the draconian sleep strategy could have increased his mental vulnerability once his equilibrium was threatened some twenty years later.

The next photo to catch my eye, as I sifted through the photos now scattered around me on the lawn, was taken three years after that German Christmas. It shows Robin in his swimming trunks, standing on edge of the Gatineau River in the province of Quebec, Canada. It is not a very friendly riverbank and he is standing in the middle of a random pile of logs. This was a logging river and these had escaped from the massive timber rafts that corralled the logs as they floated down to the sawmills in nearby Ottawa. In the foreground I can see his inflatable swimming ring. You can only see a small segment and yet suddenly my memory sparks and I can see it so clearly. It was yellow and green and shaped like a crocodile and was called Swishy. Why should this bizarre but detailed recollection have popped out of the murky depths? It is as if I cannot separate my brother from his buoyancy aid. And maybe that crocodile is the dominant memory and the boy himself is out of focus.

In the photo he is looking out of the frame, he seems wary but then his body looks well formed, firm and tanned. I rummage through the pile to see if I can find a photo of me in my swimming gear. I want to compare our bodies. Already I am convinced that he was a better-looking child than I was, but there is no evidence, merely my assumption. But the absence of a photo to prove a point also seems significant: I was there, perhaps just not too photogenic.

In 1955 my father had been posted to Ottawa as part of the British military mission to the Canadian Government. So in January the four of us set off on The Media, a Cunard liner that combined shifting 7000 tons of cargo with transporting 250 'first class' passengers from Liverpool to New York twice monthly. We were a family embarking on an adventure at a time when crossing the Atlantic usually meant a five-day voyage rather than a seven-hour flight. I remember little of the voyage itself but I have a residual sense of the sheer exhilaration both Robin and I must have felt: the extreme contrast between the unimaginable glamour of the voyage with the grey dreariness of post-war Germany.

But most significantly, the next eighteen months were to be the happiest of my childhood. It was family life as we had barely experienced it before and never did again. My mother and father were present: no nannies, no military manoeuvres, we were intertwined, as a happy family should be. The warmth of this familial proximity has meant that I have more clear memories than at any other time in my childhood. As ever, the details are sketchy but the emotional residue is potent and most of the fragmentary glimpses that I can excavate from that time are uncomplicated, even joyous.

We moved into a rented cottage by the side of Kingsmere Lake. A ramshackle holiday home that had its own jetty, a beaver dam in the woods just behind the house, maintained by some predictably busy beavers. We went to the local school but then it burnt to the ground and so it seemed that the summer was uninterrupted: swimming, boating and enjoying the seemingly constant presence of my mother.

I remember what must have been Robin's birthday party in that first summer cottage. Kool-aid, hotdogs and jelly and my father organising games of hide-and-seek in the woods. These are childhood memories as they should be. Innocent, happy and physically liberated. And yet, as I recall that party, and dimly my own party two months later when we had moved back to winter in the city, I realise now that this was the zenith of my birthday experience. Since my birthday falls in the middle of November and by the following year I was to be at boarding school, I was never to have another birthday party at home. Robin, on the other hand, was born on the 1st of September, in the school holidays, and so wherever we were, his birthday was always celebrated with fun and games. A cause for resentment? I fear it may have played a small part in defining our relationship. As I look back now, I find it very hard to think of the next ten birthdays, where the best I would get were a few cards, a small parcel and, if I was lucky, my name read out in assembly, without some feeling that despite being the older, I had drawn the short straw.

As I start to navigate my eighth decade, I find I am indeed more affected by the absence of childhood birthdays than I ought to be. Until I met my partner I realise that as a young adult I underplayed birthdays, but she came from a family that did the opposite, and so for our own children birthdays have been big on celebration. As I recall my brother's birthday parties I feel a disproportionate sense of grievance in the contrast between my brother's birthday fun and that of my own children, and my own muted celebrations separated from those I loved.

* * * * * *

We spent the winter of 1955-6 living in Ottawa where the snow was cleared away regularly and we could go to the reassuringly brick-built Muchmor Elementary

School just around the corner. We could walk to school on our own and I imagine that I would have tried to hold Robin's hand, but I am almost certain he would have rejected it. I feel that already he was standing up for himself and I was probably a non-essential guardian.

The following May we moved back out to the country, this time to the Gatineau Valley where we took another summer cottage. It was in the woods above the river and it was almost impossible to prevent the racoons from raiding the garbage. I have no idea whether we went to school. If we did I have no memory of it. Once again, I have no one to ask and can only fall back on my hazy recollections distorted through the prism of my incipient jealousy.

I have one powerful memory from those otherwise carefree days on the waterfront. Resonant and unsettling, it was triggered by that photo of Robin standing with Mr Swishy amongst the escaped lumber. I confess I am engaged in an act of transferral. That look of wariness and anxiety belongs to me not to him.

On the next-door lot lived Major Hurd, a military colleague of my father's who had a bigger cottage and a motor boat. He taught us both to water-ski and we thrilled to the speed and spray and sheer exotic adventure of it all. After one of these sessions, still heady from the exhilaration and still in our swimming trunks, my brother grabbed a water pistol and started to chase me. I ran, laughing but still competitive. I was after all the older brother and I needed to prove my superiority. First, I ran in circles around the lawn, then up the stairs and across the wide porch and, rather unfairly, into the sanctity of the Major's house, where my mother was sharing a gin and tonic with him. Robin wasn't going to be able to soak me in the confines of the Major's well-appointed sitting room. To impede his passage and give me some breathing space, I slammed the door as I ran into the house. It was a glass door and as Robin lunged across the porch, he failed to see the door in his path and ran straight through it.

A door like that today would have been made of tempered glass and he would have bounced off. Even if it had shattered, prudent health and safety regulations would cause it to break with little damage to the human form. But this was 1954 and a cottage in the country, and the glass smashed and shattered as his small, bare body burst through it.

I turned at the sound of breaking glass just in time to see my brother's face distort with the shock of impact. His eyes widened and his mouth opened but no sound emerged. Then the blood began to flow from what seemed, at that moment, like a thousand gashes in his firm brown skin. He stood stock still, arms akimbo, frozen in the awful anticipation of what was to come. Frozen that is, apart from his gaping mouth from which emerged a howl of anguish, shock and retribution.

Within seconds my mother was up and rushing to his side. But there she froze too, in a state of panic, of indecision and desperation. She could not hold him, she could not immediately staunch the bleeding; she was helpless. Then the Major arrived with a reassuring first-aid kit. Robin was led to the sofa, a large towel laid out and his cries subsided. Order was restored. There were far fewer wounds than the flow of blood would suggest. My mother too was empowered at last and began the process of swabbing and bandaging. Robin had her full attention and loving devotion, and as I cowered in the corner where my feeble whining apologies were ignored, I was both humiliated and jealous.

There was nothing tragic about that incident. It was shocking but hardly cause for any permanent sense of retribution. Even his scars seemed to heal well enough, with little outward sign to remind us in his later years.

In fact, as I recall, the whole incident faded and was barely ever mentioned. On the other hand, as I dive back into that early moment in our family history and recreate the sights, the sounds and my hapless role in our modest sibling drama, it awakens a new sense of disquiet. It triggers a complex set of after-shocks, many of which seem to reverberate across the years. That photo had unlocked an emotional nexus, which told me something about our relationship. Reconstructing that scene caused me to contemplate how that incident reflected who I was and who I was to became.

First, I connect with the guilt. I had, however unwittingly, done my brother harm and I can recognise that sense of guilt because it pervaded much of what was to follow. Then there was the jealousy, as I was pushed to the margins of this Technicolor drama, diminished by my foolishness. I wanted to be on the receiving end of all that succour.

I cannot recall any attempts by my mother to mitigate my shame and comfort me. Robin was the wounded star and centre of everyone's sympathy and concern. My mother came to his aid in a way that I felt would not be available to me. It was my first clear memory of competing for her affections, and I had lost. Try as I may, I cannot recall any similar moments when I was to be the focus of such intense ministrations. When I fell and gashed my knee, some years later, and required forty stitches and weeks in plaster, I was at boarding school, a thousand miles from her and her sympathy. And finally, I stop to wonder where my father was. He was absent and that in turn resonates with his absence from so much of the important moments in our lives.

This incident was an exception to the totality of those halcyon days. My predominant recollection is of a family at ease with itself and a childhood interlude full of lightness and joy. There was a physical freedom and a warmth that liberated us all from our North European assumptions and expectations. Robin and I had a mother and father on hand. No untoward displays of affection but a quiet certainty that we were loved.

As that summer on the river started to fade, we packed away our modest possessions and headed back to England. The cosy family paradigm was about to be shattered. We arrived back in the first week of September and by the end of the month I was sent off to boarding school. I was still only seven years old.

DISTANCE TO DESTINATION IS 5782 MILES.
ESTIMATED ARRIVAL TIME 11.14.

So now the cabin is really dark. There are flickering screens all around me. One in each seat back. It's crazy but true. Each passenger has their own cinema screen and they can watch films and TV series and even play computer games. Still over 5000 miles to go. I see from the moving map we are passing over Sri Lanka where three days ago there was a horrendous series of bombs that have killed hundreds. I really think some things have changed for the worse since your day. These massacres are all too common. A month ago it was Christchurch. You stopped off in New Zealand on your way to Australia in 1969. This time a right-wing maniac kills fifty-one in a couple of mosques. At my lowest I think you may be well out of it.

We are off to school. And once again you're going to have to put up with my account. I hope you will recognise the place and that my hard-won recollections have at least some resonance with you.

You see, I haven't yet come clean about one of my ulterior motives. I appreciate that suicide usually has a multiplicity of causes and it is almost impossible to pin down any one. And yet, they also say that you can often see some early warning signs. I will try not to make too much of whatever our boarding-school life did to our heads and our hearts, but I hope you would agree that it is a legitimate line of enquiry.

77

5. Major and Minor

If you tell these stories today outside the milieu that used and still uses the boarding schools, it is the mothers that people wonder about first. How could they have done it? How could they part with children so small, give them up to the care of strangers? And then ignore their distress?

Alex Renton, Stiff Upper Lip

I head back to that jumbled photo collection and there is another photo that starts to clear the mist. It is hard to date exactly, but I think it is likely that this is Robin's first day at school. In the photo you see us both dressed in uncompromising grey serge suits with substantial shorts and long woollen socks topped with the school colour: a no-nonsense red. I can see the colour quite clearly although it and all my photos of that time are black and white. We are holding our school caps and someone has helped us tie our ties. They are fit for purpose.

Already I am towering over my brother. I must have been five foot ten. My suit jacket sits uncomfortably on my elongated frame. There are creases in all the wrong places. My knees peer out white and vulnerable, waiting for that encounter with the concrete playground. My shoes seem large and weighty and the shine is dull. It is a picture that makes me wince, in the memory of just how my frequent growth spurts gave me unwanted height, but none of the other signs of maturity. I was uncoordinated and slightly flabby.

Robin on the other hand fits his jacket. He is in proportion. There are few unsightly creases. His body was on the way to developing strength and poise. His shorts seem somehow more appropriate. He seems at ease with himself. He is pleased to be going to school. He knows he will do well. And I know he will probably do better than me.

I am sure that there is an unseemly degree of over-projection, but I feel that the picture encapsulates the differences between us: differences that were going to haunt our relationship, or lack of it, for many years. Robin was to be the person I could never be, or so I thought. He was the golden boy, the apple of my mother's eye. The one she found easier to love.

I have no doubt that the objective reality belies that assumption. He was not a lot happier than I was and, in my own way, I eventually defined a persona for myself that was distinct and free from that debilitating comparison. But at that time and whilst we were at school together, although I was Bethell Major and he was Bethell Minor, that was not how it felt to me.

* * * * * *

In September 1956, just a few weeks after we had arrived back from Canada, we were staying with our grandmother in mid-Wales and I stood at the top of the stairs and looked down on my brand-new tuck box and the school trunk with brass corners and a cabin-lock lid. I feel pretty sure that my heart was not full of cheerful anticipation of the larks to come; rather, I would have been experiencing what I now describe as a 'nameless dread'.

In his book Stiff Upper Lip: Secrets and Crimes and the Schooling of the Ruling Class, Alex Renton explores the relevance of attachment theory to the experience of boarding-school education most particularly in the young. Those engaged in helping the men and women who find themselves suffering from what is now described as 'Boarding-School Survivors' Syndrome' argue that this early separation can be catastrophic:

'They see the abrupt breaking of attachment that happens at the door of the boarding school as unique and provably damaging. A key issue is that the child suffers the catastrophe with the knowledge that their trusted primary carers thought this was good for them... This may be very traumatic. The boarding school door is often the place when a child realises that adults' love has its limits.'

Renton is sympathetic but not wholly convinced that this is always the case or that it necessarily has long-term implications for adult mental health. From my experience the word 'catastrophe' is far too dramatic: for me it was a painful though muted realisation that love has its limits. I accepted that at the age of seven I needed to shift from looking to my parents for love and support and instead focus on securing my own survival.

Renton writes about the process that occurs once the tuck box and trunk are unloaded and an emotionally subdued farewell has been engineered without any embarrassing signs of distress, then:

'The child's energies turn to coping and survival:

*new patterns of behaviour that will shape their future
selves and indeed their lives.'*

Of course, I can be reasonably sanguine about
the longer-term impact of what must have been a
traumatic separation with its congruent acceptance
that I could no longer rely on my mother's day-to-
day love. I cannot deny that it has had an impact on
my emotional transactions from then on. I have no
doubt that my survival skills, whilst they did me proud,
also curtailed my emotional growth. But I survived! I
have made it into my seventies, sustained a primary
relationship through thick and thin, helped bring up
my children who still speak to me and have, to the
best of my ability, been on the receiving end of an
unconditional love.

Whereas Robin did not survive. I will need to
consider the impact of his early separation on his long-
term mental health. But for the time being, in 1956,
he had two more years to enjoy my mother's singular
devotion. What is more, he was then thechosen one.
His big brother was out of the way. He could enjoy
the singular warmth of his mother's love, without
distractions.

It is very important to say, at this point, that our
prep school Tockington Manor was not a bad school;
indeed, it would sit at the more benevolent end of the
spectrum of prep schools in the fifties. Alex Renton was
motivated to embark on his, essentially even-handed,

review of the British boarding-school experience by his time at Ashdown School, probably the most notorious of prep schools, with an unequivocally evil headmaster who enacted and condoned sadism and sexual exploitation of the worst kind. And there were other schools that were just as bad. But Tockington was not like that, which is why, inasmuch as I have salvaged any memories at all, they are largely benign. Not unproblematic when seen through the prism of a life devoted to the stable home-based family and the state-education system, but lacking in any obvious trauma.

Although I know that the headmaster, Gordon Tovey, did beat the boys in his care, I do not recall having received a beating from him. I was inclined to give him the benefit of the doubt. Much later in this quest, however, I met Jim Singleton, who, bizarrely, had tracked Robin from prep school to public school and on to the University of Western Australia. He had a very different view of the headmaster at the time Robin was there.

'If we were seen as "not trying hard enough", we had to carry around a card onto which for each lesson teachers had to record our behaviour with a tick or a cross. I found it all very difficult and regularly received too many crosses. At the end of each week, he would beat me. It happened again and again. I must have been eight or nine. I was devastated, but could not tell my parents, although when the family doctor questioned me, all I could do was to howl "It's not fair".

Of course, I was a conformist and emerged remarkably unscathed. Physically that is. My one major indiscretion was when I was caught stealing other boys' tuck from matron's store room, for which the head did not beat me, but stopped me taking part in the swimming gala where I was destined to excel. I think in retrospect I might have preferred the beating.

In trying to trace Robin's education, I knew that I really only have my own experience of the schools we both went to as a guide. I like to think I was supportive, but I know that the caste system in a boarding school was driven by age-derived status. You kept to your own and, I fear, it was considered to be 'soft' to be seen to care too much for your younger siblings. As a result, I have precious little to go on when it comes to Robin. Like the recollections of our childhood, the story is turning out to be my story not his. That is disappointing and yet there are clues to be found and I want to believe that as I connect with my past, whilst at school at least, our paths and our emotional development will have had enough telling similarities to make it worth the journey. So I needed to chase down those prep-school years and there was only one way to do it. Like all cold-case investigators, I needed to visit the scene of the crime.

* * * * * *

I had not been anywhere near Tockington Manor since the day I said goodbye in July 1961. Some fifty-seven years later I was parking my car outside the main door. My satnav informed me, 'You have reached your destination.' That was a little premature, because I had no idea what the destination of my temporal journey was likely to be. I knew the place would still harbour some ghosts, I was less sure as to whether they might haunt me.

Before reaching the front door, I recognised the open courtyard that had served as our playground. Then I looked down and the first vivid flashback hit me. The surface was old rough concrete that was as uninviting to the human body as it had been some sixty years earlier where, on that very spot, I had I tripped and fallen and lacerated my knee. I had been chasing another boy who no doubt was well balanced and light on his feet. I was the opposite: tall and uncoordinated. I was frequently losing my balance, bumping into people and things. That same concrete ripped a gash which, when I finally got to A&E, required forty stiches and put my leg in plaster for weeks. As I stood on the same spot sixty years on, almost expecting to see remnants of my blood (there had been a lot of blood), I thought back to the incident in Canada when Robin had been the chaser and it was his blood that had flowed. I could not stop myself from recalling the absence of my mother's care just when I needed it.

I mentioned the incident to the headmaster as I shook his hand and commented on the state of the concrete today.

'Funny you should say that, only yesterday we put out a tender to get the yard tarmacked.'

'And about time too' I said, but not out loud.

'I imagine you would like to have a look round. Bring back memories and all that?'

'Yes, please.'

First stop on the tour was the library, now well stocked with carefully labelled age-appropriate texts, all at child level. I seemed to remember having to climb up a rickety set of Victorian library steps. Apparently, it had been removed some time ago, clearly a health and safety nightmare. Once up the ladder you could access shelves full of dusty desiccated volumes; I certainly remember rows of G.A. Henty's 19th-century blood-and-thunder accounts of colonial derring-do, with their guileless racist representation of the indigenous populations of the Empire. Perhaps there was a set of Biggles, more derring-do, this time in Spitfires and with a fiercely Eurosceptic view of the German nation. I think that Enid Blyton, my favourite at the time, would have been considered too frivolous.

I noticed where my locker would have been and suddenly had a vivid memory of the one act of violence I fell victim to. I had managed to annoy a boy called Lambert (surnames only), who was known to have a short fuse, but still took me completely by surprise when he lashed out with his fist and hit me on the jaw. It was the sort of blow that I had only ever seen cowboys deliver on television. It was not so much the pain I remember but the shock and outrage at anyone breaking the fourth wall in that way.

Then on to the dining room, which was just as I remembered. Smaller of course, everything is always smaller after that long a time lapse, but the ornate wooden caryatids holding up the fireplace and the high Georgian windows looking onto the garden took me straight back to the meagre meals that failed to fill my rapidly growing body (I was a lot taller than my age group from the moment I got there). I looked across to what I suddenly remembered was the 'Babies' Table' where the formidable Mrs Bull kept tight control over the new boys. At first it rang no bells, but then suddenly I was overcome by a powerful reprise, confirming my thesis that it is the moments of high emotion that trigger the sharpest recollections.

It was the day of my eighth birthday, the first away from home and just a few weeks into that first term. We would receive our letters at the breakfast table. I had a modest pile of generally anodyne cards: one from my godfather contained a five-pound postal order. My mother's was a jolly card with an upbeat inscription peppered with slightly frantic exclamation marks. I coped with all those. I was amongst my peers, who were suitably impressed with the postal order. But then I opened the letter from my father. He had taken the time to write several pages in his tiny military handwriting that was hard to read, and so as I scanned the pages it was no threat to the equilibrium. But what did for me was a series of tiny sketches of us on skis, and riding in a horse and sleigh, all describing our long-lost pleasures in Canada. That was too much and I could not contain my tears. I sobbed and sobbed. This was my father who had always kept his distance now suddenly reaching me, as he never had before. I knew I had been separated from my mother's love but this made it clear that I would also feel the pain of being isolated from a father as well.

Then we went up the broad central staircase, which required a flourish of defiance to overcome my instinct that knew its use was forbidden to us children. I had asked to see the dormitories. I knew exactly where I was going. The dormitories were all named after birds and the new boys were to be found in Snipe. To my astonishment the sign with its wooden painted bird was still there, and I knew exactly which bed had been mine.

The only clear memory I can dredge up is of lying in my bed on that first night after matron had turned off the light and feeling the inexorable build-up of a primal wail. Wanting to howl but knowing that it had to be contained like a sneeze in the theatre. And then, to my surprise, finding some solace in the muffled sobs that were coming from the beds all around me. That was a rite of passage indeed: discovering that my comfort would rest with the confederacy of fellow sufferers. I certainly wept that night and for many more nights. I learnt how to do so without disturbing the others. I was quickly inducted into the common pact that showing your grief was very poor form even in the suppressed solitary moments before falling asleep. I wanted to ask Robin whether he could remember his first few days in Snipe. Was he able to make sense of this wholly unfamiliar environment with its mysterious expectations and rituals? Surely he must have felt the same sense of abandonment. I am still uncertain as to how that experience impacted my long-term emotional health. As for Robin, I can only speculate.

Further down the corridor I came across Falcon: a dormitory that elicited another highly charged recollection. I was ambushed by its clarity and then suffused by its emotional wake. As I stood staring at the space that had been occupied by the prefect's bed I re-lived an incident that does not haunt me anything like as much as the contemporary orthodoxy might predict. I was ten years old and my dormitory prefect was an awe-inspiring thirteen years old. He was a gentle soul whose body was definitely post-pubescent. Once the lights were out and matron had repaired to her sitting room at the other end of the corridor, he would, in a totally non-threatening manner, invite us younger boys into his bed to feel his extraordinarily enlarged and erect penis. I have absolutely no sense of coercion and am certain that it was just an appreciative feel rather than anything more vigorous. I remember experiencing nothing more upsetting than a wild sense of awe that he was in possession of such an inexplicably firm and extensive appendage.

I have no memory of any other homoerotic incidents during my time there. It may have been going on and I was just excluded from the action. I certainly had no conception of myself as a sexual being, which might have protected me. Looking back at my experience from the perspective of the current climate, where historic abuse has been rightly exposed and its damage acknowledged, it might appear that I was just blind to the implications, but I take a more benevolent view. I think mine was a school where the prevailing atmosphere was not overly exploitative. I think I was lucky. I know that others were not and I am not arguing for complacency, merely for a recognition that not all sexually charged encounters between young boys lead to long-term damage. I do of course wonder whether Robin had any similar experiences and whether he would agree with my benign assumptions.

As is so often the way, however, the common survival code that kept us all in thrall to the boarding-school regime worked for me. I have worryingly few clear memories of my first years at Tockington, largely I suspect because I was at heart a conformist who quickly learnt the survival codes and fitted in. I went along with the predominate culture and met most of the expectations. I was still pre-pubescent, with an impossibly uncoordinated body that seemed to be growing by about two inches a year. And yet I got into the school football team as a goalie and used my size to appear effective at rugby. It was conformism rather than natural talent: I had learnt how to play the game and it stood me in good stead for the rest of my education and, I suppose, my life.

Meanwhile Robin was being educated in a very different environment. My father was by now stationed in Münster in Germany and Robin attended the British Army day school in Portsmouth Barracks there, where my father's regiment was based. According to my mother, he was very unsettled, wetting the bed and generally giving her cause for concern. I have very little evidence for just how good or bad his school was and whether the bed-wetting was the result of the poor quality of care in the school or a very early manifestation of some mental disturbance. What I do know is that our mother did not feel she had any way to alleviate his apparent distress.

My mother was definitely a woman of her time. She told me that she was convinced that Robin would be better off at boarding school. She was sure that a stable environment would ease his symptoms. However, in trying to seek out reasons for his subsequent illness and death, I know that she did agonise in retrospect over that decision. Army parents from the officer class were faced with that dilemma: it was either the substandard education offered by the Army Education Service or a boarding school back in England. The expectations and institutional rituals of the time offered reassurance that separation was the best course of action. The Ministry of Defence made a handsome contribution to private-school fees through the Continuity of Education Allowance, and also subsidised flights for boarders to join their parents during the holidays. I can imagine how, in that context, when finding that my son was showing signs of disturbance and unhappiness, I might well consider the certainties of boarding school as a reasonable solution. Unhappy children make desperate parents and I now accept that my mother was desperate.

So Robin was also equipped with a tuck box and a trunk, and set off to boarding school with carefully labelled vests and pants and, it has to be said, an elder brother who should have been there to help him take the plunge. But, now, as I try to recover any memories of how helpful I was, I am once again faced with a gaping empty hole. As I look back at the photo of the two of us, I like to think I was on hand to provide some reassurance, but Robin would have been all alone in his bed in Snipe and stifling his own tears.

Jim Singleton did recall Robin. He had a positive memory. He described him as 'buoyant'. He was struck by his body language which was assured. He remembers that Robin had an intense focus on whatever he was doing.

'Did you see any signs of distress or instability?'

'None. He seemed a lot more comfortable in himself than I ever felt. I was really miserable for most of my time there. But Robin seemed to thrive. He was an amazing swimmer.'

'That would have been our time in Canada. I think he swam across a 600- metre river at the age of five.'

I have little else to go on. I am assuming that he developed those survival instincts, and his mind and body suited the environment. If he was distressed and wetting the bed in Germany, it looks like my mother's prep-school experiment had worked. There seems to be little here to inform a narrative of incipient mental vulnerability. And yet like me he had been cut off from his mother's love. He must have felt that dislocation and underlying resentment. He was a survivor. We both were.

* * * * * *

I had cause to reassess my assumptions about our relative qualities when I returned to the headmaster's study for tea after the tour. He got out the compendium volumes of the school magazine. The Tockingtonian was a dry affair compared to the glossy multi-coloured overly designed contemporary annual record intended to reassure parents they were getting their money's worth. We turned to Robin's valedictory account:

'R.A. Bethell 1958-63 Head Monitor from Sept '63, 1st XI Soccer '61, 1st XV colours '62-'63, 1st XI Cricket. Swimming X 61-63 (Cup '62, First Class), Boxing weight '63. Set IIa. To Sherborne'

Then in the April 1963 magazine there is a review of the school play: Treasure Island. *'Long John Silver (Robin Bethell) led – and at times controlled – his infamous shipmates with cheerful vigour.'* And I now have the photo to prove that he did indeed lead in that first foray onto the stage. There seemed enough here to confirm my recollection that he was the successful one and I was the laggard. However, we tracked down the brief, bald account of my own career on leaving the school some two years earlier. I was shaken to find that far from being the under-developed, awkward underachiever of my imagination, I had done rather well at prep school. I may have been in Set II, when all the scholarship boys were in Set I, but I had been a swimming champion (I thought I had been banned from the gala) and won the Coogan Cup, which I was assured was awarded to *'The Best All Round Boy of the Year.'* And I too was in the school play: Toad of Toad Hall.

'Andrew Bethell played the leading role with tremendous enthusiasm. The splendid moment with his imaginary car was unforgettable. Only a prep school boy could have been so realistic.'

I found a photograph of me driving the imaginary car and I was certainly putting that tremendous enthusiasm to work.

Evaluating my time at prep school and a success that belied my disjointed and competitive memory of myself as the 'minor' character has taught me to be wary of my developed sense of inferiority. But I know that I felt diminished when I consider my brother's qualities and the esteem in which he was held by my parents. Nevertheless, I need to be wary of overplaying the sympathy hand. I held my own at prep school and continued to do so as I preceded my brother through education and into real life. As I left Tockington Manor and headed for Sherborne, I was bemused by what would become a theme of this journey of re-discovery: a strong propensity to undervalue myself and over-state the attributes of my brother. I am wondering how much of this is a true reflection of our respective personalities, or whether I am, rather late in the day, finding the source of my own underlying sense of inferiority. Those who know me would say that my every action, throughout the rest of my life, speaks of an almost unseemly over-confidence in my own abilities. But then I have always been good at disguising the near-permanent sub-strata of doubt beneath my own capabilities. It needed a trip round my old school to bring that awareness into clearer focus. It was not to be the only time that my evaluation and investigation of my brother would reveal a deeper understanding of myself.

Dear Robin,

We have reached the Indian Ocean. I have my headphones on, playing a bit of Springsteen, as the baby has woken and is not happy. Tried some Bach, but you need the heavy beat to drown out the wailing. Not sure whether you'd be up for a bit of 'Dad Rock'. I'd like to think you would. Bruce was hitting his stride when you left.

So now we are off to public school. Sherborne, as you will remember from the school song, was founded by Edward the Sixth: 'Vivat Rex Edwardus Sextus'. Again, I am lost for any decent memories of you and I there, together. I do have a trace of your voice in a few letters you wrote me after I had left, giving me the gossip. It is clear that we had a common frame of reference, so I don't feel too bad to be extrapolating your experience from mine. When you got back from Perth, you told me that you were keen to send your own children to Sherborne. I was baffled then. Could you have had such a different experience? It makes me worry that you might reject my outrage at some of what we went through. It was only when I started to piece together the fragmented recollections that I realised quite how barbaric the place was in those days. 'Didn't do me any harm' does not cut it with me. I think, in retrospect, you might have come to the same conclusion. However, the truth is that your two boys, Oliver and Alun, did eventually go to Sherborne, but by then it was a very different place and they lived nearby with regular visits back to their mother. They did well and have none of my antipathy to the place.

So, once again, you'll need to accept that this is another very partial account with a heavy bias towards my own hang-ups. Really, your role in the story only comes into focus when I contacted your best friend 'Charley' Brown. He brings your school days to life, in a way I never could. And yet, it is not all plain sailing. There are a few elusive hints of trouble to come but I will try not to make too much of them at this stage.

6. Muscular Christianity

...that morning cold bath, which foreigners consider as young England's strangest superstitions. With a clean skin in healthy action and nerves and muscles braced by a sudden shock, men do not crave for artificial stimulants.

Charles Kingsley, Great Cities, 1857

The ethos of our public-school experience in the 1960s can be summed up by the fact that there were no doors on the toilets. It reflected a surveillance culture that assumed personal privacy was a threat to the higher goal of moulding you into a compliant member of the entitled class. It allowed older prefects to catch sight of you with your trousers down and thereby diminish you. It eliminated the only potentially private space available to you. You may have wanted merely to cry in private but you were denied that option because a greater power needed to guard against the spiritual and physical jeopardy of masturbation.

In trying to understand and appreciate Robin's experience of public school, like so much else, I have only my own experience to guide me. Robin joined three years after my own initiation into the oppressive regimen of Lyon House, one of the six boarding houses that accommodated the pupils of Sherborne School in Dorset. I cannot have offered him much support; the system kept us apart. I might have caught sight of him from time to time, but you were not encouraged to engage with your younger siblings. It would be perceived as 'soft'. The system perpetuated itself. What I went through would have been exactly what happened to Robin three years later. They only put doors on the toilets some six years after he left.

When you arrived at Lyon House as a new boy aged thirteen, there was a lot to learn and one of the most immediately bracing lessons was a Spartan ritual known as 'Up-in-Seven'. As a new boy you had to learn the early morning ritual and learn it fast. On hearing the bell at seven a.m. you had to immediately get out of bed and run to the communal bathroom where a helpful prefect had run an ice-cold bath. Along with your fellow 'new bugs' you had to take off your pyjamas and wait in the queue, naked and vulnerable, until it was your turn to lower yourself into the freezing water.

'Shoulders under!' shouts the fox-faced prefect who lounges in a warm bath in the corner with a clipboard to record the daily humiliation and identify any shirkers.

You did not linger in the bath, especially in the winter. Once out of the bath, there was no time to dry yourself, you merely wrapped the towel to cover what little modesty you had left and ran back to the dormitory. The clock was ticking. Back by your bed and locker you needed to get dressed in double quick time. No easy feat at the outset, because we had to wear shirts which stuck to the wet body and had detachable collars held on with impossibly fiddly collar studs.

Once dressed, and with bed made, you grabbed your shoes and ran to check in with that vulpine-faced prefect with clipboard and stopwatch who would confirm whether or not you had completed the task in under seven minutes. If you failed or your tie was not properly tied or the bed not properly made, then you were sentenced to 'Up-in-Three': the following day the entire process had to be achieved in under three minutes. If you failed that challenge, then you were likely to get beaten in the dormitory by a prefect with a slipper, which wasn't really a slipper, more a hard-soled house-shoe.

If Tockington Manor School was at the more benign end of the boarding- school spectrum, Sherborne School in the 1960s was located at the other extreme. It was a school that had prided itself in toughening up the sons of the upper-middle class (the upper class would go to Eton or Harrow) to prepare them for careers in the armed forces or the colonial service. As the Empire disappeared, the colonial service was less of an option, but the methodology lived on. It was considered the ideal preparation for serving your country on the rubber plantations of Poona or coffee estates of Tanganyika. The regime was deemed appropriate for both Robin and me in the 1960s: more than a hundred years after it had been developed and when the Empire was rapidly disintegrating.

I arrived at Lyon House in September 1961. It was the same school, if not the same house, that my father and his brother had attended in the late 1930s. It was the accepted way: the privations of the fathers should be visited on the sons. Although there may have been a little less overt cruelty and inhumanity, the systems and structures that would have engendered fear and distress in my father and his brother were still alive and flourishing. Our housemaster was a man who, whilst purporting to be a benevolent guardian with our best interests at heart, actually condoned and facilitated the barbaric customs and traditions that were supposed to transform you into 'a man'. There was little regard to the long-term consequences.

As with prep school, it was survival that trumped all. There was simply no space to protest, and the assumptions were so deeply rooted in the system that cooperation was guaranteed. In your first few years it would never occur to question or challenge these rituals. There was an inevitable camaraderie, for we were all in this together. But it was also fiercely hierarchical, and the hierarchy was one to which you aspired. The power dynamics that went with it were self-perpetuating and you willingly signed up.

It is true that I wasn't bullied, and strangely I was not aware of much physical bullying around me. But bullying was superfluous because the system itself exerted its own dominance and humiliation: whether it was the panicky early- morning race against time, the dormitory slippering by boys who were only a few years older than you, or the enforced athleticism that had no respect for the fragility of adolescent development. All of this kept you cowed: you didn't need the school bully to beat you up behind the bike-sheds; the institution did a far better job.

The prevailing ethos was 'every man for himself'. It was part of the survival strategy that you dared not become too dependent on anyone else. There really should have been more bonding in adversity, and yet when I look back at those early days I can think of no one particular friend. We tolerated each other without becoming close. We were terrified of revealing our own frailties and misery, and so studiously avoided identifying it in others. It was, for much of the time, a cheerful fellowship. We were not, on the whole, corrupted into barbarity by the barbaric system we inhabited. We developed a wary acceptance of each other's foibles, knowing that we were all as vulnerable as each other. But it was a shallow bond and did not teach us very much about the qualities or potential of genuine friendship.

In retrospect I can see that those first few years at Lyon House must have had a longer-term impact on my emotional development. I was a survivor and a conformist and that stood me in good stead. But it meant that I buried my anxieties and smothered my discomfort. It taught me to adapt and survive, but it failed to give me the emotional tools to reconcile the surface compliance with the emotional frailty beneath. I can only assume that the same was true for Robin. But as with so much else, I really have no clue as to how Robin felt about his time at Lyon House. I do have letters that suggest he had fully assimilated. One written in his final year has a jocular tone:

'Well life here has been running along the same tracks that it has been for the last 987 years[3], nothing unusual for the odd bloke beating it from the place and holing up in his granddad's garden shed 'cos he got stage fright! Also assorted cases of homosexuality that spice the life here.'

I am disturbed by the way he makes light of a boy who is clearly so unhappy as to run away and then get 'stage fright', and suggests that life would be 'spiced up'

---

3   *The original school was founded in 705 AD by St Anselm.

by the discovery of homosexual behaviour. This seems to suggest a boy who has been well conditioned to deflect the harsher side of life with further breezy chat about seven-a-side rugby and the teacher who 'in a cheerfully optimistic fashion predicted a comfortable fail in French'.

The tone of that letter, and indeed my own experience of a very similar assimilation, seems to accord with another observation from Alex Renton:

'Whilst appearing to conform to the system, a form of unconscious splitting is acquired as a means of keeping the true self hidden. Nick Duffell has identified this as "the strategic survival personality".'

We were both fine examples of that personality type. It took me forty years to begin to understand how the 'unconscious splitting' had far-reaching implications for my emotional health. Prior to that I was rather proud of my ability to split the pleasant from the unpleasant. I considered it a valuable attribute. I now know different and see it as a detrimental legacy (amongst many) of my boarding-school upbringing. But I have had a lifetime to work it through. Robin had just twelve years.

* * * * * *

As I discovered online, Sherborne School has its own archive and even its own archivist. I contacted

Rachel Hassell on the off-chance that there might be something in the archive that could help me to locate Robin and his time at the school. I was surprised to receive a warm response and the offer of help to provide any information she could find. I was not overly keen to return to Sherborne. In contrast to my feelings about our prep school, I felt little nostalgic attraction for the place, and had resolutely resisted any attempts to inveigle me into participation in the Old Shirburnian Society. I felt that those who made regular visits back to their old school were unlikely to be the sort of Shirburnian that I would want to encounter. Overt nostalgia for the old school has always struck me as a mark of failure to grow up.

But Rachel was clearly going out of her way, and so on a sunny April morning I found myself walking across the expansive quadrangle, known as the Courts, with my hi-tech visitor's badge on a brightly coloured lanyard round my neck. I had not come here to be seduced into a rosy nostalgia for the old days, but I had some time to kill before my appointment, and I found myself, against my better instincts, taking the worn sandstone steps up to the school chapel. It felt very, very familiar, which was not surprising. We attended chapel every day of the week, twenty minutes daily with an hour on Sundays. In my five years at Sherborne I must have climbed those steps over five thousand times.

I had spent a lot of time in that chapel and it was exactly as it had always been. I was taken aback by how the place got to me. I associated it with boredom and tedious Anglican low-church ritual. There was no reason to feel anything but relief that I had survived with my atheism intact. And yet, as I stood there I could not subdue the pangs of regret for a long-lost innocence. There were three numbers on the hymn board and I found myself checking which hymns they were because I did enjoy bawling out the well-worn favourites and still do. They had three stonkers that morning: 'Guide Me O Thou Great Redeemer', 'Love Divine, All Loves Excelling' and 'Now Thank We All Our God'.

As I set off back down stairs to the cloisters and headed across the Courts to the Archive, I recalled the phrase 'Muscular Christianity' and realised that my association with the chapel chimed with that concept of a Christianity that moulded young men through:

'a belief in patriotic duty, manliness, the moral and physical beauty of athleticism, teamwork, discipline, self-sacrifice, and "the expulsion of all that is effeminate, un-English, and excessively intellectual."'... a Victorian philosophy which permeated every aspect of life at Sherborne in the sixties.

I had very low expectations of my visit to the archive; I feared there would be some dry records and perhaps some entries in old editions of the school magazine. I also assumed that Rachel would be a proud advocate of the school and its ethos with little sympathy for my sceptical attitude. I imagined I'd be back on the road in half an hour or so.

The archive was housed in an old cloistered classroom tucked into the boundary wall beneath the imposing west wing of Sherborne Abbey. Once inside I was distracted by a life-sized cut-out of Benedict Cumberbatch leaning against an imposing shelf of leather-bound volumes that took up the back wall. He was in the role of Alan Turing, who was currently the most famous Shirburnian. I had cause to remember that, for far too long, the school had denied Turing's very existence, and accepted the shameful national repudiation of his remarkable contribution to the war effort and computer science. I was also a little puzzled that the school should be celebrating The Imitation Game in which Turing, whilst a boy at Sherborne, is seen badly bullied and buried under the floorboards. I can remember watching the film ashamed of my old school.

Rachel, it turned out, was not only a fine archivist but also in tune with my unease about the public-school education that Robin and I had received. She was no proselytiser for the boarding-school ethos and she was wholly sympathetic to my distaste for the privations to which we were subjected.

She directed me to a table where she had laid out the fruits of her research. Far from dry and sketchy, it was rich and revealing. She had found our school records, and the Lyon House Yearbooks, which detailed the termly activities that added depth and context to my fragmented recollections. To my intense surprise I was quickly putting names to faces and recalling obscure rituals and obsessions. The hierarchies of arcane responsibilities were laid out in painful detail: J. Heald i/c Chinwaggers, Paulson-Ellis i/c Bike Shed and Aggers. I am afraid to say that the arcane jargon made perfect sense. With the right catalyst, it seems the memory can be prompted into vivid recall.

And what of Robin? Rachel handed me a fat envelope: Sherborne: a Photographic Essay by Robin Bethell. Inside, a collection of mounted photographs of the life we led: clever witty pictures of the dormitories, the tuck shop and even a saucy sequence showing boys leaning out of the top- floor windows to ogle the Housemaster's daughter sun-bathing in a bikini in the gardens below. It was both technically competent and lightly subversive. It matched my image of him as the creative rebel who would later be pushing the boundaries in other ways.

There were photos of him in the house play, and one of him larking about posing as a member of a faux 19th-century darts team in waistcoats and boaters. All good fun. Then a photo that gave me a disconcerting jolt: an extraordinary action shot of him winning the senior pole vault.

He is caught at the exact moment of clearing the bar. He is strong, balanced and in complete control of his body. The picture seems to encapsulate everything I felt then and still feel now about the extreme physical contrast between the two of us. I know that I was never able to pull up my own weight, leave alone lever myself up on a pole and fly through the air. I lacked coordination and stood a gawky six feet seven inches tall. I was firmly anchored to the ground and banging my head on doors, whereas Robin could soar through the air and fill out a T-shirt with well-defined musculature. I am not proud of the realisation, but if I am to fully understand the dynamics of our relationship, I need to acknowledge that I was deeply envious of his physical prowess. It should not matter, but of course it did and it does. That photo added a little extra salt to the wound.

Next up were our respective school records. Clearly retained to provide raw material for the writing of subsequent references, they were mostly dry shorthand lists of our achievements. There were copies of our Housemaster's termly reports as they were sent out to parents, mostly bland generalisations about needing to try harder and be less careless. He comments on my wayward physicality: 'Once again he has been dogged by ill-health, but I am glad his strength is beginning to catch up with his stature.' The records also included brief more private notes: an aide memoire to what the Housemaster actually thought of you. Mine read: Honest, pleasant, tremendous trier, Gauche. I could not argue with that assessment. I was fairly honest, perfectly pleasant, I had to try very hard to keep up and I was certainly gauche.

I was about to move on to Robin's record, when Rachel stopped me.

'I should warn you, I was pretty shocked by what I found in Robin's report. You need to be wary of his Housemaster's notes.'

Forewarned, I started though the sheaf of papers. First his public reports: mostly predictable and bland, although there was more than a hint of negativity in his final report: *'Sorry to see him go before his time, the school could still have done something more for him character-wise.'* But then I turned to the private notes and saw what the Housemaster really thought: *'Able. Selfish. Left early. Spoilt by father.'* This was not what I expected to find when I blithely asked to see what the archive held.

This man really did not like my brother and I think I know why. He was someone who thought he understood the 'young chaps' in his charge, but his assumptions were lazy and predictable. If, like me, you towed the line and fulfilled his narrow definition of the male adolescent, he could be generous and supportive; but if you strayed from that narrow path and you challenged his belief system, he would be churlish and, as we see in that brief note, vindictive.

Robin managed to stick to the script in his first few years. In December '65 the Housemaster wrote: *'A sincere adult personality is beginning to appear and I did not expect to see it so soon.'* But in Dec '67 he has changed his tone: 'He knows that I am critical of him in some ways and I know too that he will find it difficult to support me.' Robin had gone off script. He was not playing the game of aspiring to climb up the house ladder to take responsibility for disciplining his juniors and sustaining the structures of control. Instead of throwing himself into team sports he was opting for individual ones: cross-country running, athletics and golf. He was a member of the school golf team for all four years he was at the school, which surprises me because I do not think he was a particularly good golfer.

On the other hand it was the perfect way to escape the oppressive 'jock-strap' team sports that defined what the Housemaster considered to be character-forming. It was a sport that celebrated individual guile not team spirit, but I also think Robin realised that you could enjoy a few illicit beers at the nineteenth hole.

I turned to Rachel and explained that this unpleasant codicil to Robin's Sherborne record confirmed my belief that I was the conformist, the one who had fully adopted the survival strategy and so was adjudged to have 'stood out by virtue of his enthusiasm and integrity'. Whereas Robin had learnt all the essential survival strategies, but had managed to retain his individual spirit, and so was seen, by our Housemaster at least, to be a little lacking 'character-wise'. I took the opposite view: he had asserted himself and emerged stronger and certainly more attractive.

'But of course,' replied Rachel. 'That's what always happens: the first-born plays safe which allows the second son to sparkle and surprise.'

I have to admit I did not expect the archivist to provide the defining analysis of our sibling relationship, but she had nailed it. That is exactly what had happened. I would eventually find a way to release myself from the clutches of conformity, but whilst at school I willingly succumbed to the dominant orthodoxy. Robin had found a way to survive without surrendering his independence and with the confidence to fly high and free. Of course he left early; he knew what was good for him. Whereas I had dutifully completed my full sentence.

When it came to the assertion that my father spoilt Robin, my first reaction was to reject it out of hand. How could my father possibly have spoiled either of us? He was hardly ever there and seemed to know very little about what we were doing. He would praise and offer support, but from a distance, and would only engage with us on his terms. This was not neglect; just the way it was done. We connected with our father via the activities and interests that he promoted: fishing, shooting and golf. Both Robin and I were happy to learn from him because that made him happy. We fished, we shot live birds and were pleased for him to take us to the golf course. But these were not our hobbies, they were his and as time went on we rejected them all.

That was my initial reaction, but then that green-eyed sibling rivalry began to niggle at my assumptions. I realised that for the last two years of his time at school I was away in Canada and I didn't really know very much about Robin's life. At that time my parents were living less than an hour away from the school in a commodious vicarage, owned by the army, my father's employer. It seemed that when not at school Robin was the beneficiary of a settled family life and a proximity that had I been denied. During the school holidays, Robin had the run of the house and direct access to my mother and father. I was the one who had maintained the physical distance from my family. He writes about buying and overhauling old motorbikes, going scrambling and trips to the local pub. There are parties and adventures with local girls. For me, school holidays had none of that allure. They were fragmented and often spent in remote army bases. Could it be that he got a better deal between the age of 16 and 18 than I had had? The Housemaster accuses him of *'leaving early.'* Could he have been close enough to our parents to have asserted his independence and persuaded them that he needed to leave before his time, in a way that I had found impossible? I hate the word 'spoilt' when applied to children; it stinks of superior moral judgement. However, it did, I regret to say, cause me to feed a lingering resentment at the way my parents may well have promoted his happiness whilst I was off the scene.

I was determined that the Housemaster's nasty little note was not going to sour the impression I was building of an enviable individuality. There was enough in the archive to feed my jaundiced view that Robin was better than me, but I was aware that I had failed to capture what he was really like at school. I needed the testimony of his friends. I was not certain, but one of the boys posing with him in the spoof darts team photo did seem very familiar. The caption told me it was Martyn Brown, and that triggered a line from one of Robin's letters about 'Charley' Brown in which he describes how they had consumed 30 pints in three days while on a cadet corps camp. I asked Rachel if she had contact details and before very long I was in touch with him. Charley was his nickname, but he was very pleased to hear from me:

'I think of Robin as my best friend at Sherborne and I was shocked and saddened by the news of his suicide… I will be very happy to send you my memories of him.'

Two days later I received a well-crafted account of their time together at Sherborne. The last three paragraphs offered me an inspired encapsulation of what my brother was like and why I both admired him and envied him.

'We were mildly rebellious as a group, covertly challenging some of the petty rules and regulations – often in those days to do with hair length, growing sideburns, and the width and length of our trouser legs. We started to mock the so-called privileges of prefects, for example being allowed to unbutton suit jackets (!), and wear coloured waistcoats, traditions that appeared increasingly anachronistic and rather pathetic. We found a friendly landlord in The Travellers Rest (a nearby pub) and ventured furtively to the backroom where he would serve us pints of bitter. We smoked Woodbines behind hedges. Meanwhile we started to notice that the wider world was changing, this was 1967/8; we blasted Jimmy Hendrix on our record players.

I remember Robin as a great friend; he was cool, but not one of a clique; he was single minded and determined; it seemed to me that he knew who he was and where he wanted to go. I admired his strength and determination.

We left school horribly and dangerously innocent of the world – girls were from another planet, sex was a prize to be bragged about; drugs (other than tobacco and alcohol) were largely unknown. We were unprepared for the new found freedoms of life beyond school in 1969.'

That was the Robin I too would have liked as my best friend.

Dear Robin,

It is starting to get light. I have tried and failed to get some sleep. Despite the legroom, I do not sit easily in an economy seat with its hard edges. I cannot bear the embarrassment of leaning my seat back into the person behind. So I sit upright. Squirming into ever more contorted versions of discomfort. I look at the moving map. We are right in the middle of the Indian Ocean. Nothing but sea in every direction. The map says we are passing over the Chagos Trench which is one of the deepest in the world and where they think the Malaysian Airlines Flight MA370 ended up after vanishing out of the sky. Not too reassuring.

You will be relieved to hear that, at last, the story reaches Western Australia. It has taken a while to get there, but it will be worth it, I promise. This is the hot stuff. This is where you take off. And best of all, I have letters. We are going to hear your voice. Your version of events. Admittedly these are nearly all letters to our parents and so only partly authentic, but still your vibrancy and love of life leaps off the page, as does your beautiful handwriting.

I have a confession to make. Those letters, all fifty of them, were gathered and protected by our mother.

They were a touchstone for her. A link to her absent son. She so wanted me to share her appreciation, but I refused. I had nothing to do with them. Not until she died, and by then she had given up on me and handed them over to your younger son, Alun.

You will want to know why. Well first, I was a coward. I knew that if I succumbed and read those letters she would want to talk about them. Talk to me about you, and I was terrified of her unremitting grief. I could not collude in her desperate need to remember. Second, I was bloody angry. You had managed to take over the moral high ground. You had become the lodestone for our family's emotional life. There is nothing like a suicide to grab the attention. I did not want to know what a great time you had in Australia. The fact that our mother was so desperate to bring me into her web of remembrance was a double irritant.

The only mitigating factor I can offer you is that once she had gone, I devoured those letters. God, you had an amazing four years. And it was the letters that set me off on my cold-case investigation. Names, dates, places, and a rich brew of anecdote and incident. They were the catalyst for this crazy venture. It's why I am in this Dreamliner flying over the Chagos Trench and heading back deep into your history again.

I say 'again' because, as I have explained, I first came to Perth five years ago. That's when this journey really began.

7. Brits Abroad

*They go forth into a world that is not entirely composed of
public-school men or even of Anglo-Saxons, but of men
who are as various as the sands of the sea; into a world
of whose richness and subtlety they have no conception.
They go forth into it with well-developed bodies, fairly
developed minds, and undeveloped hearts. And it is
this undeveloped heart that is largely responsible for
the difficulties of Englishmen abroad. An undeveloped
heart – not a cold one. The difference is important.*

E.M. Forster, Notes on the English Character

When the pukka sahibs made the journey from
England to Bombay in the 1920s they would take a P&O
liner from Tilbury to Bombay. The journey lasted three
weeks and they would stop off at Gibraltar, Marseilles,
Port Said and Aden. At the end of January 1969,
Robin boarded the P&O liner Oriana in Los Angeles,
bound for Sydney. It was a two-week journey stopping
in Hawaii, Fiji and Auckland. The cabin which he

shared with three other strangers was way below the waterline. He does not mention the contrast between his journey and our family voyage to Canada twelve years earlier where we had rather more luxurious cabins on the top deck. He ends his first letter home by confirming that his heart may have yet to be tested, but his public-school confidence and social skills were already standing him in good stead:

'I needn't ramble on any further about shipboard life as you know the story but I must have accumulated at least twenty complete life histories along with assorted medical cases and enough tall stories to beat the Empire State Building. However, all good fun and I have given as good as I have got to keep things going.

As you can see it has been a fantastic voyage – it is quite inappropriate to just say thank you for all you have done for me. – This is not the place to ramble on about my feelings, but even now I cannot believe I will not be seeing you for so long. But I shall get back sometime.'

It was to be four long years before he did return home. As the Oriana sailed under the Sydney Harbour bridge, he was bursting with energy and anticipation. He, like me, was a proud product of the British public school, setting off to distant parts. He would assimilate and thrive. Spread his wings and expand his mind.

* * * * * *

He was not the first to go to distant parts. As I came to the end of my time at Sherborne I knew that I was not considered 'Oxbridge material'. This meant that in the eyes of the institution I was destined either for a 'redbrick university' to study law, or for the army to follow in my father's footsteps. I am pleased to say, although still a conformist, that I did realise there was more to life than either of those rather unappetising options. It was 1966 and although the swinging sixties had largely passed me by, the zeitgeist had made a faint impression on my privileged expectations. I began to wonder whether I could jump the rails that had me heading inexorably towards a future of mediocre predictability. So, when I saw that The Worshipful Company of Drapers was offering handsome scholarships to pay all fees and living costs to any Commonwealth university, I saw a possible alternative path in tune with the itinerant gene that was my inheritance. There was no exam, just an interview to assess whether you would be 'a good enough chap' and 'not let the side down'. I applied and put down Canada as my preferred Commonwealth destination, attended an interview and a few weeks later learnt that I had been awarded a three-year scholarship. Although I was taken by surprise at the time, I can now look back and realise that I was exactly the sort of person they were looking for. I was a survivor. I had not exactly flourished at Sherborne, but I had stuck it out. I had played the game and learnt the rules. There was an outward confidence that would have impressed the panel: I had that public-school fluency combined with an apparent self- sufficiency that would play well in the Commonwealth. I fancied McGill University in Montreal, which seemed to be the happening place, but the Drapers Company directed me to Toronto, then a byword for dreary provincialism, and the most traditional college in the unappetising University of Toronto. Trinity College was built like an Oxford College and was the destination of choice for the offspring of affluent Anglo-Canadians. I arrived in September 1966.

Some two years later Robin too applied for the same Drapers scholarship. As I had done, he put on his best suit and tie, took the train up to the City of London, where he had a low-key interview and a formal lunch in the gilded hall (were they checking his table manners?).

A month later he received the welcome news:

'Dear Sir,

I have pleasure to inform you that you have been awarded a Draper's Company Commonwealth Scholarship of £950 per annum to the University of Perth, to read for a degree in Geography. The company will also meet the reasonable cost of the outward passage to Australia. The scholarship is for a period of three years, commencing with the Australian academic year which starts in March 1969.

I should be glad if you could confirm that you accept this award.

Yours faithfully,

Hugh Farmer, Clerk'

Reading that letter, to my shame, I once again experience more than a twinge of resentment. Somehow he had managed to steal my thunder and devalue the currency of my modest act of rebellion. Made it look easy. And where I had gone some three and a half thousand miles away from hearth and home, he opted for a more impressive nine thousand miles away. He thought he would be heading for Sydney, but the good Mr Farmer, Clerk to the Company, had a different idea. The University of Western Australia in Perth is about as far away from his family as he could possibly get!

* * * * * *

As we have seen, our family myth was that my brother Robin had started to take drugs in his last two years at the University of Western Australia, which had started him on a slow inexorable road towards schizophrenia and eventual suicide. Inasmuch as I had allowed myself memories of my brother they were informed by this myth. When he returned, he was a sad shadow of the man we hoped he would be and this vision, mixed in with my guilt and anger, created a toxic brew. Any grief was locked down and I would not allow myself to challenge the myth. For my mother the myth was sacred. It helped assuage her own insidious guilt and I was not going to deprive her of that cold comfort.

Once she had gone, to my surprise I felt a strong desire to connect with my two nephews. For thirty years I had failed to play the part of supportive uncle. They had felt uncomfortable with me and I resented the way my mother had devoted herself to their wellbeing. Our encounters had been stilted and formulaic and I had certainly done little to help them come to grips with the implications of their father's death.

By 2007, the year my mother died, it was no surprise that my nephews were abroad. They had inherited the Bethell roaming gene. Oliver, the more cautious one, was practising law in Brussels, whereas Alun was working in Africa. To my relief I found that my mother's departure had caused a similar release on their part; they were keen to meet up and connect. At first a trip to the Congo was beyond me, but I did take the Eurostar to Brussels

On my final evening with Oliver, enlivened by more red wine than was probably appropriate for an uncle to be sharing with his nephew, and after I had done my best to describe his father's mental illness and after I had stretched my inadequate knowledge of schizophrenia beyond credibility, he took me by surprise and asked, 'So what was he like before he became ill?' A simple enough question to which I should have had a decent answer. But as the waiters started to stack the chairs around us, the scale of my ignorance hit me hard. I could only answer his questions with platitudes, and replay some of the family myth about irresponsible drug use and a hippy lifestyle. Hopeless. As we strolled somewhat unsteadily across the Grand Place I promised him that I would investigate those absent years and make sure that he and his brother had a more accurate and rounded story of their father's life. I told him that I would go to Australia.

It took me another five years before I was able to carve out the time to fulfil my promise to Oliver. It had to wait for my enforced retirement and the slowly dawning realisation that my high-flying aspirations had lost momentum, so that I reluctantly accepted that I could devote some time to myself. That public-school imperative to keep on achieving had started to fade, leaving space for me to fulfil my obligation to Oliver and Alun. I thought my motive was all about filling the information gap for them, but of course it was so much more than that. I needed to fill in the gaps and rediscover my brother. It was more a selfish intent that an altruistic one.

Heading off to Australia sounded like a grand plan, but it was more fraught than I had originally imagined. Over forty years had elapsed and there was no evidence that I would be able to track down anyone who could give me the insights I sought, and without additional testimony from those who knew him, my venture could be an indulgent waste of time. In addition, and perhaps more significantly, it would be just as much about rediscovering and understanding my own story. There was a good chance that this aspect of the journey could prove a lot more unsettling.

A more pressing problem was that there was remarkably little to go on. Perth really is about as far away as you can get from England and he was there at a time when communication was limited and slow. He had written letters, about once a month and mostly to my parents. My mother kept them and, after his death, used them to feed her own need for connection. She had tried to persuade me to take control of them and I had rejected her advances. The letters were more than I could handle. As a result, she had handed them all over to Alun and now they were under his bed in Kinshasa, a place both dangerous and short on connectivity. Despite repeated requests, Alun had not managed to get the letters to me before I left on my journey. Indeed, I started to think that perhaps he resented my land grab of his father's history and was deliberately holding onto the evidence. In truth, I favoured disorganisation as a motive rather than conspiracy and that judgement was confirmed when a couple of days into my trip, I received a stream of images via email that turned out to be random pages of those letters laid out on a hotel room bed and photographed on his iPhone. It must have taken him hours.

Opening up those files and seeing Robin's elegant handwriting, I felt I was on my way at last. The physical journey was one thing, but his words, and there were lots of them crammed onto the pages, re-ignited my quest and gave it substance. This was his voice fixed in time but resonating across the years. His illusive persona was coming into focus: dim and distant but palpable. Here were dates to create a chronology, places to locate him and the names of people I could contact: rich pickings for the cold-case investigator.

'1st March 1969

Perth – Friday morning eleven o'clock. I got a taxi to St George's College. What a beautiful city. I really thought to myself as I drove up to the college: 'No! I haven't made a mistake.'

Wonderful as these letters were (and when I did get my hands on the full collection there were over fifty) they were not going to be a window on his real feelings especially as time passed and life got more complex. These were letters written to his parents. Self-censored and circumspect. He would not have wanted to offer much cause for concern. He knew how to feed my parents' hopes and expectations. I could recognize the code because I had used it myself in my own letters from Canada. Nevertheless, I felt confident that I could read between the lines and there was now a much better chance I could get access to other witnesses and their testimony.

* * * * * *

Marcus Collins, however, did not feature in those letters and I had low expectations of him. I had been given his contact details by a family friend, who seemed to think that Marcus had been at university with Robin. He had been slow to respond to my email, but eventually, I did get an encouraging reply:

'I knew Robin reasonably well as part of the 'English Contingent' at UWA. The late 60's and early 70's were halcyon times to be at UWA as they probably were in many places. He was very much part of the same social set as I was and for several years I saw a lot of him. The Robin I remember looked the spitting image of Michael Yorke and had a lovely personality (and was a very good rugby player).'

But there was a further paragraph that offered a premonition of what was to come and reminded me that this journey could lead me into darker terrain:

'I do remember Robin was smitten with a Perth UWA student who may have led him astray with drugs and I always thought that it was the drugs that caused his later problems.'

Notwithstanding his hypotheses that matched

the family drug-related narrative, Marcus was fully engaged. He told me that he had been spreading the word amongst his alumni friends and many of them had memories of Robin. Apparently, they had responded to his emails with a surprising enthusiasm. He wanted to meet up and show me the results of his research and then told me he had taken the liberty of inviting a few of the respondents around to his house to reminisce and wondered if I could face joining them. He thought it might be hard.

This was a remarkable development. Suddenly what had felt like a self-indulgent foray with few prospects was transformed into a collaborative venture that could result in access to a rich vein of recollection. It gave a new status to my quest.

Three days later I arrived in Perth and met up with Marcus; first, in his architect's office where he presented me with a folder. On the cover was a photograph of Robin taken at a rugby match. He is not playing but watching. Long hair and with those very same Michael Yorke good looks. He is watching the photographer with a wry confidence. I was, once again, taken by surprise. This was the Robin I had come to find, the Robin I had lost. I was far more affected than I ever could have predicted. He was so damned handsome, so poised: I felt the faintest flutter of a love that I could never have predicted. This journey was going to unsettle me, and my certainties.

The folder was a treasure trove. Marcus had been busy. He had grasped the role of investigator with remarkable enthusiasm. He had found all Robin's college records, including the application correspondence and a curt request that he should pay his overdue bills. And then in a second section he had printed out all the replies he had received from those who knew Robin. The men reminisced about his prowess on the rugby field, whilst the women had a different, more nuanced perspective:

I remember him zooming round campus, very flamboyant and very active in the drama society and so damned good looking. Thinking about him takes me back to the 60's, it was great at the time but I am pleased I came through unscathed and happy to have moved on. I always think of Robin as one of the 60's victims.

Marcus told me how surprised he had been by the

response to his exploratory email about Robin. These did not seem to be people who were particularly close to Robin and yet they seemed perplexingly engaged by the prospect of sharing their memories of him. Marcus suggested two reasons for this: first, it did seem as if Robin had a charisma that was as attractive to men as it was to women. They may not have been his close friends but it seems that they wished they had been. Second, he suggested that here were people who had been young then but were now more than sixty years old. They had lived full lives but were keen to revisit those days when everything seemed possible and the pleasures and the heartbreaks seemed so life-affirming.

Next, Marcus took me for a tour of the university. First up was a visit to St George's College, where Robin spent his first year in residence. He showed me Robin's college room, and I stood on the spot where, Marcus told me with some relish, Robin had bet that he could throw a rugby ball across the quad. He failed and lost the bet, but in me it caused an unsettling time warp to my own early days at a foreign university when I too had been pushing my luck.

St George's was a new-world red-brick facsimile of an Oxbridge college. Eerily reminiscent of my college in Toronto. Like Trinity College, Toronto, it had a porters' lodge and a faux-Tudor dining hall. This was where the Drapers Company sent their public-school scholars destined for Australia. In fact, a little later I discovered a letter written by Robin whilst he was still making plans in which he said he hoped to be going to university in Sydney. This set me wondering how he ended up in Perth. A letter in Marcus' folder from the Drapers Warden to the Provost of St George's explained why.

'I do hope that I am not crossing the line when I suggest that it would be a good thing if he started in at St George's.'

It seemed they had an arrangement with St George's which, it turned out, was not surprising as the Clerk of the Drapers Company had gone to university with the Warden of St George's. The old boy network. This was clearly the same network that had re-directed me from the far funkier McGill University in Montreal to the downbeat University of Toronto. Those Drapers knew the right sort of place to send a well-bred public-school boy. I do have cause to wonder whether Robin's story would have been any different had it played out in the cosmopolitan Sydney rather than what he later describes as that *'cultural backwater,'* Perth. It raised a similar query in my own past: how might I have reacted to the cosmopolitan and far more radical world of Montreal where the French Canadians were flexing their independent muscles and Leonard Cohen was writing the poem that would become the song 'Suzanne.'

After St George's, Marcus drove me around the campus, pointing out all Robin's haunts. We passed the imposing library building where he did his work in the first year because the childish hi-jinks of his fresher contemporaries, who he discovered were mostly one year younger than him and acted their age, were not conducive to concentration. Then on to sports fields where he played his rugby and found the surface 'like concrete' and unforgiving to his bare knees. We stopped off at the student bar where Marcus remembers long evenings consuming large quantities of beer with the rugby boys. I remember a line in a letter:

'I find those kind of get-togethers OK for a while, but the conversation is limited viz: girls, beer and for the slightly more sophisticated, cars.'

Finally, we head out to the residential area where Marcus has identified the house at 123 Marmion St, where Robin moved for his second year. Now transformed into a stylish well-appointed home for the professional class, it did not take much of a mental leap to imagine it as a dilapidated student rental costing, as I discover, $22 a week.

Marcus left me with instructions on how to get to his home. I was expected at around seven thirty and he suggested that around twenty-five or so people would attend. I had not anticipated such a crowd and I found my own eager anticipation to participate in this shared retrospection began to waver as the hour approached. I was uncharacteristically nervous as I knocked on the door and was invited into a room full of strangers all looking to me for permission to share their memories of Robin and, it transpired, of their own lives and loves. The men talked about Robin's prowess on the rugby field and the women about how much they fancied him. I found myself speaking about my brother to strangers in a way that I had rarely allowed myself to do with my own family. These people were fascinated by my search for answers; it seemed to chime with theirs.

But just below the surface there was an under-current of unease. Many had their own stories of close relatives who had succumbed to personal tragedy and mental illness, much of it rooted in those febrile times. My narrative had given them permission to do their own excavations. Maxine told me the harrowing tale of her sister whose life had been enlivened by heavy drug use then blighted by mental-health problems. She suggested that Robin's suicide might have spared us a prolonged and increasingly chaotic decline. She had no illusions about the liberated Seventies, and reminded me that I shouldn't either.

Robert had been my brother's neighbour in his first year living in college. He spoke of his exploits on the rugby field and cavalier approach to dirty laundry. But after a few moments the bravura world of young lads at play gave way to a heartfelt account of his own brother, now suffering from severe mental illness after sustained recreational drug use in the 70s. He told me his brother was extensively medicated and had no joy in his life.

Robert's and Maxine's stories further galvanised my need to put the past in order – and stirred up another well of guilt. Should I have worked harder to persuade Robin to control his psychotic incidents with medication? Would he be alive now? The treatment available in the mid-Seventies had been crude, but perhaps that was just an excuse. There was so much more to find out.

After an hour or so of these intensely personal and provocative exchanges, Marcus drew the room to order, and asked me to say a few words.

I heard myself try to explain how for thirty years my anger and guilt had stood in the way of exploring Robin's life, and most particularly the part of it that had happened here in Perth.

Someone called out: 'What was Robin like at school?'

I gave the best answer I could.

'Did he have children? What do they feel about their father?'

Perhaps this was the moment to step back and let the party resume, but I had had a couple of glasses of excellent red wine and I answered. Haltingly at first, but then with more fluency, I was drawn into the intense engagement of the whole group. I explained that Robin had left his wife Carole and two boys, one three years old and the other a mere six months old, sons that were then in their thirties and had been the catalyst for my quest.

It felt a little unsettling to be sharing my stumbling recollections and half- formed assertions with strangers. But it served an important purpose: it gave my venture a broader context. This was not merely a parochial bit of family business, it was emblematic of a generation's search for reconciliation with a very particular time. Everyone in that room had a story to tell about their 'sixties', and it put mine into perspective.

* * * * * *

The majority of those at that party had known him in the first year or so and their anecdotes made it very clear that Robin was a busy guy. As I read through his letters from that time, that seems like an understatement. In his first year at St George's he certainly hit the ground running. In a letter dated March 21st 1969, just three weeks after the start of his first term, he is telling his parents about what he has been up to, so far:

'The extracurricular activities have been the most time-consuming. These include rugger, University Dramatic Society, photography for Pelican *(the*

university magazine), freelance work for a photo studio in Nedlands and taking one of the major roles in the Freshman Production for the entertainment of the college gentlemen. I was the judge in a take-off of A Trial by Jury, *which was good fun and seemed to go down quite well.'*

He has bought a moped, which is irritating him with a series of punctures. And there is also reference to 'my new girlfriend Ann' whom he appears to have got off with at the Freshers Camp. He writes *'Ann is a really sweet girl with a good face for photographs'* and he has persuaded her to act as a model in a photo assignment he has secured:

'We were lent a $60 Christian Dior catsuit in black crepe and Ann dressed up in it and she looked fantastic. We went down to Cottesloe beach and I got some great shots of her on a sand dune with the sea in the background.'

He stays up all night in the darkroom developing and printing the pictures and the next day the boutique, which had commissioned him, seemed pleased and used one in its advertising. It was the start of just one of his many photographic ventures that would feature in his letters for at least two years. Ann, on the other hand fades from view later in that first year when, as we will see, Diana takes over as his model and the object of his affections.

I am stunned by that letter of the 21st March. It is

made up of two aerogrammes which in his tiny, tidy writing runs to around 2000 words. He has been in the country for less than three weeks and yet he is already engrossed in a frenetic range of activities. He seems to be bursting with creativity, vitality and, evidently, virility. I am in awe.

Whilst that whirlwind of proactive engagement takes my breath away, as I sit here, in my seventies, imagining how he could possibly have found time in the twenty days available to embed himself with such energy in so much, I have to pause and compare his whirlwind exploits with my own. I too was a public-school boy abroad and three years earlier I had arrived in my mock medieval college with its old-world traditions and new-world freshman frolics. And I too had what I now recognise was a similar impact. Within a week I had been elected President of the Freshman Year and had led my male peers to victory in the Cake Fight, an initiation rite that required me to lead the troops in a battle with the second years defending the narrow gate to the quad. The Freshmen had not won that fight for over twenty years! A leader of men, as my public-school headmaster might have put it (but never did). And on further recollection I realise that I was almost immediately involved in a college drama production and playing rugby for the university. I could not compete with his photography and, of course, I didn't have a girlfriend I could call my own until many months later (and she jilted me a few months after that).

So, what is it with these over-achieving public-school boys and their frenzied levels of social engagement? Well, we were fine examples of what the public-school system was set up to achieve. We were fully equipped to hit the ground running in foreign parts. We had been trained to take on the challenge of strange cultures and triumph. We had been imbued with confidence and charm. We were not backward in coming forward. We felt entitled to be masters of our own destiny. But then again, I have to ask: at what price?

I found I was easily beguiled by these accounts of Robin's first year in Perth. They helped to build up a positive narrative, one that not only made me envious but caused me to underestimate my own experience. As I compared our experiences I could not stop myself from putting aside my own successes and focusing on my vulnerabilities. I started to recall how I possessed a resilient carapace of confidence and endeavour, which was too often undermined by a soft fleshy underbelly of uncertainty and self-reproach. I was trying very hard to live up to expectations that had been set by an elite education system and endorsed by my father. If I look back at my letters from that time, I too was aiming to impress. To sell an image of myself that would satisfy all parties. As I read Robin's letters it brings it all back.

He too was determined to fulfil expectations, and yet as I dig deeper I will find evidence that Robin too had a very similar duality: a shell of dynamic vigour and creativity protecting a profound uncertainty.

* * * * *

By the end of his first year Robin was finding the constraints of college life irksome and before the end of the year he was plotting his escape.

In October 1969, he writes:

'The Drapers have said I can move out into a house next year which is good. Rent is pretty reasonable here and I should be able to live for well under what it costs to live at college, especially if the rent is split between three or four of us.'

In fact, just three of them ended up in that house on Marmion Street. Robin, Rob Speechley and Piers Partridge. Three British public-school boys revelling in their new-found freedoms and determined to live life to the full.

On my return to England, after my first trip to Perth, I set about trying to track them both down. I heard that Rob Speechley had been through some hard times and now appeared to be living in Thailand. A couple of attempts to contact him via Facebook drew a blank, but sometime later he did eventually reply and his only contribution was a rather unhelpful tale of meeting my brother for a drink back in England and how Robin had accused him of hitting on his girlfriend: not what I was after. Piers Partridge on the other hand was a lot easier to track down and turned out to be a fine witness.

Piers makes music on his own and with others in the straw-bale music studio he built for himself in his back garden. Before moving to Somerset, he was part of the North London psychotherapeutic community and, having been to boarding school himself, he had shown a special interest in the plight of those 'Boarding School Survivors'. But perhaps the most engaging lines in his lengthy Linked-in profile refer to his table tennis prowess where: 'I use a standard bat, stand well back from the table and impart an unreasonable amount of spin.'

His emails had been full of insight and I was thrilled to receive, once again, such a warm and responsive welcome. Like so many of the friends I had met in Australia he was more than ready to roll back the years to help me understand my brother, but Piers was able to add an extra layer of understanding of the psychological issues at play.

He took me for a walk through the woods. It was late spring and there were bluebells in abundance. I felt I was in safe hands and plunged straight in:

'That house on Marmion Street, it must have seemed like a dream to a bunch of public-school boys?'

'It was exciting, yes, but we were so very unprepared for this drastic change in our young lives. We knew nothing. I don't know how we managed really, except that to manage things on our own was what we'd had always done. Automatic pilot.'

That struck a chord with me. I should have realised that this was just as much about me as it was about Robin.

'Yes I recognise that in myself. I flew on automatic pilot for years in Canada. Somehow Sherborne had programmed us for survival but not much else.'

'That's the ex-boarder pathology – highly socialised, capable, charming, articulate, independent and a bit lost.'

'Hmm. From his letters he seemed so bloody active and yet if what you say is true then I have failed to get an honest picture of him.'

This was an important moment for me. Piers had such acuity and his memory was clearly a lot sharper than mine.

'Well, Robin had that sweet ex-boarding school open-faced naivety about him. A lot of us ex-boarders never quite grow out of 'the boy' – maybe because the natural processes of evolution are interrupted. Very good looking, and a sweet charm mixed with a paradoxical remoteness.'

A bit lost, a bit remote? This was another side to that hyperactive charmer I had read about and heard speak of.

'You are not the first person to mention that. My father had the same quality. Nobody quite felt they "knew" him.'

'No, I never felt I was really getting to know who Robin was. But he might easily have said the same about me. Neither he nor I were in any way qualified to take on the job of looking after ourselves in the mad tumble of late 1960s Perth. It was a massive gamble with our lives.

'I suppose you could say that for Robin, the table turned against him... eventually.'

We have circled back to his cabin in the woods and he invites me for lunch. As he warms up the rough vegetable soup, I realize that we cannot go delving into the past without reflecting on the present. Piers reminds me how lucky we public-school survivors are to have made it this far.

'My body has a lot going wrong with it and sometimes I feel sad to have lost the ease of younger days. And then I remind myself that I'm simply lucky to have made it back in one piece. A sodding miracle.'

Cottesloe, Western Australia.
Time since arrival: 23 hours 10minutes.

Dear Robin,

I am back in Perth. It is almost six years since I was last here and met up with Marcus and a group of your St George's friends. You may ask, 'How come the long delay? If you were that interested in finding out more, surely you would have got on with it.' It's a fair point and you could argue that my procrastination was a mark of a fickle loyalty to your memory. But in my defence I could say that writing is a lot harder than I thought. Not least because I had underestimated how much this damned book was going to be as much about me as it is about you. I was on a journey into my own past and it was proving pretty unsettling. I took my time but once back on the case it got richer and richer. I chased down some hot leads and that got me going again. Then I knew I had to return to the scene of the crime.

It may have been a sixteen-hour flight, but they still managed to land half an hour early. I was expecting some debilitating jet lag, but the bright sunshine and the anticipation wiped away the tiredness and I am buzzing with energy.

I am sitting in a café looking out over Cottesloe beach. The sun is still shining and you are on my mind.

149

Seems like a great place to be writing to you. Once you had left the hallowed halls of St Georges, this was your place. A suburb with benefits. A great beach and the first stirrings of a bohemian lifestyle. I am not sure you would appreciate the 'developments' that have taken place over the last fifty years. There are odd glimpses of the relaxed slightly run-down place you knew, but generally it has been ruined with a rash of high-end condos and expensive restaurants.

I know you swam on this beach because I dug up a photo of you right here. Naturally it is not just you: you are leaning intimately on the shoulder of a slim young woman, smiling into her eyes. She has a great body and, confirming all my shameful envy, so do you.

I had dinner last night with Vic who, as you will see, I met on my first trip and has since become a good friend. I showed him that picture. 'He was a beautiful boy,' he sighed, and as a gay man, he was only partly talking about your beautiful mind! As we will discover, he did fancy you, but you turned him down.

This next chapter reflects my dishonourable interest in your love life. I need to apologise now. It is unseemly, but it is an essential part of your story. I have had to deal with so many women telling me about your good looks, but when I press them on the matter several have assured me that it was not just your 'pretty face' and long blonde hair. You had a sensitivity that was so very different to the average

Australian male. These women were not used to dealing with men who could respond to and talk about feelings. In the words of one, 'We used to say: he's very sensitive, is he gay? No, he's English.'

8. Women Beware Women

I knew also that popular culture, films and television, was still somehow delighted by the notion of naive but charming public school characters, who would prove terribly attractive to women, before letting them down.
Nick Duffell, The Making of Them: The British Attitude to Children and the Boarding School System

The get-together at Marcus' house had left me with a mixed set of emotions. The warmth and depth of the responses had provided a validation of my venture. It felt like I was involved in far more than a selfish quest to assuage my guilt and disinter some respect for and love of my dead brother. But I remained haunted by the way so many of that group had such mixed feelings about that time and that place. As Piers Partridge wrote to me after our meeting:

'Perth was in its full-blown, slightly delayed, 60's explosion. Everything was coming off the cultural walls. When I first arrived people would stop their cars, wind

down their windows and shout at me to "get my bloody hair cut". Two years later and they all had Status Quo style hair-dos themselves. Cheap dope, some of it laced with all sorts of weird stuff, was pouring in from Asia and there was a lot of experimenting going on.'

We will come to Robin and the cheap dope from Asia later in the story, but during those innocent early days the three heroes of 123 Marmion were still growing their hair, pushing their boundaries and enjoying their freedom.

One of the men I met at the party was Jim Singleton. His name had not cropped up in the letters but, as we have seen, he had been both to Tockington Manor and Sherborne and then come to UWA a year after Robin. He told me how he was totally in awe of the Marmion Street gang of English musketeers with their creative enterprise and social confidence. They represented everything that he aspired to and which, he modestly acknowledged, rarely achieved. He was envious of Robin in other ways as well. Later on, that same evening, he sheepishly told me of an occasion when he met Robin sitting in the sun outside the library. He looked jaded. Jim asked him what was up. 'Oh,' said Robin, 'I went to a party last night. Near the end, most people had left, but I seemed to hit it off with this gorgeous woman. I went home with her and we made love all night. Didn't get a wink of sleep.' Jim remembered the interchange word for word some forty years later. Together we debated whether this was just braggadocio or whether he did indeed have an enviable sex life.

In our different ways we both wanted it to be true and then again not true. Jim was painfully honest in recognising his own hesitant beginnings in that regard, and I was less forthcoming but nevertheless sympathetic. I had none of Robin's physical appeal. In my late adolescence, I was very tall and it had taken years for my body to catch up with my stature and its very excess restricted my sad attempts to be stylish. From the days of my prep-school shorts through to my misshapen corduroys that were never quite long enough, I rarely felt comfortable in my clothes or my skin. I felt sure that I could not cut a dash. Whereas Robin had one of those bodies that made anything he threw on look 'right'. That photo on the front of Marcus' folder seemed to sum it up. Fi Nattrass, who had taken the picture, did so, she told me at the party, because 'he was so spunky looking'. Nothing particularly stylish, just obviously at ease with his physicality, and she recognised it right away. Like Robin, I could use my English accent to good effect and could chat up women, but rarely got much further. I lived vicariously through my best friend Dwight who had already fathered a child and was both experienced and highly desirable to the very women that I had hopes of attracting. I would eventually make headway with women, but like Jim, I would have been threatened by Robin's insouciant recollections of a random night of passion. But at this stage in my investigations I cannot not deny that I had a possibly unhealthy interest in Robin's life as a successful Lothario.

One of the women at the party was someone who had featured in my early research. Diane LeFroy was the daughter of a couple who ran a sheep farm 100 miles north of Perth. Robin had been introduced to them through a connection of my parents, desperate to offer him some fixed points in his solitary odyssey. Diana's parents did indeed welcome Robin and both they and the sheep farm they ran would prove very important to Robin later in the story. But it was Diana who featured most in my memory. She was always described as 'a model' and I have a couple of photos of her, taken by Robin, which demonstrated that she definitely had the look of a model: she was radiantly beautiful. I remember seeing those pictures very early on while he was still in Australia and, of course, I assumed that she was his girlfriend. That, on the other hand, was only my assumption. It was never specifically stated and it was clear that, whatever romantic relationship they may or may not have had, it did not last.

I did however know that she was important to Robin during his early days in Perth. Because of the parental connection, my mother had talked about Diana, but she had made maternal assumptions that assumed a platonic friendship. Whilst I on the other hand have to confess to an almost prurient interest in exactly what sort of a relationship it had been. So when, at the party, I asked her whether she would be interested in a longer chat, I have a feeling there was a faint trace of my twenty-year old self who perhaps hadn't quite given up hope of joining the fun.

She was happy to meet up. Her tone at the party was a little cooler than many – a timely reminder that simply because I was on much more than a sentimental journey, it didn't mean that everyone else would sign up.

My interpretation of Diana's initial coolness was

subsequently confirmed when, once we were making arrangements to meet for lunch, she made it clear that she would come with her husband. That was definitely not what I was hoping for. I wanted us to be alone and for her to be free to share some intimacies about her relationship with Robin. I felt the presence of her husband would change the dynamic. It could only be a polite run around the course, untrammelled by any of the emotional honesty that I craved. Clearly, she did not see this as anything more than an innocent stroll down memory lane, one that she would be happy to share with her husband. Who was I to use the emotional leverage of a dead brother to change the terms of the encounter? But she had said that she had kept Robin's letters to her. Perhaps they might add something new.

We met for lunch. Diane and her husband Ross duly appeared in a large white Range Rover. They were, of course, warm and welcoming. There was a hint of something more than social bonhomie in the hug that Diane gave me, but perhaps I was imagining it. They suggested we head to Fremantle, a few miles down the coast.

We chatted about jobs, children and holidays. They had a barge in France, and cruised the canals of the Midi each summer. She had been married to Ross for forty years. They lived and worked on a sheep station that was a few miles from Colvin – her parents' place and Robin's safe haven.

As I tucked into the caramelised calamari in Piri Piri sauce Diana brought out a file: photos of her own children, to start with, and the French barge. The tone changed when she spoke about Robin's son Oliver who had visited during his gap year. The final photo, slightly faded, was of him working in the sheep pen, looking back over his shoulder, with a look almost identical to that in the photo on the front of Marcus' folder.

I was silent for a moment. 'My goodness... he looks... just like his father...'

And for Diane and Ross, that was the end of it, the kind of comment we make all the time about other people's children. But for me it was a stark reminder of the distance I had to travel. Looking at that picture I realised what a very bad uncle I had been. I had almost certainly been told about his visit to the sheep farm – my mother would have wanted to tell me – but I had taken only the most cursory interest. I had gone AWOL, evading my duties as a brother and an uncle.

Out came the letters. She had gone to a lot of trouble to photocopy them. I was touched. As she handed them over, I recognised his cramped but elegant handwriting and caught snatches of his confident prose. One was written in September 1970, eight days after his twentieth birthday. A couple of sentences leapt out at me:

'...this is an effort to formalise some thoughts on a special subject which happens to be... you.

...you see, something has taken place – rather inevitably, for we have seen quite a lot of each other – which leaves me in a cold vacuum – I don't know which way to go...

... I am not trying to suggest that there should be something there, and at the same time I am not trying to make a pretty friendship into an embroiled affair, but the unfortunate complicating factor is that you constitute a little bit more than just a friend...'

I abandoned any attempt at politeness and read the whole letter. It was a declaration of love. And a tortured, convoluted, circuitous and terribly British attempt to find out whether she loved him. It showed a lack of confidence that flew in the face of my image of him as the confident Lothario. It was an acutely painful cry from a heart that, if not broken already, was flinching at the imminent possibility.

I glanced up. 'Diane, this letter... He's telling you that he loves you, isn't he?'

The downward flick of her eye told me that we were not going there. We were sitting at a table outside the Mussel Shed, looking out over the industrial harbour of Fremantle, with her husband in attendance.

'I don't... I really don't think so. We were just good friends.'

I probably should have left it at that, but I had a feeling that because I had delayed so long, the clock was now ticking loudly. 'He... He was telling you he loved you, and wanted to know whether you loved him...'

At that moment I did see something more in her eyes. It may have been another attempt on my part to reconstruct someone else's narrative, but I was pretty sure it was the dawning awareness that this might have been a turning point, and she had missed it.

Robin and Diane continued to be friends and he retained more than a fondness for her. In another letter he revealed a recent failure in his love life. However, it is very likely that at the moment of the declaration in that letter, she may have taken the view that he was not going to be an easy ride. He was intense and fiercely introspective at times, and she in turn may have chosen not to see it, as a means of self-preservation, rather than merely missing the message altogether.

Later that evening, sitting on Cottesloe beach as the sun set into the Indian Ocean and waves rolled in, I read the letter again more carefully. It was not just a sad tale of unrequited love, but was intensely redolent of the boys we were. This tortured obfuscation brought back all the unsettling memories of my own first stumbling efforts to form relationships. Our public school had equipped us with a surfeit of confidence when it came to plunging into new circumstances; we could swiftly adapt and excel. We both had made an impact 'zooming round campus'. And although I came a poor second to his charismatic appeal to women, I knew that a British accent could turn heads. The trouble was that our public school, by depriving us of the direct love of our mother and denying us daily interaction with young women, had left us wholly lacking in confidence when it came to emotional engagement. We covered this up with our own particular brand of convoluted self-effacement. In Robin's words:

'The reason for the of lack of substance to my feelings, may be that it is wholly my construction and is not mutual, in which case my uncertainty is all my own fault and I must attribute it to my own lack of sensitivity.'

* * * * * *

There is a coda to my encounter with Diana and husband. Some years later, on my subsequent trip to Perth, I met up with them both and stayed in their farmhouse. Ross was outside preparing the cattle for market and Diana appeared open to further exploration of her friendship with Robin. I took the opportunity to bring out the letter and to ask her once again whether she realised that this was declaration of his love for her. This time her answer was very different. Yes, she knew he loved her and indeed she came to love him, 'but only as a brother'. She was frank and open. She had never found him sexually attractive. She was still recovering from a disastrous relationship with her previous lover. He had totally captivated her and, she told me, set the bar high for what she found attractive. She had been devastated by his rejection, but could not deny her intense attraction. Robin was never going to replace him.

Once again I had to alter my hasty assumptions about what had happened. This about-turn reminded me that I simply could not take the first-hand testimony from fifty years ago as an accurate account of some objective truth. It is obvious, of course, that in matters of the heart there is only a shifting subjective truth. What I could tell from this second encounter was that Diana was re-living an intense version of that truth. She may not have been certain about the exact timing and she could not be sure exactly how she reacted to Robin's declaration, but she was sure of one thing, emphatic in fact: she had had no physical feelings for him. I could not decide whether I was sorry for her or for Robin.

My encounters with Diane had been both poignant and salutary. Poignant because it revealed a painfully vulnerable side of my brother, a side that was never going to be revealed in his letters to my parents. Salutary, because it struck me that I did have to be wary of the pernicious impact of sibling rivalry. So far, I have been content to indulge myself in a sense of my own adolescent inferiority; and it was his physical prowess that weighed heaviest. Seeing that photograph of him winning the pole vault had struck a particular nerve. Yet it was an unwarranted indulgence. As my investigation progressed I was condoning my own jealousy: wallowing in self-pity for my younger self. Finding out about Robin's success with women, his charisma and the apparent vibrancy of his life caused me to diminish myself in his aura. I was searching for an affirmative narrative to share with his children and mine, but in so doing I was allowing myself to pick away at the frailties of my own lengthy adolescence. This was an unintended and unwanted backwash from the excitement of the chase. There was also an undertow of an unsavoury prurience that pandered to my seventy-year-old sense of diminishing potential. At the time it did not make me feel as uncomfortable as it does in retrospect, but looking back at my enthusiastic pursuit of his love life and the sad comparisons I make with my own experience, I am not proud of myself. It feels a little grubby, if I am honest.

The date on the ill-fated letter to Diane was 9th September 1970. There would be few clues in his letters to his mum and dad on that aspect of his life, but sometime later I did return to the issue when I finally got round to digging out his letters to me. I had been in denial, so when I eventually checked through my own papers I was shocked to discover a little cache of that correspondence. These were naturally somewhat less self-censored and drew back the curtain just a little on his love life. I checked the dates, and sure enough, in a letter dated August 1st, just five weeks before his heartfelt appeal to Diane, he writes to me:

'Life is strangely disconcerting – I am having an odd relationship with a 25-year-old nymphomaniac (I think), which I have yet to work out but it's springtime so what the hell.'

This appears to be a throwaway line, and of course my mind went straight back to Jim Singleton's anecdote at the party. Could this be the same woman who had kept Robin up all night? More significantly, what had happened to mean that he was so determined to declare his love for Diane just five weeks later? So, back to the parental letters. One dated 24th August mentions that he has been invited up to the sheep farm in Colvin for a break. Maybe that was the moment he realised that he loved Diane. He writes his proclamation two weeks later. It would seem that he was seeking a more profound relationship, even if he was able to secure less committed relationships with some ease.

But then I notice that in another letter to me written five weeks later, in October, he makes another throwaway reference to *'Not getting my bit. It has been a long season without rain.'* However, that was a letter of introspection too; in the same paragraph he writes, *'I am sure I would still be living in the Sherborne-inflicted smog of unreality if I had stayed in England.'* Then, with yet another disconcerting swerve, he describes:

'This week the secretary of the local Communist Party came onto campus to sell copies of the banned 'smutty, salacious, obscene' *(I quote the Daily News, the Chief Justice and the Police Commissioner)* Portnoy's Complaint. *Despite police efforts, they managed to dispose of 300 copies to students, nearly all, reading it for the wrong reasons.'*

Clearly the good citizens of Perth still had a way to go before the sixties sexual revolution would be readily accessible to all. But that did not seem to be constraining my brother or many of his female friends. He was however going to have to wait another seven months before he experienced what I would call 'the real thing'.

There is so much evidence of his attraction to and involvement with women that it seems perverse to raise the question of his sexuality. However, there was a line in an email from his friend Piers Partridge that has caused me to at least consider the matter:

'I sometimes wondered if he was sexually ambivalent. He was very good looking but in a way that was neither heavily male or female. I'm sure he would have been attractive to both sexes. This was unusual in heavily testosterone 1969 Perth.'

This apparently bi-sexual attraction must have been confusing for him. He would have emerged from Sherborne and indeed from St George's College with all the rituals of a firmly heterosexual orientation (despite the allure of the homoerotic sub-culture of the boys' boarding school). However, he was quickly drawn to the theatre, and his friend Paul McGillick, a theatre director who worked with Robin, wrote to me about the 'camp' theatre scene:

'There was a sub-group, what we called the camp group, now more commonly the gay scene. In Perth this was centred around the theatre and the university. We all got on, but it suggested two quite different cultures. I have always been an unreconstructed heterosexual, but a number of my young male contemporaries – quite frankly due to predatory behaviour by older homosexuals – experimented with gay life only to end up straight.'

As we will see, he rebuffed the advances of one of his best friends, who did make a pass, so we must assume that he did not succumb to those 'predatory' older homosexuals. Nevertheless, it must have been perplexing and could have caused him some identity confusion. Paul also wrote that his memory of him:

'...is of a lovely, gentle, generous and urbane individual. But even then he seemed to be emotionally labile, a little delicate.'

I shall hold onto that word 'labile'; it seems to resonate with several other descriptions of Robin at university. The OED defines it as 'liable to change, easily altered'. That is a quality that could have a bearing on my cold-case inquiry into his eventual demise.

Meanwhile, as 1970 ended, I found a letter dated November 20th, which seemed to suggest that those gay thespians had certainly not diverted him from his dominant path. He writes 'Exams are over, weather incomparable, life very very, very beautiful AND have just met a wonderful girl and every moment of living is worth it.' It was scrawled in large letters and the joie de vivre springs off the page.

If 1970 was ending with a flourish, 1971 was going to spring some surprises. Big changes are afoot.

I have decided to capture some of your spirit by writing this at the university library. You seemed to have done most of your academic work here; not that this chapter has much to do with that side of things.

Now I have got to be up front about this envy. As you will have gathered from the previous chapters, I am pretty unresolved about the fact that you seemed to be a better person than your elder brother. That sounds a bit blunt, and I am sure I did not feel it so strongly at the time, but re-visiting our childhood and school days, and even those first days at university, has caused me to see all my frailties, in stark contrast to all your qualities. Of course, I am preoccupied by the physical differences between us, which is reinforced by all I have found out about how both woman (and men!) were attracted to you. But it goes deeper than that. In this next chapter we are going to see how you threw yourself head first into the Age of Aquarius. You wholeheartedly embraced the sixties, even though it happened in Australia in the seventies. But what hurts is that I really was a child of the sixties and I was in North America for the real thing. And yet it bloody nearly passed me by entirely.

Do you want the evidence? Well, in my mother's pile of letters from me, from Canada during my first summer break, I found a postcard dated July 1967 and postmarked San Francisco, CA. I was writing from Haight-Ashbury. I was bloody well in the scene, right there, during the 'summer of love'. So what did I make of it? Well here's what I wrote on a postcard:

'Met some really interesting people – long hair, no shoes, and drugs – but very interesting to hear them talk. We stayed at the University of Berkeley – another very interesting place. The ad on the front of this card is for a jazz club in S.F. – the most famous – we went to a jazz concert here lasting six hours!! Please keep the card. The main thing is DON'T WORRY'

Well that 'jazz club' was the Fillmore Auditorium and the concert was Cream. Ginger Baker, Jack Bruce and Eric Clapton. Played for six extraordinary hours and I WAS THERE. I could pretend that I was stoned and use it as evidence that I did the sixties. But the truth is, as the card shows, I hadn't a clue. And Berkeley was a hotbed of radical protest, and all I can say is it was 'an interesting place'.

Can you wonder that when I found out about what you were doing in 1971, I felt a little jealous?

9. Finding Victor

'Fantasy' is a word Kesey has taken to using more and more. It is a good word. It is ironic and it isn't. It refers to everything from getting hold of the truck to some scary stuff out on the raggedy, raggedy edge.

Tom Wolfe, The Electric Kool-aid Acid Test

Marcus Collins, his research and his hospitality gave me the opportunity to meet and to hear first-hand from so many people who could remember Robin as he was in those early days: the hyperactive, rugby-playing photographer who had a way with the women. But, as I prepared to leave Perth, I knew that I had failed to connect with the person who had shed at least some of his public-school persona and started to explore the alternatives. I needed to connect with the people he got to know in 1971 when his letters had taken on a very different tone. At the start of that year, in a letter to me, he writes:

'At risk of appearing like an archetypal dilettante,

I will say that my intellectual sensibilities have been pricked into frenzied activity and my reading and thinking has become incredibly interesting and worthwhile.'

He then quotes from Marshal McLuhan, Herbert Marcuse and Jean-Paul Sartre and not surprisingly there are signs of an incipient politicisation. In the same letter he describes his decision not to register for the Australian National Service where, via a ballot, one in twenty were called up to fight in Vietnam or as he put it 'kill anything that's dark and moves':

'Anyway, I refuse to subscribe to 1) a war I have no conceivable belief in 2) a law that controls the freedom of the individual 3) the system that can countenance such a law. It makes me liable for a $200 fine, two years in gaol or two years in the army.'

He recognises the risk but since he thinks over one hundred of his contemporaries in Perth are also refusing to register that 'the bureaucratic chaos that will ensue will not be untangled until I am well out of this shit pile'. This bit of news was not shared with my father the Brigadier, who happened to be good friends with the Chief of the Australian Defence Force. Robin was well aware of the irony:

'Of course if I did get conscripted it would just be a question of Dad writing a letter to General Hassett to get me off! Doesn't it make you want to PUKE.'

He may have felt he was striking out from his

schooling and his family but he knew, as did I, that the ties that bound us to our heritage are harder to break than we would have liked.

Yet Robin is clearly doing his best to break with those ties. The coming year is full of innovation and turbulence. I needed to find those who could help me shed some light on his evolving persona: the players whom Marcus could not reach, those who participated in his search for a different way.

I did have one lead. In a letter I had found amongst the assorted collection Alun had sent via his iPhone, Robin wrote about wanting to come across to Melbourne and meet up with 'my good friend Vic Marsh and his friend Carmen Lawrence who now works at the Australia Performance Group'. That name had caused me to return to one of the theatre programmes that I found in my mother's papers, most notably for a production of Sergeant Musgrave's Dance, where Robin played Sparky and Vic played Hurst. There was a good chance that Vic would remember Robin and I hoped that, if I could find him, he could tell me about his involvement in the theatre scene. I was disappointed to find that none of the 'rugby crowd' seemed to have heard of Vic or knew anything about him. They had, on the other hand, all heard of Carmen Lawrence.

Carmen was well known as a career politician in the Australian Labour Party and had become Premier of Western Australia, the first woman to become state premier in a notoriously chauvinistic country. Although she had dropped off the political radar, it was not hard to track her down: she was lecturing in psychology and science at UWA.

Easy to track down, but not quite so easy to approach. In fact, there was no response at all to my first email. But my time in Western Australia was running out so I decided there was nothing for it but to phone her office. Again, her secretary was cool. Ms Lawrence was not available. Would I like to leave a message? No I wouldn't. I was only in Perth for one more day and I would only take up a few moments of her time and the matter was personal. Eventually, after a long delay, I was put through to Carmen, and true to her reputation she was not effusive. I made my pitch and eventually she thawed somewhat. Yes, she did remember Robin but not well. Yes, he may have come to Melbourne but she couldn't remember. She remembered him as charming and a rather good actor. But she was not going any further. She was polite but she would not be drawn into my conspiratorial plea for intimacy.

However, the main reason for contacting her was to see if she could lead me to Victor, but when I mentioned his name her lukewarm manner became positively icy. No, she did not know where Vic was. Did she have an email address for him by any chance? No, not an up-to-date one. Did she have an out-of-date one? Yes, she might have. There was a silence, as if she were rummaging through her address book. 'I suppose you could try this one,' and she read out an email address for the University of Queensland. I asked if she knew where he was living and she was not sure but suggested it might be somewhere in northern New South Wales.

I had low expectations as I sent off an email to Vic. If he was living in NSW, how come he had a Queensland University email address? I was certainly not expecting a prompt reply. My brief expedition had only a few more days to run. I was heading back to the east coast, to Melbourne but as yet I had no leads and only some first cousins to visit. I was starting to feel that I was not going to make anything like the progress I had hoped in solving the puzzle of Robin's last two years in Perth.

Then, just as I was packing my bags and saying my farewells, an email from Vic!

'Yes, I am still contactable through this university e-mail, and I live a little north of Byron Bay on the north coast of NSW.

I am really chuffed to hear from you, but what a pity that it has to be around such a sad event. I remember Robin with great affection: his incredibly engaging grin, his blue eyes and his generous spirit and would love to have continued to know him as the years have passed; I am sure we would have had a lot to share. What a pity! Please send me a photo and of course we should meet.'

At last! A glimpse of Robin as he became, from

someone who knew him well and was fond of him and who was clearly willing to talk about him. This was a breakthrough. Suddenly it looked as if my journey would take me where I wanted and needed to go. It seemed like I had found someone who could tell me about the Robin I needed to get to know.

I wanted to meet up with Vic, but where exactly was Byron Bay? It sounded as if it would take me out of the reassuring and reasonably familiar cosmopolitan Sydney/Melbourne nexus. In fact, it is very small on the map and about 800 kilometres north of Sydney. Google maps told me it would take nine hours to drive there even if I went back to Sydney, which was not my plan. That seemed an impossible distance and I was reconciling myself to the thought of having to make do with a phone call, when a closer look at the map suggested that Brisbane was much closer. In fact, Byron Bay was just 120 kilometres south of Brisbane. The app suggested I could drive that in just under two hours. I did some calculations and reckoned I could allocate 24 hours of my precious few days left in Australia and was just in time to change my flight from Melbourne to Brisbane.

Byron Bay is well known in Australia. As the Lonely Planet guide puts it:

'What makes Byron special is the singular vibe of the town itself. It's here that coastal surf culture flows into the hippie tide washing down from the hinterland, creating one great barefooted, alternative-lifestyle mash-up.'

Alternative-lifestyle mash-up' sounded a very long way away from the world of St George's College, photos in the university magazine and the rugby club. The guidebook description seemed to suggest a place where people lived a self-indulgent life, deliberately avoiding the challenges of the technocratic world: a place to opt out and become citizens of the counter-culture. Could that have been Robin's destination had he stayed and survived? I liked to think that Robin was on a different trajectory, driven by a love of the theatre and an evolving radical political sensibility. I felt sure that Vic would be the one to fill in the gaps. I sent him a photo of Robin, taken around the time we would be talking about and told Vic to expect me for lunch the next day.

'Oh my, you look just like Robin! You remind me of him. He was so handsome and so young!'

Such was the spontaneity of this welcome that I immediately felt a confusion of identity. This man clearly had a powerful sense of Robin and I seemed to slip into that persona. It was, rather unnervingly, as if I had become my brother. Vic was fit and robust with a grey moustache and a cropped grey hair. His physicality caused me to wonder what Robin would have looked like in his sixties. Would those good looks have stood the test of time? And Vic too was indeed interested in Robin's good looks. He very quickly revealed that, although at the time he knew Robin he, Vic, was still hovering in the closet, Vic had known that he was gay from an early age. He explained that 'gay liberation' had scarcely penetrated even the counter-culture in the early 1970s, and 'coming out' was even more of a challenge that in subsequent more liberal times. Such was our immediate bond of intimacy, he confided in me that he had expressed his feelings toward Robin who had politely turned him down.

Now, in 2013, Vic is obviously more comfortable with his sexuality.

'I fell in love with his spirit, but it was in a very nice package. But you know he put me off in such a lovely way. Coming out in Australia at that time was a fearsome business. Had I tried something similar on a straight Australian, the response would probably have been very ugly. But Robin was gentle and sweetly told me that he was not interested in that side of me. Such a lovely man.'

I spent less than twenty-four hours with Vic and yet we become firm friends, sharing not only the details of our relationship with Robin but also the differing paths our own lives had taken. Vic described his own drug-induced nervous breakdown, which was followed by ten years as a modern-day monk on the road in East Asia and then segued into a career in television. I told him about my three-way career which began in teaching and then moved to television and finally to running a television channel. I told him about my first foray into my family's history when I left teaching to make the film about my father's escape from the prisoner of war camp in Italy: how we had retraced his 500-mile walk and how I had gone some way to establishing a relationship with this man who had kept his distance for most of my life. I described how my career in television had taken off and how I had won prizes and made films that seemed to make an impact but which had all come at some cost. For him it was the ruthless commercial ethos that blunted his creativity. For me it was the constant sense of being on the periphery of a profession that I had joined late in life. Despite some success I felt like an outsider, which seemed to confirm the nagging perception of myself as impostor. We compared notes on that capricious industry and its effect on the psyche.

Then we got back to Robin. I wanted to know

about the theatre. Vic confirmed that Robin had plunged into that scene almost from the moment he arrived. Vic believed that he had identified university theatre as way of connecting with a more creative and intellectually challenging group. I had done the same because like Robin I realised there was a lot more to life than banter with the sporting crew. Much later, I found a paragraph in Vic's own autobiography that captured what I think was the motivation of all three of us:

'The English department has a strong theatre component, and some of the lecturers encourage me to cultivate my thespian persona. Through this doorway I encounter a host of stimulating grownups whose mastery of the theatre arts bespeaks an apparent freedom from the kind of insecurities that eat away at me and, on stage – albeit briefly – working through well-rehearsed lines and movement, I can play at being a stable, coherent character.'

Vic told me how he had met Robin through the University Theatre Club and how they had got on immediately. I asked him about a production of Sergeant Musgrave's Dance which had appeared in those early letters. In July 1969, just a few months into his first year, Robin writes: *'I have learnt all my lines for Sgt Musgrave and it is going well. I feel I am really achieving something there.'* The production was destined for the Festival of University Drama, to be held in Canberra a month later. Vic had the larger part of Hurst and Robin played Sparky, his rival for the affections of Annie the barmaid. Vic remembers they worked well together and recalls the scene where they fought for the attentions of Annie. Sparky got the worst of that, but Robin and Vic went on to be close friends.

In his letter from that Canberra Drama Festival, Robin is dismissive of the other university productions:

'They all cry "Technique, theatrical technique!" They just know how to say their lines, no group feeling. But we have been brought up in Perth in the free theatre discipline. Not surprisingly word has got round that we are doing something different.'

The play was directed by Paul McGillick. I found Paul on Google and contacted him to see if he remembered the production:

'Musgrave was very edgy and a lot of emphasis was put on the group to develop authentic interaction. We did all sorts of touchy/feely exercises (many derived from Grotowski who was the God) and when we took the production to the Intervarsity Drama Festival in Canberra in 1969 we didn't rehearse as such, but played ball games to sustain group sensitivity. It was a very dark production with a fair bit of chanting, black uniforms (inherited from a production of Richard III) – completely wrong, of course, because the soldiers were meant to be in red British tunics hinting at blood.

Ours was certainly the best production at that Festival and, indeed, was voted the best by a panel of judges. My memory of Robin is of a lovely, gentle, generous and urbane individual.'

I know from Robin's infrequent letters to me (which had taken me so long to disinter) that he was embracing the radical re-invention of theatre from Europe and America that was starting to infect the complacent Australian scene. At a similar stage in my re-awakening in Canada I too was experimenting with some subversive theatre of my own. I was directing Vaclav Havel and my own version of Lord of the Flies with a cast from the poshest prep school in Toronto. I now know that we had much more in common than I had allowed myself to believe. I may have denied it for thirty years, but I now know that Robin had recognised our parallel interests. There is a postscript to one letter that reads: *'You have my new address, write soon. I want to talk about theatre.'*

I managed to excavate all that commonality of experience later as part of my determined efforts to turn back the clock. At that moment, however, sitting with Vic eating a toothsome macrobiotic lunch, I was beginning that process and I felt a wave of exhilaration. His enthusiasm and obvious deep respect for what Robin had been conjured up for me a vision of him that was totally transformative. So far, those I met had been almost formulaic in what they said and remembered about Robin: all genuine and good to hear but not like this. Vic remembered Robin in a way that I was desperate to capture both for myself and for his two sons. I wanted more.

'Tell me about his acting.'

'It was incandescent. Truly he would blow us away. He lacked some technique and was not ready for the big parts, but all of us could see that he had the makings of a fine actor.'

'Do you think he wanted to make a career of it?'

'We all thought so. We absolutely believed that when he got back to England he would have enrolled in a drama school and gone on to great things.'

I told Vic that once he returned to England he never uttered a word about his acting. Not a word. He seemed to have lost all his confidence. Vic confirmed that Robin had been working with some of the best directors.

'Several went on to be very big names in Australian theatre. These were people who were cutting their teeth in Perth and Robin was part of that. Aarne Neame directed him in a production of Edward Bond's The Pope's Wedding. Aarne became a hugely successful director in Australia. And another big name was Ray Omodei. I think Ray was a big fan.'

Vic was such an enthusiast and clearly so fond of Robin that I did wonder whether he may have been over-egging the talent. Not for the first time in this journey and not for the last, I could not stop myself from wondering whether had he stayed in Australia and built on his talent and his contacts, could he too not have had a fulfilling career in Australian theatre?

Vic lived in a modern apartment with a view out onto the Coral Sea. It was not in Byron Bay and there was little sign of the 'alternative-lifestyle mash-up'. He had a commodious balcony and as the sun started to set, Vic got out a bottle of wine and started to talk about a trip he had taken with Robin and a bunch of their friends: both hallucinatory and geographical. The story of Robin as thespian had been revelatory, but here was a new kind of intelligence, even more beguiling. From what I could see this was a mystical as well as a physical journey and I would later confirm that it marked a dramatic revolution in Robin's life.

It all started with Maz. I recalled some mention of Maz in Robin's early letters, although with few details about his provenance. He was a friend and a fellow English student. He was actually 27 and had travelled out to Australia overland and, it would seem, had not just become a prophet for the eastern-inspired alternative lifestyle but, according to Vic, he had developed a capitalist approach to hallucinogenic drugs. He had arrived in Perth from Sumatra, which had been the last stop on his trek and where he had filled his suitcase with Buddha sticks. Now more commonly called Thai sticks, this was an unusually potent brand of marijuana made even more potent, it was widely believed, for being soaked in hash oil. By the time he entered their circle of friends in 1971, Maz was, in Vic's account: *'A gnomish Pied Piper figure from the counter-cultural underground.'*

Robin and Vic were into radical theatre. However, with Maz supplying the stimulants, they felt like fully paid-up members of the counter-culture which was only now infiltrating into the alternative student body of Western Australia. So it was natural that when word reached them that what would later be billed as Australia's first alternative festival was going to be held in Canberra later that year, the newly formed gang of counter-cultural warriors, now calling themselves the Campus Guerrilla Theatre, needed to be there. And Maz led the way.

After a whip-round, Maz had raised the funds to rent an elderly Ford Transit van. He and Robin ripped out the seats and replaced them with old carpets and hessian cushions covered in ethnic carpets. Since this was shaping up to be much like the journey described by Tom Wolfe in The Electric Kool-aid Acid Test, in which Ken Kesey and his Merry Pranksters travel across America in just such a bus, I was disappointed when Vic had to admit that the bus was not painted in psychedelic colours, but a grubby dull red. What he did confirm was that Maz had laid in a good supply of those Buddha sticks and they were joined by nine other people, making a company of eleven when they set off to drive the 3700 kilometres to Canberra. It was a gruelling drive: from Perth along the Eyre Highway through the Nullarbor, down to Adelaide, up through Swan Hill and Wagga and on to the Australian National University in Canberra.

Vic read me a passage from his autobiography, which he had just finished:

'Our wardrobe was an eclectic tribute to imported ethnicity and every colour from the chemist's stocks of dye bled brightly through my electric clothing, each layer forming a counter-cultural rainbow waiting to be unveiled. Hundreds of miles passed in an easy haze as we rotated drivers. Bags of buddha sticks inspired the ride and whenever we spilled out the back of the van for a piss-stop, dopey earthy fumes clung to our hair and clothes.'

And Robin was in that van dressed in garish cheesecloth trousers and a tie-dye shirt with a red bandana around his now luxuriant head of hair. Or at least that is the way I imagined him. I have just one photo of him from that era (the one I sent Vic) and at least it confirms the headband. At the same time, it is not the clothes that focus my mind; it is the image of him reclining across the back of the van, stoned and philosophical, waiting his turn to take the wheel and presumably surviving the experience of driving while under the influence of an hallucinogenic. Luckily for them all, the Eyre Highway had few curves and even less traffic in those days.

A few months later, when I finally got hold of all Robin's letters I found his letter to our parents describing this amazing venture. As I read it I am stunned by the change in tone. This is no boarding-school missive, this is someone who throws cautions to the winds and has total faith that his establishment parents will accompany him on the ride of his short lifetime. Of course, there is no direct mention of those Buddha sticks but it was possible to read between the lines:

'It was by far the most enjoyable long-distance journey that I have ever done. Of course, you cannot avoid getting pretty incredible things happening when you coop eleven people in a red box for three days on end: there was no friction, no real discomfort and much laughter.'

He describes what they call the *'God Show':* *sunrises and sunsets. 'Celestial Promotions do a very nice line in God Shows especially over the desert, all reds and purples.'* With Vic's more honest account to help us I think we get the picture.

Although the historians of Australia's belated assignation with the world of the rebellious sixties try to suggest that the Aquarius Festivals (there was another bigger festival in Nimbin in 1973) were the antipodean answer to Woodstock, the numbers don't stack up. Half a million went to the field in upstate New York, a mere 40,000 went to the first Aquarius. But to

Vic and – as I discovered in his letters some time later – to Robin, it was a transformative experience. Vic captures it vividly in his biography:

'There were hippies, students and sundry hangers-on gathered to celebrate the dawning of a New Age of peace and I greeted my brothers and sisters as fellows from the lost tribes returning to a new Jerusalem. Huxley's doors of perception were being blown right off their hinges. Stoned-out heads streamed through lecture halls, love-ins and impromptu songfests, mingling mind, body and spirit in easy familiarity. There could be no holding back against the swelling tide rising up on all sides; they flowed together in blissful unity as they were surely meant to do.'

And Robin was caught up in that tide, his parental missive proclaims with a breathless and radiant wonder:

'There was a large gathering of people, who were all thinking the same thing and the atmosphere was electric. There was a lot of love in the air, which may seem rather trite, but it was the first time that I really understood what 'love thy neighbour' means. So much happened, not just in terms of events, but to my view of myself.'

I am jealous. My own journey into the psychedelic never-never -land occurred four years earlier and although it took me to Haight-Ashbury and Berkeley in the summer of '67, it was a very tame affair in comparison.

I did make it to a six-hour Cream concert at fabled Fillmore West Auditorium, but in retrospect I didn't have a clue what was going on and never really got into Cream. No, mine was no Kool-aid Acid Trip, and hearing about Robin's mind-altering exploits some forty years after the event merely confirmed my own unease. He may have had his 'sixties' in the early seventies, but he was a damned sight more in tune with the zeitgeist than I had ever been.

Vic had mentioned a documentary about the Aquarius Festival, and as the breeze started to cool and the mosquitos got to work, we went back into his cramped front room to dig out the DVD. Called *Good Afternoon*, it was made by Phillip Noyce, now a mainstream international director (he directed *Rabbit Proof Fence*), but as a young filmmaker he was in the avant-garde and experimental scene and keen to push the boundaries. It is an innovative multi-screen film which contrasts lingering shots of the alternative crowd, their relaxed encounters and new-age workshops with wordy interviews with key players. I felt like I was eavesdropping on Robin and his friends. Although as the juxtapositions rolled by I did not catch sight of him, it was easy to imagine him just out of the frame. Certainly stoned but soaking up the rambling mix of alternative philosophy and what, to my jaded sixty-five-year-old self, seemed like an overly self-indulgent hedonism.

For Vic being transported back to those times was a mixed blessing. After the Festival he had gone on to Sydney where some friends gave him a birthday present of four tabs of LSD which he took all at once. As he later wrote, those tabs were *'high octane fuel for blasting into the God Zone. I zoomed off into wonderland, alone.'* And alone was the operative word. Losing his connection and missing his ride back home in the red bus, he wandered the streets of Sydney in an acid-induced psychosis for several days until he was arrested and jailed overnight. Neither he nor I had any idea at the time, but this episode in his story was to prove a significant precursor of what would eventually happen to Robin.

By now Vic and I were sleepy, drained by our intense hours of reminiscence and connection. I, of course, was still hoping that I might catch a glimpse of Robin in the film that was rolling on and when I asked Vic whether he had seen anything that might fit the bill, he was not encouraging but added, 'You would have a better chance of catching sight of Cy. She was a distinctive woman. Very beautiful.'

Cy, it transpired, was one of the three women on the bus, and the one with whom, Vic explained, Robin became captivated. Although he had known of her before the trip, they got together on that journey and, according to Vic, wafted around the festival like the perfect hippy couple: in love with each other and in thrall to the psychedelic happening that swirled around them. Vic said, with slightly ominous certainty, 'They were perfect together, what a pity they weren't ready for each other.' I was mesmerised by Vic's description and by the beguiling romance of falling in love on a journey across Australia in search of enlightenment.

I had been tantalised by the oblique but poignant reference to Cy in one of the random selection letters I had received from my nephew. During my time in Perth I had asked everyone I met whether they knew of Cy. And everyone who was around in those days did indeed know Cy Geiger. The men I met could talk only about her radiant beauty and how she broke hearts across campus. The women too seemed to know of her but were a little less generous. But nobody had any idea that she and Robin had got together and nobody had a clue where she was. Someone suggested that she had converted to become a Muslim and changed her name and just maybe she was living in Melbourne.

I drove back to Brisbane to catch my flight to Melbourne and as I waited in the departure lounge, savouring the warm intimacy and resonant insights I had reaped from my brief time with Victor Marsh, an email flashed up on my phone. It was from Marcus who was continuing to research on my behalf. He had tracked down Cy who had indeed changed her name to Halimah. And he included a mobile number. Suddenly

I had a very pressing reason to visit Melbourne and was in sight of the next important step in my quest to understand my dear dead brother.

143 Broom St, Cottesloe, WA 6534.
Airbnb Number 76532.

I have been having trouble with my foot and have it looked at every few weeks. Siobhan is a podiatrist and I have told her about your story and this book. A few weeks ago she surprised me by saying. 'It must be hard. You have to keep chronological time separate from discovery time.' That took me aback. It has been a problem and I have to keep checking that you know which time we are in.

I am writing this letter to you during my second visit to Perth. As usual, I am playing around with so many different timelines. The story so far is all based on my first trip and this next chapter will show you how my detective work hit pay dirt. I am holed up in an Airbnb, a tatty annex at the end of the garden. It is pleasingly rundown, like a student gaff in the 70s and makes me feel like I am inhabiting your world.

I am just about to set off across town to meet up with Halimah: Cy to you. As you will see in this chapter I managed to track her down on that first visit. Not easy as she had changed her name and moved from Perth to Melbourne. But we did find each other eventually. She turned out to be such an important part of your story.

10.   Aquarius Rising

Coming of age in the drug culture of the 1960s and '70s led many of us to 'turn on, tune in, and drop out – experimenting with every available drug, chasing that ultimate high while looking for someone with whom they could share it. Thinking ourselves invincible, we did not realize that we were flirting with danger.

Bobby Legend, The Age of Aquarius

A few months later, when I was home in London and when I finally got my hands on all the letters that I had refused to look at for so long, I was able to read the letter written in May 1971. The one in which Robin tries to relay to his rather staid and establishment parents just some of the joyous and transformative experiences he had had at the Aquarius Festival. It included a tender introduction to the woman that Vic had told me about that evening in his apartment outside Byron Bay.

'I would like to introduce you, in as much as that is possible with a biro and a piece of paper, to Cy who is

a beautiful girl. There is little else to say that will mean anything except that she is the same age as me, teaches art, has beautiful parents and a beautiful brother and has added a completely different hitherto unexperienced dimension to my life. Why she is mentioned at this stage of the saga is that she came on the bus, I hardly knew her at all and always regarded her from the foot of an ivory tower and had never thought twice about trying to fight through the hordes of admirers, but it was just one of those things.'

* * * * * *

I had flown back to Melbourne in a state of uneasy anticipation. I had a name and a mobile number for the elusive Cy. Up to now, I had always softened the initial contact with likely witnesses via a friendly email. 'You don't know me, but I think you knew my brother… sad untimely death… suicide etc.' As well as giving the recipient a chance to absorb the news about Robin, it gave me a chance to introduce myself and my quest. I could gauge their reactions in their written response. It helped me mitigate any emotional resistance to my delving into their past. But I had no email address for Halimah. I didn't even know her second name. This was going to be a high-risk cold call. I was braced for rejection and kept my hopes in check

At first it seemed that I had been right to lower

my expectations. Her initial greeting was wary and it felt as if I might be an unwelcome intrusion. Yes, she knew Robin, but it was a long time ago and she was not sure how much she could tell me. She said she could meet me but she was busy. I had to press as my time in Australia was fast running out. We agreed a coffee tomorrow might be possible. She named a place and a time and then hung up. It was not an auspicious start. I tried to get used to the idea that this meeting was not going to illuminate anything and that I had just been very lucky with Vic. Then, as I was managing my disappointment, the phone went. It was Halimah:

'I am so sorry, Andrew. I did not mean to be so cool. It is just that you caught me unawares. Robin was terribly important to me. I have intense memories of our time together. I miss him. And I cannot wait to talk to you.'

This time the warmth in her voice enthralled me. I felt the same instant bond with the past and with Robin that Vic had elicited in that first encounter. She confirmed our date for the next day and I felt a frisson of anticipation.

Federation Place in downtown Melbourne is a modernist development, a cultural hub around a huge open plaza. I am waiting in the agreed coffee venue. I am early and I consult the guide book to learn that *'the main square is paved with 470,000 ochre coloured sandstone blocks from Western Australia and invokes an image of the Outback'*. I stare at the pattern and think of my new relationship with Western Australia. I am waiting and still waiting. Has she got cold feet? Am I in the wrong place? Then I look across the coffee house decking and there, in a corner, is a woman of a certain age, looking at her phone and all alone. Could it be?

It was indeed. Halimah had been waiting for me. She had texted me to say she had got out of work early, but my dodgy UK phone provider had failed to deliver the message. We were relieved to have met; we could easily have spent another hour in our respective corners. It was clear that she was as nervy as I was. We made desultory small talk as we ordered our herbal teas and flapjacks laced with Chai seeds. I was immediately struck by her good looks. It was not hard to see how forty years ago she would have been the focus for all that male attention. Tall and with a warm expressive face, she was a striking woman well capable of turning a few heads in her early sixties. Again, I was distracted by the subversive thought that I was muscling in on my brother's love life.

Once settled, it became clear that this was a potentially magical encounter. We fell into an easy rapport within minutes. Gently testing out our respective narratives and finding nothing but congruence and empathy. When she talked about Robin there was a wistfulness that spoke of poignant reminiscence.

'Vic told me all about the bus trip across to Canberra. Eleven of you in the back of the bus. Is that when you and Robin got together?'

'That's right. I had seen him around campus, but I wasn't a student so we hadn't really met. I had noticed that he was very good looking, and had a free-flowing charm. We had some friends in common but that was all.'

'And what about that trip? Three days cooped up in the bus? Vic suggested that you were stoned all the time.'

'Generally, I didn't do drugs. Pot made me feel paranoid so I usually avoided it, but it was hard. The rest were smoking pretty constantly. But Robin was very attentive and lovely, even though he was high a lot of the time. And he was very attractive. I remember his headband. And his embroidered bell-bottomed jeans. He did his own embroidery. I was impressed by that. I suppose I was a bit naïve, vulnerable even and he made me feel safe.'

'Do you remember Maz? Vic said he was the Pied Piper of the group, a bit of a Merry Prankster. I admit I am a little suspicious of Maz. I sense that Robin was in awe of him and I am wondering whether Maz had inducted him into the drug scene. I have come to see him as a potentially malign influence.'

'I do remember Maz. He was an influence. I am

not sure how malign, but he certainly was pushing drugs and he was charismatic. I am not sure you could blame him for Robin's introduction to pot. I think a whole gang of them were involved.'

That caused me to think back to Paul McGillick's email where after his account of Sergeant Musgrave he wrote about the splits amongst students on campus:

'Outside of the theatre I didn't really mix with Robin. And I think one reason for this was the era. This was the counter-culture. You were either into long hair, drugs, communal living and the anti-war movement or you were 'conservative' like me. I have never taken drugs, I don't like 'trooping off in a gang' (D.H. Lawrence).'

I am building a picture of Robin as a 'free spirit' but I am starting to feel that maybe he did indeed 'troop off in a gang' and that Maz was a totemic figure in that gang. There was more work for me to do in that regard. Quite how embedded was he in the long-haired, pot-smoking gang and to what extent did it sow the seeds of his later self-destructive turmoil? For the time being getting together with Cy on the road to enlightenment seemed, in contrast to those premonitions, a life-affirming venture

'And what about when you got there. To the festival. Were you an item? Vic seemed to think so.'

'Yes. We were together. We were instantly immersed in what was, for both of us, a totally new experience. We strolled around in a happy daze absorbing the incredible array of alternative styles and happenings. We slept together, but in a huge circus tent. There wasn't much privacy. It was freezing and we cuddled for warmth rather than anything more.'

When I get back to Robin's account in his letter, there is the same elegiac wonder at the multiple layers of sensual inspiration.

'The clothes, the colours, the music and the people were all incredible and added to this there was non-stop programme of events in the way of films, plays, exhibitions, readings, workshops, dancing, singing. It seemed wonderfully endless. Of course there was too much to see, but it didn't matter because just walking around was so good. It is really difficult for me to convey the atmosphere and the way it changed me.'

And Halimah had some very clear memories of their wanderings.

'I remember how he picked daisies and presented them to me with a grand flourish. And once he pressed an acorn into my hand. In return I gave him a little cloth wallet, which I had embroidered. He told me he'd keep it forever and I think he used it to keep his stash of drugs in. Did you find it in his things I wonder?'

If only I had found it. How much I would have loved to tell her that he kept it to the end and we had retained a collection of his precious objects. But I had virtually nothing concrete to remember him by: just his written words and now, slowly but surely, the words of others. Words were a pleasure but the lyrics of his story could so easily flatter to deceive.

* * * * * *

Some months later, after I had returned from the trip that connected me with Halimah, I was sitting back in my home in London and I had obtained my own DVD of Good Afternoon and had become somewhat compulsive in re-playing it, with my finger hovering over the pause button. It was a seductive act of virtual time-travel. It is easy to see past the somewhat loosely edited alternative documentary style to a remarkably atmospheric study of the festival. The DVD was a visceral connection with that time and Robin's life. It was far too easy to imagine I could glimpse him and Cy wandering hand in hand amongst the aspiring counter-cultural warriors who had assembled to parade their revolt from the Australian mediocracy. For one crazy moment I was convinced that I had seen them, walking away in the middle distance. I froze the image and toggled back and forth. Maybe, just maybe? But a cooler self asserted control over my hopeless aspirations. I let the multiple screens roll on.

A lengthy scene of impromptu folk singing was starting to bore, when in the contrasting screen I watched as what looked like a platoon of Canberra's police were moving across and into a mass of fun-seekers. It was the start of a sequence revealing that it was certainly not all peace and love. In the latter stages of the festival, the police appeared to be hell-bent on ruining the show. It seems that some of the more politically motivated attendees had decided to do a peace march on the national Parliament, and not surprisingly the authorities were less likely to 'live and let live'. There were further scenes of confrontation: fragile hippies facing macho defenders of another sort of peace.

It seems as if the organisers managed to broker a truce and the police left the festival, but it clearly soured the atmosphere. It was hard to reconcile with Robin's lyrical 'love is in the air'. So I went back to his account and eventually (it is six pages of his tiny writing) found this:

'There were radical elements in evidence too, but they didn't feature until the last day when they had their "Day of Rage" which was anti-war, anti-apartheid, anti-this, anti-that demonstration that achieved little except a few column inches that the good radical cherishes so much.'

Sentences that would, I think and hope, have offended my own political sensitivities of the time. I was no firebrand, although I was very clear on whose side I was on when it came to the Vietnam War and North American racial politics. Two years into my time at university I would not have written sentences like that, however much I was in love with the girl and the moment. In my life it was 1968, the year that Martin Luther King was assassinated, and I had high hopes for Robert Kennedy for the democratic nomination to beat Nixon, whom I despised. During my boyish drug-free trip across America in 1967, I had got stuck in Watts just a few months after the riots and then hitch-hiked through Detroit a few hours after the riots there had turned the streets into a war zone. As a student at that time it was hard not have been radicalised to some degree at least. Indeed, I think I was already formulating a position which rejected the dropout flower-power culture on the grounds that it was turning its back on the pressing political issues of the day in favour of a selfish hedonism.

I fell to wondering what had happened to the Robin who had, in his letter to me six months earlier, raged about the military draft and refused to have anything to do with a war that he had 'no conceivable belief in'. Would those Buddha sticks have permanently blunted his social conscience? Then I considered the impact of the parental filter. This was a letter that was already blowing the lid off his parents' expectations. Maybe he muted his sympathy for those 'radicals' for the sake of our father. As I move on through the story, I hope I will find that this was only a temporary surrender to the lotus-eaters.

* * * * * *

In Providence Square, Melbourne the light was starting to fade and the waitress was clearing away the cups and stacking the chairs. Halimah and I were still deep in our time-shifting voyage round my brother. It became increasingly clear that this was not merely a transient crush or drug-assisted infatuation. Her relationship with Robin had a deeper resonance. I had allowed her to roll back the years and savour what was so clearly a significant love.

'You know he proposed to me?'

'What! When?'

'During the festival. He was besotted with me and I suppose I was with him.'

'Did you accept?'

'I don't remember, but we didn't make plans to marry!'

She was laughing now, but there was sweet sadness to the humour. A missed opportunity? Surely not. I made light of the idea, but that didn't mean I was untouched by the poignancy.

'Not sure of the status of a proposal of marriage when stoned. Probably not legally binding.'

We gathered our things and made for the edge of the square, where the rush-hour traffic on Flinders Street was intruding into our absorbing rapport with the past and brashly reminding us of the harsher imperatives of the present. I was acutely aware that I was starting my journey home to England the next day at the crack of dawn. My time was running out and I knew that I was very unlikely to meet up with Halimah in any foreseeable future. As we started to make our farewells it was obvious that neither of us wanted to cut short what had been an extraordinary meeting of minds and spirits. We prevaricated. Delaying the moment. Then I chanced my arm:

'I don't suppose you are free for dinner?'

Her relief was constrained but I was pushing at an open door. I wasn't the only one who wanted to prolong the encounter.

'Well, I have a couple of things to do at home. But why don't you come round at seven and I'll make us supper. Nothing fancy, just what's in the fridge.'

'If you don't mind that would be wonderful. I think we probably have lots more to talk about.'

'Here's my address. I'll see you then.'

And she strode off to catch her bus.

Rather like my time with Victor, we had slipped into a friendship that seemed to have its foundations firmly rooted in the distant past, but was no less beguiling for that. As she rustled up an omelette and salad and opened a bottle of wine, she tried to recall what had happened once they left the festival.

'It's funny, I can't seem to bring the next part into focus. I know we went to Sydney and I remember sleeping on the floor of someone we hardly knew. Probably someone we met at the festival. We were untethered and seemed to go with the flow. I know we didn't go back to Perth for another ten days or so. I really can't remember, except I was with Robin and that was a very nice feeling. '

Sometime later I was able to fill in the blanks for her. At the time I had not yet discovered Robin's letter to my parents with its breathless introduction to his new love. However, he tells the story of what happened after they left Canberra and the festival and headed for Sydney in the red bus, Maz at the wheel. There were just four of them in the bus by that stage: Cy and Robin and Maz and his girlfriend Gerry.

Although even in those days Gymea Bay was largely made up of weekend homes for the wealthy, a group of hippies had found a run-down quarter and were squatting in a series of dilapidated houses. The group were mostly young Germans who 'lived by making clothes of crushed velvet and leather.'

'They were very peaceful and kind to us feeding us with beautiful food and as soon as we met, giving all the girls their 'uniforms' (velvet kaftans). We stayed there for about five days absorbing the peace and love after the hectic times in Canberra. They let us make things in their workshops and I ended up with a full-length purple cloak and matching trousers in crushed velvet. We were fascinated by their life-style. They were heading off to India to gather more material and skills before buying some land in Queensland to set up a collective.'

This was a seductive taste of the counter-culture that could easily have turned Robin's head and set him off on an itinerant new-age existence. But to my retrospective relief, he recounts how they bid their hosts farewell and drove the bus back to Sydney, then down to Melbourne where they gathered the rest of the Merry Pranksters (except for poor Vic, who having wandered the streets of Sydney lost and wasted by the four LSD tabs was now out on bail and forced to remain there), and by the beginning of June they were back in Perth.

* * * * * *

In Halimah's kitchen some forty years later I was finishing my salad and started to pour myself another glass of wine when she reached across and placed her hand over my glass.

'No more, you are driving.'

It's true, I was going to have to drive back that night to my first cousin's home in the suburbs before getting up at 5 a.m. to catch my plane, but I was feeling very relaxed and was wanting to cut myself some slack. I had only had a glass and a half and was inclined to bend the rules when it came to the legal limit. But she was firm and filled up a glass of carbonated water.

I wanted to know why she had changed her name and her religion.

'Well, it was a couple of years after my time with Robin. The next Aquarius Festival took place at a place called Nimbin. It was a lot bigger than Canberra and one of the headline acts was the South African jazz pianist Dollar Brand. He and I got together and it was just at the time when he was converting to the Muslim faith and he changed his name to Abdullah Ibrahim and I followed him and changed mine to Halimah.'

I remember listening to Dollar Brand in the seventies. I had been a fan and continued to follow him as Abdullah Ibrahim. I already found Halimah glamorous, but that story added yet another layer of fascination.

I must confess that my initial reaction was to judge her conversion as an impulsive act of solidarity with her famous lover and in tune with the spiritual indulgence of the time. However, as I got to know Halimah over the next few years, it was clear that this conversion was no whimsical pursuit of an alternative lifestyle; rather, it reflected her spiritual side. She took her new religion seriously. She told me that her grandmother had called her a 'seeker' and throughout her life she has continued to seek and find support and succour in the transcendental.

To deflect her from her subsequent lovers, I asked

about how her burgeoning relationship with Robin had stood up to the plunge back into the cool realities of life in Perth. It seemed that for a while it did. Robin writes that he is happier than he has ever been.

Some months after I had returned home from Melbourne, Halimah sent me a message with a photo attached:

'I am having to move and was clearing out my cupboards when I came across this: my mother's wedding dress. It brought back a beautiful memory of wearing it riding on the back of Robin's motorbike as we sped off to the Magician's Ball. I remember my hair and my dress flowing behind.'

I am easily transported to a warm spring evening in Perth where I am standing on the side of the road, probably wearing my tweed jacket and ill-fitting jeans hoping to get lucky and this good looking guy in a crushed velvet cloak and an even better looking woman roar past on a 500cc Suzuki on their way to some impossibly romantic venue where they will dance the night away and make love as the sun rises over the Swan River. Yes, I cannot tell a lie, I am distressingly jealous of my brother in those few heady months. I have nothing remotely similar to match both the fantasy and indeed the reality. He did drive a motorbike, he was good looking and he had a fabulous girlfriend who wore her mother's wedding dress as they drove to the Magician's Ball. There was magic in the air. Whichever way you wrap it up, it is a seductive package that does feed the sibling rivalry that I have only recently fully acknowledged.

Halimah too can confirm that my fantasy was not that far from the truth:

'It was very romantic and we did have a lovely time in those weeks after Canberra. We were very much in love and in tune. I suppose still quite innocent. I was living at home and Robin was very restrained in respecting my boundaries. That's what made him so different from the other men I had been with.'

But the idyll was to be short-lived. I wanted to know what happened because I had that fragment of a letter that suggests they broke up shortly afterwards. Halimah's tone changed and I realised that we were getting closer to the painful part of these reminiscences. Their relationship may have had an innocence that could have boded well for the longer term, but unbeknown to Robin there was a spectre hanging over the whole enterprise.

In the two years before meeting Robin, Halimah had been having an affair with a married man twenty years her senior. We can look back at it from the MeToo perspective and it seems thoroughly exploitative. But, as is so often the justification for past misdemeanours of this sort, it was a very different time. Halimah did not feel she was exploited, and although he never followed through his promise to leave his wife, their relationship did in fact stand the test of time. They kept in touch for many years. But in May 1971 he was off the scene, travelling in Europe with his family.

Such was our new-found rapport that Halimah felt emboldened to try and articulate how having the good looks that caused her to be desired was not such a blessing. It brought superficial pleasures but the immaturity of so many of the men in that place and that time meant that she was wary and defensive. As one woman explained to me, '*We assumed that Aussie men were incapable of empathy, sensitivity and expected them to be predatory.*' No wonder she found some peace and reassurance in the arms of an older, more mature man who was devoted to her.

Then along came Robin and she allowed herself to be blown away by his adoration and his creativity and she fed off his sheer happiness. This was something different and seemed so right. But the ghosts of the past rarely let you escape scot-free and her married lover may have been far away but he had not lost interest. Halimah described how, just as things were going so well with Robin, she started to receive letters from Europe dazzling her with a heady mixture of the wonders of Renaissance art and his love for her.

At first she kept it secret and clung on to the real-world romance she was enjoying. But it was a stealthy worm of disruption. Her married lover was still in love with her, and Halimah found it harder and harder to push him into the background. It became clear to Robin that something was up and as they approached the end of August, just three months after those heady days in Canberra, she confessed. Robin's underlying vulnerability (the flip side of all that public-school confidence) meant that he had little emotional resilience. He would not demean himself by fighting his corner. For him it was all over and although Halimah knew that her young self was likely to regret it, she slipped back into the well-worn habits of the almost inevitably unobtainable though sweet and seductive love of her original affair.

* * * * * *

It was late by now, way past midnight and I had my very early start. I was reluctant to extricate myself. If after just two hours of Halimah's memories on Federation Square I had felt a sharp pang of regret at its likely end, then after another three hours of close association to my brother's memory the leaving was going to be that much harder. But leave I did, eventually. We vowed to keep in touch. There was so much more to uncover and to celebrate.

My heart was singing and my mind was whirling as I set off towards the suburbs. What had started as a high-risk venture with a strong likelihood of a low-key result had turned into a wonderfully fulfilling experience that had transformed my feelings about my brother. I was re-running the pleasures of our conversation and my mind was elsewhere so I was a little slow to understand the implications of the flashing blue light in the road ahead of me. A policeman glowing in hi-viz was waving me into a cordoned-off lane where his colleagues were waiting.

'Good evening, sir. Where are you off to?'

I put on my best English accent and explained where I was going.

'Had anything to drink, sir?'

I gulped and my stomach turned. If this went badly I would be missing my plane home. I steadied myself.

'A glass and a half of wine, officer. With a meal.'

'Then you won't mind blowing into this, will you, sir?'

I took a tremulous breath and blew. A horrible pause whilst he passed the breathalyser to his colleague. His colleague looked, paused and smiled.

'That's all in order sir. No problem. Drive carefully now. It's late.'

I tried to dissipate my obvious relief with some gratuitous and unnecessary gratitude – 'Thank you so much, officer' – and drove off, even more convinced that my encounter with Halimah had been blessed with magic.

The next morning I did indeed make it to the airport on time. I had very mixed emotions about heading home. I had been on the road for just six days, hardly an odyssey, but the emotional journey had felt a lot longer. I had made unexpected progress in my desire to locate Robin in a time and place. He was starting to feel real and I was getting my conflicted feelings into some sort of order. However, there was a strong sense of regret. Exciting as it had been, I knew that I was only at the start of a journey and I really did not want to deny myself access to Robin's numerous other friends, girlfriends and colleagues, many of whom were already getting in contact and filling my inbox with tantalising vignettes of how Robin lit up their memories of those days. I knew there was much to do, but equally I knew my journey had fulfilled my most optimistic expectations. I was a lucky man.

And as if to validate the magical, an email from Halimah flickered onto the home screen of my phone:

'Our encounter has made me remember one of my favourite Rumi poems. Can you imagine, 800 years old & he could be speaking of Robin:

Red Shirt

Has anyone seen the boy
who used to come here?

Round-faced trouble-maker,
quick to find a joke,

slow to be serious, red shirt,
perfect coordination, sly,
strong muscled,
with things always in his pocket:
reed flute, worn pick,
polished and ready for his Talent –
you know that one.
Have you heard stories about him?
Pharaoh and the whole Egyptian world
collapsed for such a Joseph.
I'd gladly spend years getting word
of him, even third or fourth hand.

Robin's presence is quiet & surely felt & I wonder at
how things are being put right & perhaps to rest.'

It caught me by surprise, and I simply could not stop myself from dissolving into tears. I have cried so rarely in my life and I surprised myself. It was partly the remarkable resonance of the poem itself. It was exactly what I had been doing: looking for word of him. In the next few years I would indeed get word of him, second, third and even fourth hand. And although it transpired that the journey had just begun and it would be a lot longer before I came back to Australia, this was clearly a cathartic moment. The moment when I realised that I was on the right track.

COLVIN, VIA MOORA, WA 6510.
TIME 11.45 PM.

Dear Robin,

I am writing this at Colvin or near enough. It's a place you knew very well. It plays what I think is a pivotal role in your story. I felt it was important for me tread in your footsteps because as you know something happened and you ended up dropping out. I am staying with Diana and her husband Ross. I had met them both on my first trip to Perth when we had lunch and she showed me that letter where you were trying to tell her you loved her. Now on this my second trip to Perth, they have agreed to take me up to Colvin and show me around.

I am not sure Ross buys into my quest. I suppose he never knew you and this obsession of mine to take people back in time is not to everyone's taste. Most people have a few ghosts from those days that they would rather not disinter. They all admire me for trying to find out about you, but that's because you are dead. I get the benefit of the doubt. I get the sympathy vote. I cannot assume that everyone feels the same way.

I was certain that Ross was bored with my constant questions and perhaps even disapproved. He must have been aware that his wife was rather too happy to talk to me about the times when she was modelling and attracting the close attention of all the boys. But then on the drive up here this morning, he took me by surprise and started to talk about his brother. His brother John was younger, he too came from traditional farming stock and had gone to UWA just like you. And just like you, he had played rugby, joined the UDS and was an enthusiast for the student life. He was more of a conformist than you, but at about the same time as you he was beguiled by drugs and the counter-cultural explosion. He dropped out and headed off to Nimbin, inland from Byron Bay, where the Australian Love Children were gathering. He joined a commune and lived off the land. He is still there to this day, and wholly cut off from his family. So Ross knew a lot more about the loss of a brother than I ever guessed.

That set me thinking about those forks in the road. The sliding doors and how when you came back from the Aquarius Festival you could easily have taken the same path as brother John. You were in awe of those German hippies with their crushed velvet and plans for a commune. Your friend Vic Marsh spent the next ten years as a travelling Buddhist monk. Was there a chance that you too could have dropped out for good? I think it is unlikely, but you did drop out and you did seek solace in the simple life. But I now think what you were doing was saving yourself.

11. Escape to the Country

Later I would understand that modern industrial communities are obsessed with the importance of 'going somewhere' and 'doing something with your life'. The implication is an idea I have come to hate, that staying local and doing physical work doesn't count for much.

James Rebanks, The Shepherd's Life

I am the time traveller. I am sitting in a café opposite the Octagon Theatre where Robin had done much of his acting. The sun is setting over the Swan River and I am nursing a second glass of red wine. It is not hard to imagine myself back to the winter of 1971 as Robin emerges from the theatre deep in conversation with Ray Omodei. He is an inspirational director and they are good friends. The rest of the company are coming out now and Robin leaves Ray with a passing hug. I look for Vic, but he has left the scene. He is in Melbourne with his wife and child. Robin is so obviously at ease with his fellow actors: a comfortable rapport.

Then he looks up and there, across the square, he sees Cy tall and serene, her long skirt of dazzling tie-dye swaying with her graceful stride. He smiles, gives a wave to his friends and walks towards her. They embrace and kiss. Then he wraps an arm round her and they head off to the macrobiotic café. I know that Robin has the little cloth bag Cy had given him at the Aquarius Festival and in it he has the block of hash that he will later use to roll himself a joint to enjoy as they watch the sunset. Cy will have just one puff but is happy to relax into the aura.

I am just one of many who are admiring from afar. There's Marcus the architect who had been such a good friend in the early days of rugby and St George's College. He is envious of the girl but suspicious of the drugs. He'll wave and smile, but Robin and Cy are so far off his wavelength now and too entwined to allow for any idle chat about the good old days. Jim Singleton is also there with his girlfriend Helen. He still sees Robin from time to time after he moved in for the summer of 1970 with the public-school Brits in the house on Marmion St, but he too has missed out on the counter-cultural blast and is a little daunted by the sight of Robin so completely transformed from their days at school together. Like me, and plenty of others, he is very envious of the girl by his side. He and I both know that she is well out of our league.

Once the sun has set, they will take off on Robin's

500cc and head across town to another house in Cottesloe that they now share with Maz and Alan. There will be beer and music and chat. Robin, lightly stoned, is leading the way with some intense rumination on Joyce's Ulysses, as he is into his course on the modern novel. Then after a while they will head off to bed.

I am allowing myself free rein to conjure up this fantasy: My Brother in Love. Of course I am envious, but this is not the raw envy of my twenty-one year old self. At seventy years old I am savouring the thought of what they had during those halcyon days. As he wrote: *'right in the midst of love'*.

I want it to be true and I want it to go on. I want them to grow into each other and lay the foundations of a long-term relationship that will stand the test of time. I am taking a vicarious pleasure in the progress of a fulfilling love affair. His life seems so full of promise and I am cheering them both on from the sidelines. I want there to be a happy ending. But my fantasy is just that, a wishful aspiration. There are darker clouds obscuring the balmy spring sunset.

As August moves to its close and spring is in the air, Robin is approaching his birthday. On September 1st 1971 he will be twenty-one years old. Surely there are plans for a big party to celebrate not just his majority but also his newfound love? I imagine that my parents will have dispatched presents and cards, but I can find no evidence. I am looking for the clues but there are none. There is an absence of letters to his parents, which I put down to his living life to the full. He has other far more important things on his mind, for his life is humming with joy.

Then something happens: unexpected and against the run of play. He abandons it all... and my fantasy is shattered.

One day before his birthday he abandons his life in the city and heads off up the Great Northern Highway to the little town of Moora, where he turns off into open farming country. He is aiming for Colvin, the sheep farm owned and run by Mr and Mrs Lefroy, the parents of his good friend Diana. He is travelling alone. He needs a break, perhaps just a weekend, to recharge the batteries after the last three months of frenetic bliss. He is drawn to the countryside but perhaps he is looking for something else. He is about to turn twenty-one and I imagine he is missing his own family. He has met the Lefroys once before and perhaps he is hoping that they will serve as surrogates at this time of transition.

The idea of a break and the attraction of surrogate parents makes sense, but then I look through his letters and it turns out that he will spend four whole months at Colvin. He has abandoned his friends, his theatre and his love. This is a screeching handbrake turn, a sudden transformation from the man who was so inspired and invigorated by his mind-bending and life-changing experience at the Aquarius Festival into a ghost of his former self. What the hell happened?

I start to scrabble through his letters from the farm looking for clues. His style and tone is radically altered. His handwriting has become even more dense and precise. He is detached and ruminative. I imagine he is trying to reassure his parents but, as I read them now, the letters are worrying. Has he had a nervous breakdown? A drug overdose? Or has he seen the writing on the wall and needs to save himself?

The first letter I can find is dated 5th September, just five days after his birthday and a week after his sudden exit from his life in Perth. He refers to a letter that has clearly gone missing from my mother's collection (perhaps it was too distressing?)

'I realised that my last letter will not have stopped you worrying. In fact it probably made it worse. But it is all true especially the bit about being happier now than I ever have before. Now there is no doubt about what I am doing. It is all my decision and I know you will allow me that right for as Dad has said to me when he was twenty-one he was fighting against the Germans in Africa.'

He goes out of his way to dispel their inevitable fears. He will be doing his work for the exams in November and it will be easier with no distractions. *'I am confidently expecting high grades.'* He is certain that all his friends from Perth will come up and visit him. He also suggests that Cy might come up and live with him later, as she has finally made the break from home and her overly possessive mother. It all sounds very plausible. He seems confident that he will persuade his parents that his sudden volte-face, just three months before he is scheduled to complete his degree and fulfil his obligations to the Drapers Company, is perfectly comprehensible. I am not fooled and nor, I suspect, were they.

He confirms my doubts when he finishes his first letter from Colvin with a disconcerting flourish:

'I celebrated my 21st birthday up here with the Lefroys. It was my first day in the country and the beginning of a new life for me, in which I am endeavouring to refine the art of living down to the point where nobody gets hurt, worried or anxious and harmony and honesty are the corner stones.

Peace and God be with you both,
Robin'

That sign-off causes me to ask whether there has been a spiritual shift. Has he imbibed the Kool-aid? Is he now an acolyte of the hippy priesthood? Is he consolidating his conversion with this escape from the city and its materialist demands? And yet he is also in love, which should cause him to be counting his blessings not seeking solace elsewhere. It is confusing.

I then turn to his next letter, written a month later. He has beautiful handwriting but when he is happy it expands and flows. Now it is small, precise and cramped. The tone has changed again. That philosophical sign-off has mutated into a fully-fledged rumination on the meaning of things. Again, I am imagining my father reading this over breakfast as he sits there in his Brigadier's uniform before heading off to the Staff College where he would be lecturing officers in the art of war. But I now see that this letter is addressed to my mother only, which makes sense.

'Dear Mum,

My life has slowed down and I am able to feel the deep rhythms of nature much more, and they calm me in my moments of solitude and uplift me in my time of joy. That demon loneliness that plagued me not a little during my first weeks here has been vanquished and now I feel neither happiness nor unhappiness, joy nor sorrow, but a deep quiet peace and I wait for what the future will bring me with certainty, certainty in the innate goodness of things. The evil that we create for ourselves, is no more than our narrow vision of our own selfish appreciation of events.'

And it goes on. And on. Until even he realises that he may be pushing the tolerance of my mother who is, of course, endlessly tolerant of her younger son, but who must by now also be beginning to wonder what has happened.

'I hope you don't mind this contemplative sort of writing, but I have had less of the art of the conversation.'

If she had managed to plough on, however, she would come across some genuine revelations about his state of mind and the causes of this upheaval:

'The major price I had to pay for jettisoning myself into the country with such precipitate haste and thoughtlessness (about others) was my relationship (a terrible word!) with Cy. This was the result of the entry of a third party into the game. There was a little pain and sadness, but one learns to accept the quirks of Fate, just as here the farmers accept the wind that flattens their wheat harvest.'

So all that optimism about Cy coming up to live with him has vanished like wheat chaff in the wind. That 'third party' is her married lover and so it came as no surprise to me. Whether the alarmingly understated emotional impact, 'a little pain and sadness', will have convinced my mother, I will never know. As an ex-public-school boy myself I know for certain that the dissolution of such a promising and fulfilling relationship (not such a terrible word) must have caused him intense pain and despair. I have a letter written to my mother from Banff Springs. My first real girlfriend was working in the famous eponymous hotel. I had hitchhiked three thousand miles to join her, only to find that she had dumped me in favour of the hotel lifeguard. I too had written to my mother alone and I too was diluting a howl of pain with public-school platitudes about other fish in the sea. And for

Robin it was no quirk of fate, it was a desperately sad conjunction of circumstance and his devious vulnerability.

The break-up with Cy must have contributed to his evacuation to the country, and yet there is a still a problem with the timeline. He abandons Perth the day before his birthday; five days later he is writing to explain his actions and is reassured that 'Cy could be coming up to live with him.' He would not have written that if he was in a state of deep distress, because the relationship was over and he was running away from the consequences. So surely his sudden self-imposed exile must have been precipitated by something else. I went back to the letters in search of any clues. His parental letters offer nothing new. I then turned to a letter he sent to Diana.

As I've written earlier, I had met Diana at the start of my first trip to Australia and I had been easily distracted by Robin's putative love letter to her and her apparent failure to recognise his cri de coeur. She had also caught me by surprise with her photo of my nephew Oliver with its startling similarity to his father, standing in the sheep pen on the same farm that Robin had used as an escape hatch from his turbulent life in the city. Those two distractions caused me to forget that she had given me a number of other letters. Although he had not been her lover, he was still very close to her and was naturally much more open to her than he ever

227

would be to his parents, or even to his brother.

Sure enough, I found a letter written on October 6th 1971, again just a month after his precipitous arrival at Colvin.

'Well here I am working happily and peacefully at your home – don't ask me why I am here because I really don't know – I suddenly found some part of me driving here to say hello to your dear family and then another part of me offering myself as labourer in exchange for food and keep. I sailed out of Perth, and the intensive social requirements of city life on an enormous burst of energy. I was in the midst, right in the midst, of love – but those links between people are so tenuous – and it dissolved without my body there to nourish it: much pain and sadness for a while but trees, sheep, birds and sky understand and accept your pain so much better than humans, and now all is well. An overwhelming experience, pure love: one must respect the energy.'

There is a definite change of tone from the letter to his parents. *'Much pain and sadness'* v. *'a little pain and sadness.'* We hear that he drove up to Colvin but only to 'say hello' and then ended up taking on the job of labourer. And then he writes that *'he sailed out of Perth... on an enormous burst of energy'* to escape the 'intensive social requirements'. This seems to contradict the *'drove up and stayed-on-a-whim'* explanation. He had demonstrated that up until the end of August he had thrived on those *'intensive social engagements.'* What had caused him to suddenly find them intolerable? This is an important turning point and a critical moment that requires explanation if I am to put it into the context of his longer-term journey into mental illness.

I needed to dig deeper and that meant getting back to Halimah. I had been so captivated by her story and it seemed such an appropriate culmination of my first Australian trip. I had been luxuriating in an inspiring narrative that had fired up my imagination and my envy. Yet, when I try to make sense of what happened later in the year, I realise that my fantasy projection was not going to give me the answers I needed. I knew from Halimah that their apparently idyllic love affair had a canker at its core in the form of the travelling lover and his persistent intrusion into Halimah's consciousness. She had explained how Robin had eventually realised that, in the well-worn royal cliché, 'there were three of us in this relationship, so it was a bit crowded'. But the dates do not add up. The break-up seemed to happen well after he left the city, and his reasoning for the decision seems to be very much about himself. I needed to push for more information. So I contacted Halimah and arranged a Skype conversation. In preparation I sent her message saying, *'I want to ask about the end of your relationship. Do you remember when Robin left town and migrated to the country?'*

It seemed as if she too was suffering from that same

memory shortfall as had bedevilled my memories of Robin and our time together.

'I really cannot remember exactly how it all came to an end.'

'He said you had just moved out of your home to get away from your possessive mother and moved into the house that he had been living in. Do you remember that?'

'Well I do remember moving out but I can't remember where I ended up.'

'And you can't remember him leaving the city and going up to Colvin. It seems like it was very sudden and I am trying to work out whether he was running away from you and the knowledge that he had a rival for your affections.'

'No it is all very vague. But I can tell you that he changed. He changed a lot during that period.'

That seemed more promising. Although things seemed to be taking a very different tone from the euphoric message about the wedding dress and the Magicians Ball.

'Changed in what way?'

'Well he became more and more frenetic. I am certain that he was taking more drugs and dealing as well, I think.'

'Taking and dealing?' That was a new and rather shocking development. I assumed a rather benign use of recreational drugs in tune with everyone else. But dealing? I thought his friend Maz was the dealer.

'Oh yes, I really think he was dealing. But the real problem was that there were more and more occasions when he couldn't settle, he'd suddenly seem distracted, even frantic. I was missing the calm Robin, the one who made me feel secure. Thinking about it now I can only assume it was the drugs. I am not sure which drugs and I don't think he was taking LSD. But he was definitely starting to change.'

When I pressed her, she jumped forward six months to early in his last year, some six months after the escape to Colvin. In early 1972, Robin's last year in Perth, she had misgivings about sticking with her married lover who, although back home in Australia, was showing no signs of leaving his wife. Cy began to realize that if she was to be happy she would have to shake him off. He was most unlikely to fulfil any sort of sustained relationship. So she tried to go back to Robin. They met up by chance and quickly slipped back into the rapport they once had.

'We had a really nice evening. He seemed his old self. Very warm considerate and caring. It seemed like we were back in tune. I was delighted. I realised that my other affair was a distraction and that I could easily fall back in love with Robin. If I'd ever fallen out of love with him. At the end of the evening we went back to his place. I think it was his place, maybe mine. We made love. I felt it was a beautiful night. Just like it had been. We fell asleep in each other's arms. Then in the morning something happened. Robin was very different: cold, hard and unresponsive. He turned his back on me. Got up and had a shower. He said nothing. I was vulnerable and confused. It was like he had flicked a switch. He hardly said a word as he got dressed and left. I was shocked and baffled. I felt angry with him for leading me on.'

'Did he contact you again? Explain?'

'No. Not a word about that evening. I saw him around the place. I started to work in a vegetarian café on campus and later in the year Robin would drop in. But he was quite cool.'

'The last time you told me that story you said that you thought it was the drugs that had changed him. But then we agreed that it might have been self-preservation, he didn't want his heart broken again.'

'I am still not absolutely sure. He may have had second thoughts, but the old Robin would have been gentler. He would have talked, explained, been sensitive to what I was feeling. This Robin was so cold. He literally turned his back on me.'

'So, going back to the break-up in September, did you see signs of that change back then?'

'As I said, he was frenetic but there were occasions when he was his old self and we had some lovely times. But I think, and I really can't remember clearly, that he was changing and because I wasn't really into drugs in the same way, I think we may have been drifting apart.'

I was perplexed by the way the narrative could shift with each re-telling. I knew my own memory was not to be trusted but that did not seem to stop the easy acceptance of what others recalled. I was happy to find credence in their narratives, especially if it fed my own wishful thinking. I was trying to confirm a story in which my brother was not significantly changed by drugs. I felt I had gathered sound testimony that he was a fully functioning, active, creative and inspiring figure for all who knew him. I wanted his mental illness and eventual fate to be an unlucky confluence of luck and circumstance. Not a slow and inevitable decline.

Now I had two strands of the narrative that could threaten that hypothesis. First, Halimah suggesting that drugs were already impacting his behaviour eighteen months before his departure back to the UK. Second, I am having trouble working out just what happened to cause him to suddenly drop everything and abandon his lover and his life to escape to a reclusive alternative in the country. Could it be the first comparatively minor mental breakdown, which foretold a more catastrophic crisis a year and a half later? We know that he has strong survival instincts, developed in the harsh realities of a boarding-school education. Could it be that he saw the writing on the wall? That the frenetic demeanour that Halimah identified was in fact the first signs of disturbance that he recognised and so decided to take remedial action: to withdraw and regroup?

I cannot help thinking that this rural time-out is highly significant and that I need to persevere in my efforts to understand exactly what happened. I contact Diana and ask whether she has any memory of what happened and why. She was away in London at the time but knew exactly what I was asking about and finished her message:

'I must add that I have aerograms, also, written by my Mother when I was in London from Dec 1970-72. Quite a few mention Robin being at Colvin Sept 1971 onwards but her writing is shocking. There is much detail as to what was happening on the farm and plenty of unlicensed advice she felt free to issue me from a distance!'

Another voice from that time that might just add a further insight; assuming that we can decipher those letters.

* * * * * *

It is a few days into my second trip to Perth and I am travelling up the Great Northern Highway. I am in a car with Diana and her husband Ross. I am in the front seat of the Range Rover, a little cramped for my elongated frame, but nevertheless I am feeling a sense of liberation. I am, once again, on the physical trail of my brother. All those letters and second-hand testimony from those with fluctuating memories have got me so far, but I have convinced myself that retracing his route and seeing what he saw might help me to understand how he felt. Diana has arranged for me to visit the farm at Colvin. I am going to see the cabin where Robin spent four months over forty years ago. It is an indulgence, as I do not believe in ghosts. I was able to conjure up the spirits of the past when I visited our old schools because I had been there too: it was our joint history. This is Robin's place and time. I am the intruder. But I want to re-read those lyrical descriptions of his rural isolation and bring them to life through my own experience. Things will have changed of course, but less so than much else. Farming is slow to move with the times.

It is a three-hour drive to the small town of Moora and Ross was in the driving seat. Ross had been a bit of a dampener on my first encounter with Diana six years before when I had confronted her with that declaration of love in the restaurant in Fremantle. I tried to be polite and communicative whilst what I really wanted was to put myself into Robin's place at the wheel of 'Mollie', his battered Austin A40, as he drove up this same highway the day before his twenty-first birthday in 1971.

We drive up the Swan Valley past vineyards, past Pearce aerodrome where the Australian Special Services practice anti-terrorist manoeuvres on a derelict Boeing 747. The road narrows and it is just two lanes and now I am seeing very much what Robin would have seen. Gum trees line the road. There are numerous varieties depending on the soil. My favourite is the Salmon gum whose the peeling bark reveals a smooth trunk in delicate shades of pink.

Now the landscape is opening up. It is the end of a long summer and the grass is brown. Not a trace of green, although when Robin drove up at the end of August, the start of spring, it would have been verdant and there would have been water flowing in the dried-up streambeds. I ask about Colvin and whether it had changed much since then. Diana grew up on the farm:

'In those days there would have been more than 10,000 sheep grazing the 30,000 acres. We would have had three or four men helping my dad. It was a hard business but they made it work in those days.'

Ross, who still farms their own place not far from Colvin, tells me how the Australian Wool Corporation ruined the industry with incompetent price fixing.

'The last good year for wool was 1981. It's been downhill ever since. Diana's brother Jeremy has sold off all the Colvin stock and has leased the land for grazing.'

We are going to meet Jeremy at the farm. I recognise the name. He is Diana's much younger sibling. In a letter to her, Robin had written:

'Jeremy and Dwins (his younger sister Edwina) are

as painful as ever – not nasty of course – just a pain in the neck. By themselves they are delightful, but together they continually contend for affection and attention.'

Jeremy is now over fifty and did not take to the farming life. He meets me at the door of the old house, where Robin will have arrived, out of the blue, and to the intense surprise of Diana's parents. Later I will read Betty Lefroy's letters to her daughter which described his arrival:

'Yesterday evening I was attacking the usual mound of washing, when very suddenly Robin Bethell came into my mind & I thought… "well we have seen the last of that rather casual young gent". He had not answered my letter and I knew he had got it because it had not been dead lettered. At 6.30 he walked through the door having left Perth with a tent and a bag of brown rice to go north and think his thoughts so to speak. He says he thought of the Lefroys and decided to drop in. But to cut a very long talkie story to the minimum, it is arranged that he is going to work here for nothing but his board and lodging.'

As we sat round the same kitchen table having lunch, I asked Jeremy what he remembered of Robin.

'Well, I was only eight at the time, but he made a real impression on me. I can clearly remember going over to his little house and he had this incredible collection of fine-nibbed coloured pens. I was fascinated by the intricate patterns he would draw. He was always very warm and gentle with us. He seemed to have a lot of time for us.'

That was reassuring. It does not sound like someone recovering from a nervous breakdown. And yet this was the testimony of an eight-year-old.

Jeremy was keen to show me around. We jumped into a battered four- wheeled buggy and we headed up the gentle hill over the rock strewn parched earth. I wondered how sheep could have ever survived on this inhospitable land. We stopped and got out and Jeremy led me into what he described as a paddock and I would call a field.

'We don't usually name the paddocks. There are far too many of them. But this is the exception. It's called Robin's Paddock. My mum and dad named it after he died. He used to come up her in the evenings to meditate.'

Later that day, I came across this passage in Betty's letters.

'He has an altar in one of his rooms and follows some mixture of a religion of his own with a bit of ritual and fortune telling. His fortune of course. Sometimes I think he is as nutty as a fruit cake!'

From subsequent letters I think I reassured myself that she did not really think that he was mad. She may have been a justifiably bamboozled by his new-age spirituality but subsequent letters show that she grew very fond of him. She nurtured him with healthy meals and wise counsel.

We are back in the buggy and Jeremy is taking me to the ramshackle cottage where Robin stayed for those four months. I have read about it in his letter.

'My little house is very comfortable, with my record player, a heater and three carpets and all the kitchen things I need to cook. I have a gas stove and wood fired hot water system. The water is pure rain water. The Lefroys are good people and have my livelihood at heart. Fresh eggs, honey, bread, in fact all my food and a cooked meal whenever I want it.'

I enter an empty shell of a building that has been left to decay. Jeremy points out where the white ants have eaten away at the rafters. I wander around and try to conjure up the ghost of my brother and to work out where he would have set up his shrine. It is hard. There is no trace of his life. Why should there be? My feeble attempts to bring his letters alive achieve little. But it is not a wasted pilgrimage. It feels good to be where he was. Like Cottesloe and the Octagon Theatre and even St George's College. It matters that I have walked in his footsteps. It is my homage to his memory, but I cannot pretend to be transported back there. I walk past what might have been his vegetable patch, but a busted fridge and a rusty empty oil barrel break the nostalgic spell. We have all moved on and in so many ways this is not the place it was in 1971.

That evening over dinner I read out some of the

florid passages from his letters. His accounts of the working life are nicely written, full of charming detail and make for a celebration of his time there and his talents. He had taken to the country life. He was happy to learn how to be a farmer. I recalled a line in a previous letter: *'I can see myself as a farmer. It suits me.'*

'Today we put the ewes with the Rams for mating. Mr Lefroy calls the Rams the 'workers'. There are eight rams for 400 ewes! Ewes are pretty stupid animals really – so frightened. If a ewe gets tired it just lies down and looks pathetic, but not the ram. I was driving this particular mob of rams too fast and one of them decided it was too much bother and stopped. I went forward and gently nudged him with my front tyre. No effect. I tried again. Same response. The third time, it took exception and turned and faced me. Then it came at me and the bike. Head down, a solid clunk as he butts the front of my four-wheeler and moves me back about five feet. Next time you talk about people behaving like sheep, make sure you specify the sex!'

Robin stayed at Colvin for four months. He did indeed take his exams, driving the 100 miles back down the Northern Highway. Despite his early protestations to his parents that the solitary country life would be good for revising, Betty has a different story.

'Bethell got back this afternoon after taking his exam. He reckons he "ballsed it up". Apparently, he had prepared for the wrong paper. Was writing about books

he hadn't read. Really he is so vague!!'

When he eventually does leave for good, Betty reflects on what was clearly more than a simple boss-and-worker relationship:

'I was sad to see him go as we've all got on very well really. Dad got on with him very well indeed: perhaps an attraction of opposites. He was very pleased with a little piece of paper Dad gave him, shook him warmly by the hand and gave me a kiss. We couldn't help thinking and wondering if and where and when we ever meet him again. So ends the first edition of Bethell.'

So what does all this add up to? Am I any closer to understanding what went on? Was he running away or saving himself? I am inclined to opt for the latter. After all, as public-school boys we had been taught how to look after ourselves when the going got tough. I want to argue that he glimpsed the alternative life and he realized the pitfalls it embodied. He fled to the bosom of someone else's family, to his surrogate parents, because he needed time to work it out of his system.

Betty's farewell may have marked the end of her *'first edition Bethell,'* and she was right to doubt whether they would ever meet again. However, there were several more editions of his story still to come.

Dear Robin,

I am back on the Dreamliner heading home. Not quite as much fun as the journey out. Even though I have the leg room again, this time I am centre seat and to my right a very large woman who spills into my already limited space and on the other side a man who sleeps most of the time with his elbows denying me an armrest. Not much room to type and this time it takes seventeen and a half hours. Going home is never as much fun as setting out.

I have got to your fourth and last year in Perth. You are twenty-one years old and still at university. You only signed up for a three-year degree but for reasons I still cannot fathom you had to take two more courses before you could graduate. But it is a hell of a year.

You will have to excuse me because although throughout the journey so far I have been on the lookout for any clues that might explain your death, I am especially vigilant during this stage. I am asking everyone about the drugs. You know why I worry about the drugs. I really don't want that to be the reason you had such a dreadful time in the end. I am

243

keeping an eye out for clues that you might be losing it in other ways. And yet I feel sure you would think that it is not a good look to be asking everyone, 'Do you think my brother was mad?'

As you will see, the good news is that all of them give you a clean bill of mental health. You seem to have cleared your head in Colvin. You have seen off the seductive allure of an escape to the fields of Nimbin and the hippie dream of an alternative reality. I am glad about that, it was touch-and-go, but you made the right call. Those four months in Colvin paid off. As you say in your last letter from there: 'I think I am a little closer to finding out who I am.'

1972 is your last year in Perth and although it took a while to hit your stride, it was a good year. You were calmer. Fulfilling your potential. Raising all our hopes that you had an amazing career ahead of you. You are a shining light. So full of promise. Growing up in style.

12.   Living Experiment No 87

Don't expect theatre to satisfy the habits of audience,
but to change them.

Bertolt Brecht

In the mid-sixties the French government moved their
nuclear testing from the Sahara Desert to the Mururoa
Atoll in the South Pacific. There were immediate
protests from the New Zealand and Australian
governments, and by 1972 the protests had moved
onto the streets. There were regular marches and the
protest banners were blunt in their condemnation: 'We
Don't Pee in the Atlantic, so don't Shit up our Pacific'.
Some even took direct action, and French banks were
a popular target.

Simon, a friend of Robin's, was a political radical
and determined to bring direct protest against the
nuclear tests to the streets of Perth. He decided to
target the newly opened Banque Nationale de Paris
in St George's St. His idea was to create a disturbance

with a smoke bomb thrown into the lobby of the bank. He was a solo operator but realised he needed wheels and a getaway driver. He knew Robin had a Suzuki 500cc motorbike, but was less sure how much he was committed to the cause.

Robin's activism tended to be on the quirky, artistic end, but was seduced by the idea of a potentially exhilarating adventure and agreed to help make it happen. Together they bought the biggest marine flare they could find. They hoped it would cause a stir without any damage to life or limb. Simon remembers that when they got the flare home, Robin insisted on decorating it with CND symbols, flowers and peace mandalas. These were not crude daubs; he spent the evening before the raid lovingly painting each symbol.

Early the next morning, wearing helmets and masks, Robin drove Simon through the business centre of Perth and stopped outside the bank. A few early arrivals were standing outside but seemed unmoved by the sight of two masked raiders hovering with intent. Simon leapt off the bike broke the seal on the flare and lobbed it into the doorway. Red smoke started to fill the lobby and billowed out into the street. It was a satisfying sight but Simon did not linger. He was back on the bike and Robin set off at speed. It was a cool hit-and-run and they were both elated. As they emerged from the business zone and into the suburbs they probably didn't hear the sirens, but there were

some satisfying headlines in the local paper. There
was no mention of whether Robin's decorations had
survived the detonation. They seemed to have got
away scot-free.

Was that a true story? I did some research to find
that there was a newly founded branch of the Banque
National de Paris on St George's St, and the French
were definitely testing nuclear bombs in 1972. But I
could not find the newspaper reports. However, it fitted
my new-found image of Robin. If it did happen, it was
a risky venture that could have had very unpleasant
consequences. It showed he had flair and a lot more
courage that I could ever muster. The Perth police were
reacting badly to the protest movement in the early
seventies. A court case and even a prison term might
have changed the course of his personal history. But I
wanted it to be true. Like the vision of Cy on the back
of his bike in the vintage wedding dress on the way to
the Magician's Ball, it fed my fantasy. If it did happen, I
was proud of my brother.

I had met Simon in a bar. It was late and we had
had several beers by the time he told me that story.
I pressed him for details but the Fosters and the late
hour had clearly blunted his memory. When I rang
him the next day to see if the cool sunny morning had
revived his recall, he was no more forthcoming; in fact,
he had lost his nerve.

'I have no problem with you using the story, but

I would prefer it if you kept my name out of your re-telling.'

And that is why Simon is not his real name and I really do not know how much of it is fiction. If I was on a cold-case investigation and was evaluating the evidence, I would say that the detail of Robin decorating the flare has the ring of truth about it. The rest seems a little far-fetched. But it feeds my growing vision of a brother to be proud of and I want it to be true, so there you are.

* * * * * *

On the 4th of January 1972, Robin is still in Colvin. He has been there for over four months and writes:

'Four months up here has given me time to solidify many things that before had not been tested by experience. I think I am a little closer to finding out who I am and what we are all are doing here on Spaceship Earth. Solitude has been a fine panacea to an over-worked and over-loaded system, but I look forward to the renewed contact with the energies of other people and events that appear faster and more furious in the city. My plans are vague at the present.'

The next time he writes he is back in town. It is February and it is the summer holidays, which means that life is far from 'fast and furious'; indeed, he seems disappointed with the city.

'I am starting to feel the smallness of Perth. Most of my theatrical activity has revolved around a small group of people and they have fragmented and gone their different ways. It is hard to find others who are willing to get involved, it may be the time of year or it may be that I have lost touch with everyone during my country sojourn. So you can see I am feeling a little frustrated at the lack of outlets for all my creative energy. A rather boring letter, but things should pick up slowly as I get back into the city games.'

He may be critical of the parochialism of Perth and the absence of his erstwhile theatre chums, but he sounds pretty stable to me. If I am looking for clues to suggest that there has been a dramatic change of character or deadening of his previous vibrant self, then I can't find it in these letters. He seems poised to embark on his last year with much the same energy and sense of adventure that had driven him in his first three years. He should have finished his course and be on his way home (the Drapers Scholarship was to cover a three-year degree). It is not clear why he had to stay on. In one letter he confesses to having failed a critical part of his degree in his first year. Whatever the reason, he needed to pass two more course units to complete his degree and graduate. He has chosen a course on *'Shakespeare and his Contemporaries'* and a third-year unit on *'Chinese History from 1850 to the present day'* which, as he explains to his parents *'should* be really interesting with China now beginning to enter the Western consciousness.' He goes on to comment on the heavy workload that he claims to prefer as *'theoretically it should prevent me getting involved too heavily in numerous other bits and pieces.'* On past form I would rather doubt that he would turn theory into practice.

There is already a spring in his step by the time he writes again later in February. It is a light-hearted letter laid out in a series of colourful patterns that match the jaunty tone, even when he has to report that he is recovering from a nasty fall:

'I was sitting in a deck chair counting customers (my temp job to raise money to pay my fees, I do miss the Drapers) when a red balloon chanced to be blowing past me in the light afternoon breeze – and who can resist a red balloon? I leapt from my chair and pursued the balloon. My Indian sandals, not designed for city travel, failed me on the corners and my feet disappeared. I think I am just healing now after festering for a couple of weeks.'

He is living with someone called Alan and they have taken over a derelict house and have been given free rein to decorate it, an opportunity which they grasp with gusto: *'the ceiling of our living room has orange and white stripes and sports blue walls in varying shades.'* It would appear that he has left the self-obsessed introspection back in Colvin. He sounds much more like the man of those earlier days; certainly not someone who has damaged himself with drugs or wild living. I like to think that the country sojourn may indeed have been a survival tactic rather than an indicator of any incipient mental illness. He seems to be heading for another good year.

On the other hand, I must be vigilant. We are now less than fourteen months away from his return to England and during that period something will happen to fatally damage his mental stability. I want him to enjoy this last year. I want him to thrive and excel, but I will be testing my hopes along the way. I am lucky because there are several witnesses who will help me to assess his state of mind.

It is another month until my parents hear from him again. He has fallen out with Alan over decorating styles: *'our aesthetic preferences clashed.'* He is moving in with two girls and he is quick to reassure his parents:

'Do not be alarmed! Bethell is not moving into an orgiastic ménage a trois, but rather, a very pleasant uncomplicated friendship. There's Sue who is long brown and beautiful and works as a secretary to the Director of the Perth Film Festival and the other is Cheryl a final year double honours student in History and politics, and an ardent latter day suffragette! So there it is Bethell Living Experiment No 87!'

I set about finding Cheryl a few weeks after my return from that first trip to Perth. The initial attempt to contact her had gone unanswered and I was resigning myself to the possibility that she simply did not want to engage with me and my disruptive delving. But it turned out that she no longer monitored those addresses and my emails had lain dormant. Then I did get a reply. Far from reluctant, she sounded very interested and indeed had heard about that first Australian excursion. Yes, she was happy to talk but was currently moving between Italy and Cairo. She was Head of Conservation and Preservation at the Egyptian National Library as well as leading a conservation project in Italy. She certainly remembered Robin:

'...as fun, committed, intelligent and supportive during the time we shared the house. Always on the go, quite theatrical, plenty of ideas and friends...a couple of affairs – one quite serious, he was engaged and engaging.

Yes, he took drugs – it was not so uncommon in those days and yes, he was politically-active, in an agit-prop kind of way, but he also studied for tests and exams (which he passed), wrote papers and lived a pretty normal student life.'

So, no suggestion she had either introduced Robin to drugs or that he was using in a way that would have presaged his downfall. The letters I have from 1972 would largely substantiate her view that his was a *'normal student life.'*

It was to be another six months before I got to

meet Cheryl. She did in fact have a lot more to tell me about Robin, but in the meantime she suggested that I should try to contact Roger Hudson, a friend of hers who had known Robin well during that last year in Perth. She did not however have his contact details.

Roger was one of the many names I had collected in the aftermath of my first Australian trip, but my good intentions to gather yet more intelligence had faltered under the pressures of real life. It took me another couple of years before I did a speculative search of Twitter. To my intense surprise (there were one hundred and fifty Roger Hudsons and I had picked one almost at random) I got a reply to my Direct Message and an email address. His first email was a more nuanced account than Cheryl's with a slightly different take on his drug use.

'I am very happy to chat with you sometime on Skype about what I remember of Robin in the time I knew him in Perth. I don't remember thinking that he had any mental problems, he just seemed intellectual, sophisticated and very artistic (much more so than me), but a bit of a loner. We did have some good times together, but when I look back now (and with the knowledge acquired over the intervening years) perhaps there were some underlying issues. From memory he did seem to have and use quite a lot of psychedelic drugs – I would say more than most other people I knew.'

It was reassuring to hear that Roger could not

identify any mental problems although I was intrigued by his description of 'a loner'. I would need to explore that a bit further as prior to his Colvin interlude I am pretty certain no one would have described him in that way. Where Roger did diverge from Cheryl was on the matter of his psychedelic drug use. He seemed to think that Robin was further along the spectrum of usage than she did and using more than most of his friends. This was clearly a contact I needed to pursue.

Skype is not the ideal way to meet anyone and, even though I discovered that Roger worked in computers, his wifi connection was not the best and my view of him sitting in his Sydney home was a bit murky. However, the lack of clear visuals did not stop me, almost immediately, recognising a man of warmth and sensitivity. Like so many of my connections with Robin's friends, there seemed to be an almost instant rapport. Once again I felt the force of his character leaping across the decades.

'I didn't get back to Perth until 1972. I had been away travelling in Europe and the Far East. I was very politically active in those days. It was the height of the Vietnam protests and I had been an enthusiastic participant. But coming back to Perth, which had never been a hotbed of political activism, I felt a bit out on a limb. But I had known Cheryl well and so it was natural to visit her in the house on Bulimba Road and that's where I met Robin. We got on immediately.'

That didn't surprise me, although Roger sounded as if he was not sympathetic to the apolitical hippy scene. I wanted to know more.

'He didn't seem very politically committed. I got the sense that he was a bit of a hippy. The year before he had gone to the Aquarius Festival and was into embroidered jeans.'

'No, he didn't seem to be a hippy at all. I remember he dressed in a restrained relaxed way. I thought him very dapper. He was quite reserved, charming but not pushy or overly assertive.'

'In your email you describe him as "intellectual, sophisticated and very artistic".'

'Yes, that's right. He could be intellectually intense and as for his art, I initially got the impression that he was somehow OCD.'

'In what way?' As ever I was on the lookout for any aberration.

'Well, when I first went to the house in Bulimba Road I noticed the extensive and stylish decorations. According to Cheryl he'd done it all. And he had painted tiny pictures of birds and flowers on the walls of the front room. I thought they were printed but turned out he had painted each one individually. Seemed a bit obsessive to me. I wasn't into that sort of thing. But he was also very generous.'

'In what way?'

'Well he was generous with his time and his

possessions. I remember one time when there was a girl I wanted to impress. She lived way out of the city and my car was off the road, so Robin leant me his car for a couple of days. Didn't impress the girl much but I was really grateful. He had a pretty fancy car. A four by four that although basic was better than most of us could lay hands on. I was struck by the fact that he seemed to have more money than the rest of us.'

I was surprised to hear that he appeared well-heeled. Many of his letters to my parents dwell on a shortage of cash and the need to pick up odd jobs to make ends meet.

'You said he seemed to have more money than the rest of you. This seems strange to me as I know he had to scrape around to pay his university fees, or at least that's what he told his parents.'

'Well, I can't be sure, but I had a feeling he was dealing in drugs as well as using them. That would explain the money. I certainly remember there was never a shortage of drugs. I can't remember what drugs exactly but I was certainly using psychedelics at that time. But if he was dealing, Robin was very discreet and in every other way he didn't seem to be diminished by them. In fact, he was incredibly active.'

That was probably the most credible indication so far that Robin had been an active user of psychedelics and indeed was even dealing in drugs. But at the same time neither Roger nor Cheryl seem to think it was having any discernible detrimental effect on his psyche. Once he moved in with Cheryl and Sue, his letters suggest that he was indeed incredibly active creatively, intellectually and even politically. Roger remembered Robin's particular brand of activism.

'I remember he became very involved in setting up and performing street theatre. And it was political. I remember there was a show protesting about Nixon's bombing of Cambodia.'

'Yes, he writes about it. I wish I could find someone who could tell me more about that. I have found people who know his straight theatre work, but he mentions the street theatre several times in his letters.'

'Well, you should get in touch with Phil Thomson. I am pretty sure he knew Robin and he did a lot of political theatre in those days. I'll try and find an email address.'

In a letter written in May 1972 Robin writes about his street theatre activity:

'Nixon's blockade of N. Vietnam prompted more street-theatre which we did once on the Uni Campus and again in front of the US Embassy. It was well received by the crowd, but got a bad reception from the police who are manifesting all the signs of brutality that the American police meted out on their demonstrations.'

It crops up in several other letters where he is keen to persuade my parents of the relevance of and reason for a more immediate and democratic form of theatre:

'Our main productions at the moment are political, because they are easier to do somehow, but soon I hope we will be able to do little sketches about anything and everything, full of mystery, wonder, excitement and JOY! And people can accept it so much more easily when they don't have to consider themselves as an official audience in an official theatre. I think Shakespeare understood all these things.'

In fact there is mention of his *'unofficial theatre'* in virtually every letter from that last year. It was an important part of his life and yet I had no first-hand testimony. Roger's suggestion that Phil Thomson might know more offered me a lifeline, and I was delighted when a few a few days later he sent me another message to say that he had tracked Phil down:

'He told me that Robin was a huge influence on him (and his twin brother John). They did street theatre – anti-war stuff - with Robin as well as some conventional and experimental theatre on the stage. Phil is very happy for you to contact him.'

And I did and he confirmed that he wanted to meet if I got back to Perth:

'Be great to go back in time. Your bro helped put me on my path to a life in art.'

* * * * * *

I met Phil Thomson mid-way through my second

trip to Perth. He had suggested the Bib and Tucker. It sounded pretty down and Aussie, but actually the place serves over-priced fancy fusion fare with a great view of the sea. Phil on the other hand is very much the Aussie bloke. A solid head, bright blue eyes, a face that was lined and lived in and an accent that proclaimed his heritage without apology. I liked him immediately. He was a contrast to so many of Robin's more refined friends and I had a feeling he would add rich colour to my story. And I was not wrong.

'Look, I have got to tell you that Robin was such an influence on me and what I became. He was my mentor and without him so much of what I eventually did with my life may not have happened.'

'Wow Phil, that is quite an accolade. Tell me how that came about.'

'Well, in 1972 the campus food was foul but some people had set up an alternative whole-food café on campus. It sold cheap veggie food and it was great. My twin brother Jon and I used to eat there.'

'I know the one. Did you see Cy Gieger, a striking woman wearing an embroidered kaftan serving food?'

'Didn't know her name but there were so many bloody beautiful women. I mean it was where the fabulous people hung out. Way out of our class. But I said to Jon, "How do you get to be like them?" He didn't know, nor did I. But one day we saw a little poster on the wall in the café. It said *"Rock and Roll Theatre"* and if you wanted to join come to this address at 7p.m. Well, Jon and I thought "Rock and Roll Theatre" sounds pretty good. The address was miles off campus. It was dark when we got to this little house. We rang the bell and a guy opened the door. Now we had an expression for the hippy types, we called them the Fabulous Furry Freaks. And this was one of them. Turned out it was Maz. He was surprised to see us but took us into the back room where there were about a dozen Furry Freaks sitting round. One of them was Robin. Maz said, "It's two new people and they're twins!"'

'I know Maz was pretty freaky, but did Robin look like a Furry Freak?'

'No. He was dressed pretty normal. Long hair of course. Anyway, they were all part of an alternative theatre group and they were planning a series of political concerts and wanted some new recruits. We were the only ones that turned up. Robin was definitely a leader and he immediately made us feel at home. I think he must have recognised us as outsiders. He was an outsider too when he first got here. With his help, suddenly, we had joined the "fabulous people". Neither Jon nor I ever looked back. I devoted the rest of my life to alternative culture, theatre, writing and travelling. And it was Robin that made it happen.'

'Robin writes about the Anti-Vietnam War protests.'

'Oh yeah, whenever there were any big protests

we'd turn up. I remember the big Vietnam Moratorium March. We stayed up all night making costumes. Robin was to be Tricky Dickie and made a tall cardboard hat with the stars and stripes painted on it. Next day we were on St George's Terrace waiting for the march to reach us, when six cops turned up on motorbikes and grabbed hold of all our props and ripped them up. Bastards! Robin was very much the leader and tried to stop them. He had real presence. To me he was the older dude. The leader. And I've got something to show you.'

He reached down and pulled out a series of newspaper cuttings stuck to a piece of card. They were from the Perth Sunday Times, August 27th 1972. There were two pictures on the front page. Both had Robin dressed as an old- style British bobby. The caption story read:

'A funny thing happened in the Hay St Mall today. A group of university students calling themselves The Illuminating Magic Travelling Troupe put on a short play. The plot revolved around a group of strolling players who are continually harassed by two policemen played by Robin Bethel [sic] and John Thomson. All went well until two real police came on the scene to take their names and move the actors on.

"Those two policemen really helped the theme of the play," said Bethel. "One of them told me to put away my truncheon. Said it was an offensive weapon."'

'Of course it was Robin who tipped off the police. He knew how to get publicity. Another thing I learnt from him.'

* * * * * *

If I was looking to prove that during this last year in Australia Robin was destroying his brain with psychedelic drugs and a hippy lifestyle, then all the testimony is pointing in the opposite direction. He appears to be firing on all cylinders. It may have been a slow start after the Colvin retreat, but there seems to be more and more evidence that he had knowingly rescued himself from that downward spiral by escaping to the country. He has re-discovered a mental stability and that has unleashed yet more creative energy. He may be more circumspect and centred, which to Roger appeared as being 'a bit of a loner', but Phil's testimony makes it clear that he was a leader and a mentor and capable of injecting his energy and ideas into any venture that he chose to engage with.

While he was clearly committed to Phil and John and the street theatre, in another letter he reveals that he had not abandoned traditional theatre. In April he writes:

'Later this month I am going to have to cut down my commitment to the street theatre since we go into rehearsal of a major production. It's a good play about

a middle-aged couple, who get lost in the S. Australian desert looking for their brother, whose plane crashed. Aileen and I are playing their two alter egos who appear personified as a result of their diseased imaginations. My good friend Ray Omodei is directing and it is the biggest part I have ever got and I am getting paid!'

I found a photo of him from that production and it seemed to sum up so much about his stage presence and intense engagement with the part.

Then, in a letter in June recounting the whole experience, he writes that *'the play constituted the most important theatrical experience of my life.'* It was the second time I had come across Ray Omodei's name. Vic Marsh 1had mentioned him when we first met, so I got back in touch and asked whether he could help me track Ray down.

'Yes I do have his address and phone number. I don't know how old he is now, but it has been my experience that he doesn't feel obliged to be very communicative, unless it suits him! He doesn't have email.'

More research revealed that Ray is now 84 and is coming to the end of a very successful career in Australian theatre. I found evidence of over sixty different productions and his name crops up in every survey of the Australian theatre scene. However, Vic was right and at the outset at least he did not seem overly communicative. But when I got to Perth I tried to phone him and he did pick up, but he seemed to have just woken up and was incoherent. I eventually managed to explain that I wanted to meet him. It was not too promising, but we made an appointment for the next day.

The day before my assignation with Ray, I met another friend of Robin's. She had not been on the Marcus email list back when he threw that party at the start of my venture. But I did contact her prior to my second visit some six years later, and in her email response it was clear that Jenny Hetherington remembered him fondly and was excited at the prospect of seeking out the memories.

I met Jenny on a sunny day next to the beach at Cottesloe. Close to where Robin lived and almost exactly where he had stood with that lithesome girl causing me more pangs of envy. I mentioned my appointment with Ray Omodei.

'Oh I would love to meet Ray again. He ran this workshop in 1971. It was an incredible experience. He had just returned from England where he had been immersed in the radical theatre scene: Grotowski, Marovitz and Peter Brook. His workshop put all that thinking into practice. It was immersive, lots of improvisation and self-exploration. We meditated, we chanted, we danced and found ourselves. It was totally transformative. None of us had done anything like it before. It changed my whole perspective and caused me to go on to teach drama. Ray's ideas affected my teaching and my approach to theatre. He was inspirational.'

I had Robin's letters in my rucksack and we looked out his reference to the workshop. In a letter dated April 1971 he writes:

'Life seems to be revolving around a theatre workshop that has started here under the leadership of a superb director Ray Omodei, who has just spent the last two years learning from a guy who learnt from Grotowski. We work about four nights a week three hours a night. So with that and course work there is not a lot of time left over.'

Three hours a night and four nights a week. If it was as intense as it sounds, no wonder it changed lives. Vic had talked about the workshop and it dawned on me that it was taking place just before they all set off to Aquarius with Maz and his Buddah sticks. Judging by Jenny's sense that it was so transformatory, it would seem that Ray and his ideas had sown the seeds for Robin's subsequent flowering into the full-on counter-cultural voyager. All that improvisational self-discovery set him off on a spiritual journey. It changed his life too. Ray was an important part of the story. I was looking forward to meeting him.

I got to Ray Omodei's flat in good time. He was a little surprised to see me, but invited me in. The opening gambit was easy because he took me into the front room, which had an expansive view over the down-town office blocks: glass and steel headquarters of the mining conglomerates that had exploited the iron ore to bring temporary prosperity to Western Australia, and out onto the Swan River sparkling in the sunshine.

'Ray, what a fabulous view. That must lift your spirits every time you walk in here.'

He smiled, a generous wide smile that lit up his long expressive face, now sagging around the eyes and jowls but with the striking bone structure of man who had been beautiful. I knew he was gay and there were several photos of equally striking young men in ebony frames on his desk and shelves. Later I would ask him whether he thought Robin was gay. In one of the few coherent answers I received, he smiled wickedly and said, 'We were all gay then.'

I looked around the room and the walls were mostly covered in bookshelves from floor to ceiling, packed with elegant tomes on art, opera, ballet and literature. Here was a cultured man, a man with a deep connection to the heritage that had fed him. I searched for a glimpse of Grotowksi's Towards a Poor Theatre or Peter Brook's The Empty Space, but they were nowhere to be seen. The pictures on what little wall remained, however, showed that he had not lost his urge to surprise. A series of erotic prints showed a lithesome young woman removing her clothes, and above his desk a blatantly erotic painting of another female beauty in flagrante. My awareness of gay iconography did not account for this counter-intuitive cross-pollination. But they were beautiful and, as Halimah said to me later, 'Gay men just love beauty whatever the sex.'

Once he began to talk, or more accurately, try to talk, it was obvious that the incoherence that I had put down to poor telephone technique turned out to be much more. He must have had some sort of stroke. His speech was garbled and virtually incomprehensible. We could communicate but with difficulty. Eventually, after many false starts he explained that he knew what he wanted to say, but the words could not come. Instead I was teasing out the sense from a gabble of words and phrases that could have come from one of

Beckett's more challenging plays.

After I had explained my mission and said Robin's name and showed him photos of Robin and mentioned the others whom I knew had participated in those early days at UWA, he looked at me sadly and just shook his head. It had all gone. He had no memories of when his avant-garde approach to drama had, it seemed, affected a generation of young student actors. And even if he had, I am not sure I would have understood anything that he might have had to say.

There was, however, one moment of articulacy that made it all worthwhile.

'Ray, I need to tell you that you made an extraordinary impression on those students. You ran a workshop in 1971. Vic was there, Jenny and her friend Susan and of course Robin was there. Vic and Jenny have told me that your workshop was inspirational. You challenged them with radical new ideas not just about theatre but about the way they lived. It changed their lives. You changed their lives. You should know that.'

He looked straight at me as his face softened into a wistful smile that reached his eyes. I was unsure whether any of my earnest homily had struck home. He looked away, out of the window across the river into the distance and then with calm and intense clarity said, 'I think that is most beautiful thing anybody has ever said to me.'

It can't have been true. He will have had lovers and friends who will have beguiled him with far more eloquent flattery, and yet his acuity at that moment suggested that it did matter to him that he had a legacy of changed lives. As he entered the miasma of missing memory and the frustration of lost eloquence, I had touched that basic need for appreciation. At that moment it did not matter that he had forgotten Robin. I felt I had done what Robin would have wanted me to do: to show his ageing and befuddled mentor that Ray had transformed the mind of his young acolyte.

Our encounter lasted for two hours and I suppose I understood about one word in ten. But I had been warned that Ray loved to talk and I wasn't going to stop him, so I nodded and laughed and responded to each wayward baffling tale. However, as he rambled on and I smiled and encouraged him with my feigned attention, I thought that Ray stood for all our futures. It reminded me, if I needed reminding, that memory is a fickle friend who can abandon you just when you need it to shore up your sense of self and remind you of what others have given to you and what you have given back to others.

TIME FROM DEPARTURE: 3 HOURS 48 MINUTES.
MILES TO DESTINATION 7346.

Dear Robin,

We are back over the Indian Ocean just above Investigation Trench, which seems appropriate. The large woman on my right is working her way through the entire Harry Potter filmic oeuvre. Every time I catch sight of Daniel Radcliffe out of the corner of my eye, he is getting older.

In our story, you are coming to the end of your time in Perth. You too are growing up. You are making plans. Big plans for the trip home and then the rest of your life. You have ideas and aspirations, plenty of them. They come thick and fast. It is a little unnerving for the outside observer who is wanting you to demonstrate coherence and a stable self. But they are exciting possibilities and I am excited for you. I would love you to succeed. Your talents could have taken you in so many different directions. And in each you would have prospered. That is obvious to everyone. This chapter is full of hope and expectation.

It is also the chapter where I hear you speaking to me. Clearly, brother to brother. I have at times denied that we ever really communicated. Instead I have been relying too much on your parental missives. When you do get around to writing to me, in the last few months of your days in Perth, it is something very special.

271

13. Future Dreams

For the future, I shall rely only upon those elements of my character which I have tested. Who would ever have said that I should find pleasure in shedding tears? That I should love the man who proves to me that I am nothing more than a fool?

Stendhal, The Red and the Black

From the moment of his death I eradicated virtually all recollection of Robin and our sibling relationship. He was not so much a brother as a burden. He had relegated me to the role of he who was left to pick up the pieces of his life and carry the onerous burden of his absence. When I eventually set about trying to recapture my memories, I could call on his letters and the recollections of others. At the outset of that process I was wholly focused on the package of letters that had been collected by my mother and rejected by me and eventually recovered from my nephew. They had been invaluable and, despite his self-censorship, had provided a vital narrative with some hugely significant moments when his emotional state overcame his restraint and it was possible to glimpse the raw truth that lay beneath the reassurance.

It took me a long time to even ask myself the question: did he write to me? As the process of rediscovery began to unfold and my memories of him began to re-emerge from the mist, I thought to go and look through my, admittedly modest, personal archive. Sure enough, there was a thin folder of letters from Robin. They are few and by no means cover the sweep of his time away from me. But there are nuggets of uncensored insight that offer up a different perspective and I have referred to them already in this narrative. However, the first time I rifled through that file I failed to extract the most significant communication.

The reason it escaped my attention was that because of its size. It had slipped out of the file and was hiding in the other letters and papers that had been stashed away in a disorderly fashion. It took me another few months before I happened upon it.

The envelope is hand-made and is nine centimetres square. It is addressed to me at the inner London school where I was starting my teaching career. It is decorated with an intricate pattern of red and black lines, and as well as the address there is a circular instruction to 'open by cutting carefully along the diagonal lines'. I must have complied with the instructions because now the envelope opens up like an origami fortune-teller to reveal an A4 sheet folded into nine segments. Every segment is filled with his tiny writing, in alternate red and black inks. It is a work of art and, I am almost ashamed to admit, a token of brotherly love. How could I have forgotten about a thing of such beauty and significance? I have to get through most of the text before he refers to the elaborate construction:

'I haven't explained how this communication works, I hope you enjoy discovering it. I gave you a beginning but that is all. Read the squares in any order you like. I don't believe in beginnings and ends but I do believe in patterns, and harmony and the primitive essential dialectic that governs existence. Circles are important as well; circles and cycles and space and the heart beats on.'

It is a remarkable artefact as well as a revealing text, which reinforces and gives substance to much of what I have discovered so far. It also offers prescient insights onto what was to come.

The postmark is dated October 1972 and the way the letter starts adds salt to the wound of my forgetfulness. Clearly he and I have been communicating and, more unnervingly still, he appears to respect my opinions:

'Dearest Brother, while the well-spring of fraternal affection boils and bubbles so fruitfully, on re-reading your grey London letter on a clear, blue and bright

West Australian day – behold, I will give you instant feedback. Thank you for your thoughts and your partial vindication of my ideas. In Perth one often loses one's footing and plunges through the cracks of criticism, bewilderment and pure naivety into the clogging slough of inertia and uncertainty. This probably seems like madness to you, since the only indication of my present state of mind has been via semi coherent, highly précised conglomerates of my ideas in letters to the parents.'

I am saddened that I am only now reviving those *'well-springs of fraternal affection.'* But he has a letter sent by me from London and the implication is that we have been engaged in a dialogue, in which my contribution has been valued. Of course, his style has become disconcertingly prolix, but there is an elegance and even an inventiveness in his imagery that I admire. I am grateful to read his own admission that his parental letters have been 'highly précised', although 'semi-coherent' is being a little hard on himself. Those letters are often totally coherent even if they distort the hard facts of the matter.

Reading those sentences now causes me to reflect on just how often he *'lost his footing'* to plunge into the *'clogging slough of inertia and uncertainty.'* Not much sign of inertia in 1972. In June he had written: *'I am being hyperactive. There's nothing worse than mediocrity.'* But I recognise that *'uncertainty'* lying beneath the activity. Our public school may have empowered us to take on the world, but it did nothing to help us deal with the nagging uncertainty that made us continually question our accomplishments.

He then confides in me about his love life. There is a stark honesty here that has been absent from his previous letters to me or my parents:

'My life this year has been a little difficult due to the unsatisfactory arrangement with the woman I am sharing a house with. She is a strange girl – not in the sense of mysterious or illusive, but in her unpredictability, which is so destructive. We started off trying to establish a close relationship, and I slept with her occasionally, but as soon as I lowered the defences which we all carry round with us, she abused the trust one gives to someone one is close to, and then when my defences went up again she was unable to understand why. C'est la vie... but it has made it difficult with other women because she was jealous... oh god!'

When I showed this to Cheryl she replied:

'I too, was less than a year out from my first great love, and not well-placed to commit. I don't know why he wrote what he did to you. I find it difficult to believe he was so affected by my not taking him more seriously. At the time, it still seemed unresolved with Cy.'

It seems as if both were struggling with commitment after recent break-ups, but once again it confirms Robin's underlying lack of confidence when faced with ambiguity in his relationships. Reading about how Robin manages the lowering and raising of defences causes me to reflect on the sad ending of his relationship with Cy. I imagine that this process of lowering defences, building trust, then having that trust 'abused' must have been what happened when he discovered that Cy still had strong feelings for her married lover. I am assuming that he made himself vulnerable and then when he discovered that part of her was not available to him, he would have closed down and retreated. Then, some six months later, when she lowered her defences to open up the possibility of a rapprochement, he was not prepared to take the risk.

This paragraph also reminds me of that first love letter to Diana, written three years earlier, where he tries to tell her he loves her. Just a year out of public school, the tortured prose revealed how terrified he was of openly expressing his true feelings and making himself vulnerable. Here again is the public- schoolboy who has been trained to defend himself against the scourge of personal vulnerability. He is paying the price for his adolescence spent in an all-male community. I feel his pain. I too was denied the opportunity to practise my engagement tactics with the opposite sex at an age when I might have learnt some useful lessons. Not that it appears to have entirely cramped Robin's style. As we have seen, he seems to have had a lot less trouble than I ever had in convincing women to sleep with him.

In this same letter there is reference to another, apparently concurrent liaison. He has written a long paper on the role of the Fool in Shakespeare, a role with which feels he has some affinity.

Folly seems to be a motif that is once again becoming increasingly relevant in our age. In fact I have been a clown, a real one. I went as a clown to kids party the other day, the child of another complicating factor in my life, a married woman! It was an incredibly demanding event.

In a later email Cheryl remembered more about this married lover.

'She was called Marion and was the recently separated mother of two young children. She was a gentle person and Robin was very sweet with her and with her children. I met her a couple of times. I don't remember why it didn't work out, but I don't think there was any bad feeling.'

It doesn't sound like a torrid affair and the fact that she was separated makes it a lot less complicated than he makes it sound. I would have liked to get Marion's take on it all and I asked around in Perth but there were too few clues to work on.

The clown act appears to be fraught with failure:

'I had a few tricks like multiplying billiard balls, disappearing cigarettes, and flashing bow ties. Their effect was diminished by the utterly ruthless pragmatism of the kids. When the bowtie started flashing there was

the instant scream of 'I can see the wire, I can see the wire' (The wire connecting the tie to the battery in my pocket) Yet this was contradicted by some feedback I got from the mother afterwards who said that what fascinated them most was my pointing to the sky when they asked me where I came from.'

As I read on, it becomes clear that the clown act is more than just a way to please his previously married lover. It causes him to muse on how, by hiding behind the face paint, he can exploit *'the ambiguity of the gap between yes and no, black and white, on and off.'* He feels 'we are destructively linked to a binary notation in all our affairs'. And from that weighty aperçu he segues into a far more practical sequence. For the first time he is writing about his plans for the future:

'Dream number one at the moment is making it to New York School of Arts at the New York University in September 1973 to do some sort of course there. I don't know whether my mentality is adequately supplied with the necessary consciousness and survival skills to sustain a year or two in that metropolis. I especially want to work with a guy called Hovey Burgess who teaches circus techniques: he says "Circus skills enable the actor to understand the vitality, intensity and freedom that must exist under the spoken lines if the audience is not to be bored." Right on! I should like to hear your feeling on that dream. It is so insubstantial at the moment that the slightest breeze from a respected

quarter will dissipate it, so don't blow too hard.'

I cannot be sure but I really hope that far from blowing him off course, I would have given this idea a fair wind. It would be easy to dismiss this plan as naïve. A plan to run away to the circus seems like a caricature fantasy project. But then I find that Hovey Burgess had been teaching circus skills for actors on the three-year Graduate Acting program at New York University's Tisch School of the Arts since 1966. By 1972 Hovey had already built up an international reputation for his theory and practice. Robin it seems was excelling in both street theatre and traditional theatre and even clowning at children's parties. It was perfectly logical that he should be drawn to Hovey Burgess. It seems like a grand plan. I find myself grieving at the realisation that this was the last any of us were to hear of that inspiring ambition.

The red and black letter caused me to return to the parental letters and I discover that they too received a letter written on the very same day. He was clearly warming up for his tour de force to me. After a first paragraph in red ink he switches to black:

'The change to black ink is not indicative of a plunge into the nether regions of my consciousness, but rather a fondness for dual toned letters, which I hope you can share.'

It transpires that he is back at Colvin to revise for his exams.

'It is really so good to be up here again: to feel the heat and the dust, to smell the sheep and the pigs, to grossly overfeed myself, to conduct conversations about 'reality' and to feel one's feet very firmly on the ground. I can't think of a better way to prepare for the exams.'

He offers his parents a more prosaic account of his plans for the future:

'My long term plans are still uncrystallized as yet, but I would like to give acting a try for a while when I get back, before I either go on to do a Dip Ed or an advanced course in Media Studies or Design. I hope that you can understand how difficult it is to make up my mind from this end but don't worry too much about my lack of decision.'

Hovey doesn't get a mention. Presumably he felt that my father, now a Major General, was unlikely to see the point of three years of training in circus skills and his mother would have been saddened by the thought of five thousand miles separation just after she had got him back home. But luckily for me, he spent the rest of his evening carefully constructing and composing the red and black artwork of a letter to his brother, and I was easy with the thought of him juggling on the high wire.

There is only a month and a half before he is leaving Perth for good and, in his parental letter from that red and black evening in October, he finally lays out his plans for the return journey:

'The plan as it now stands is to ride my bike from here to Kalgoorie, to stay with friends of Ray Omodei, then put the bike on the train to get across the desert and the unmade roads, back on the bike at Port Pirie (you'll have to look at an atlas), then to Adelaide, then to Melbourne to stay with Vic Marsh and maybe the Dattners (first cousins), and up to Sydney to stay with Alan with whom I lived in the big house earlier in the year, then by plane to Darwin then island hop and get to Singapore in early January.'

The plan is further revised in a remarkable letter written to my father on November 8th. He is in the middle of his exams and has two more papers to complete, but that doesn't stop him challenging the General with a bracing fifteen hundred words (about as many as it is possible to cram onto an aerogramme) in his very smallest writing. He wants to explain his latest thinking about what he might do on his return, but, and I have to be honest here, in a manner that does suggest a detachment from reality that could be interpreted as a little crazy.

Lengthy convoluted sentences that start with his suspicion of the exam system: *'as a means of assessing a student's ability especially in a modern world where information is becoming so efficient technologically – computers etc.'* This rather prophetic observation is followed by a discursive diatribe about the mass media, which he acknowledges may not make much sense to his audience of one:

'I find letters a fairly inadequate way of communicating my impressions and ideas, and therefore will quite understand if this skeletal list of things I find important makes no sense to you.'

But he has good intentions: *'The reason I write them is so that my future plans may make a little sense.'*

Well, this was very far from a 'skeletal list': it was closer to a verbal onslaught and, even though he is writing about a subject that was and is of great interest to me, it makes very little sense to me either. If you stick with it there are signs of some coherent and deep thinking and I am keen not to see this outpouring as disturbing. He is making the case for pursuing a career in the mass media. References to Marshall McLuhan and the Global Village seem to inform some roughly articulated cultural theory about communication technology. Eventually he lays out two alternative paths.

'1) Theoretical: i.e. improve the theoretical grasp of concepts that are at the moment only intuitive – this means more learning probably at university. 2) Practical i.e. actually doing it and learning in the school of hard knocks! I am more in line with 1), but I also know that to function in 2) would also make life worth living. I hope some of this makes sense, Dad. I am still an idealist and hope ~ I always will be!! But idealists tend to get their fingers burnt, it's one of the risks of the

road. So I am expecting anything to happen and I hope it will too.'

When I first read this letter it did make me wonder whether it might be the first signs of a rambling mind starting to lose a firm grasp on reality. I find it impossible to imagine how this would be received by his father who, while having a sharp mind (he often completed The Times crossword in less than an hour), had very little intellectual curiosity and whose intelligence was confined by establishment values and a classical education that had been ossified at the age of 18. I wince when I think of him grappling with this letter. It causes me to wonder whether Robin was indeed starting to lose it. Or was he just in a manic phase of jumbled but inspiring thought?

On re-reading, however, I have come to a different conclusion. It is impossibly convoluted but it is not incoherent. There is an argument in there and it does reflect some serious reading and an awareness of the intellectual battles around communication and learning that were raging at that time. Indeed, I too was engaged in exactly the same space between my practical job (teaching) and the ferment of ideas around the impact of mass media and its ideology. In many ways this feels like a letter written to me, but sent to my father by mistake. And yet it was not a mistake. He wanted to reach his father and involve him. Whereas I, back in England for three years, had a far more pragmatic assessment of my father's strengths and weaknesses. I would never have engaged him in debate about the structuralist theories of Michel Foucault and Roland Barthes. Robin, on the other hand, had been away for four years and his image of his father appears to have become detached from reality. Instead of the military man with limited intellectual horizons, Robin had conjured up a fictitious father who would want to know what his son was thinking and be prepared to grapple with his uncertainties. The style and content may have been misjudged, but the intention was touchingly sincere. It may be misguided but surely it is not a sign of madness.

The letter does become much more practical when he writes about his plans for the journey home.

'Truth is I won't completely know what I am doing until I have done it. I will take all contingencies into account: weather money, health, head. So, I may fly straight home from Darwin, or go to Sumatra instead of Bali, or go home east from Bangkok or maybe west.!! Actually plans are not as vague as that. So: Perth – Melbourne – Sydney – Brisbane – Darwin – Timor – Bali – Singapore – Bangkok – Hong Kong – Taiwan (hopefully) – Japan – Vladivostok – London (Trans Siberian Railway). Simpler, cheaper quicker than the S.E Asia route.'

Despite the fluctuating lack of decision, I am in awe of the scale and the ambition of this adventure. I remember a throwaway comment in a previous letter about how he was thinking about *'taking the Overland trip'* which would get him *'back in Merrie Old England within six months.'* It was an easy sentence to write and I have found that the words 'He wanted to take the Hippy Trail back to England' tripped off my tongue in the telling without any recognition of the sheer challenge of such a venture. Of course it was a phenomenon of the time, an integral part of the alternative zeitgeist. It was what you did if you were a paid-up member of the flower-power generation. Indeed it is still an aspiration for the contemporary crowd on their gap years. But as I read through that list of exotic destinations and remember that there was no email or Skype or credit cards, I realise that this was a scary proposition and I am damned sure that I could never have contemplated such a solitary and uncertain itinerary. I did not have his courage nor his confidence.

Robin does have a clear enough sense of our father to make sure that he ends his letter with a reassuring financial and logistical briefing. I suspect my father will have skipped much of what came before but he will have landed on these last few sentences with some relief:

'Money: I have $300.00 and then the proceeds from selling my bike after I get to Queensland, about $400 = $700 =plenty to get home on and more. Also I am insured medically a scale 70/3 with BUPA, have renewed my

passport, have been pumped full of the very latest medical fluids, have a fistful of references, a gaggle of identity cards, passport photos and signatures and feel fully equipped to cope with most human problems. Of course, I am not covered against Acts of God, but who is?!'

I remember that in a previous letter he attached a passport photo taken for that renewal. He is looking very 'straight'. He has pulled his long hair back to appear clean cut and wears a shirt and tie. On closer study I see that it is his Old Shirburnian tie. Most likely the only tie he owns. He is not taking any chances. Hair length is still a potent signifier of a subversive and bohemian tendency in 1972 and he tells us that he will be cutting his hair before he sets off on his travels.

His next letter is to both parents and is dated November 17th, which is my birthday, although for obvious reasons he has other things on his mind and there is no reference to that. The exams are over and *'went as well as could be expected and no better, and in the hands of the gods now anyway.'* I was keen to find out the result of his efforts and some forty years later managed to persuade the university administration to let me have a transcript of his grades (they were not keen and demanded I show them his birth certificate to prove my provenance, but reason eventually prevailed). I imagine he would have been disappointed with his B for the Shakespeare course and his C for Chinese History. But, as he had explained to his father, he has little respect for exams as a means of assessment.

He is just two days away from final departure. He writes from the dentist while waiting to get his teeth 'through their final service, imbrication [sic], maintenance, check up, prior to the long awaited departure tomorrow'.

'The last few days have been a hectic whirl of forms, needles, stamps, money goodbyes, letters, junk, bills, receipts, camera, film, lens, etc, etc, as I try to get myself organized in every way. I think all those ends are tied up now. My luggage is down to that small tartan hold-all, that you gave me Mum and even that seems too much. It is funny that as you go to leave a place, you start to understand how you feel about it. I have a strange love-hate relationship with Perth: you have a really wonderful day on the beach but then you can't find a film to see or a theatre to visit.'

He seems at ease with himself. He appears to have managed his preparations with competence. It was difficult to both withdraw from a life and a world that he has made his own, whilst at the same time planning and preparing for an immensely demanding escapade. He is in control of his destiny. He is highly functional. His plans are carefully thought through, whilst leaving him open to the wondrous potential of serendipity. His confidence in himself is awe-inspiring. I can find few signs of an incipient mental condition, but then again I realise that I am driving the narrative in a way that glosses over all those previous glimpses of his vulnerability and self-doubt. To judge by this letter he has *'put a set of tyres of excellent quality on the bike' and is 'in short, ready for take-off'.*

As he plans his final day with a potent mixture of sadness spiked with an incipient and roiling excitement, there is no hint of foreboding. He is energised by the prospect of chance encounters and unanticipated happenings. What he has not mentioned to his parents or to me is whether or not he has a stash of hallucinogens packed away in the corner of that tartan bag. I imagine he does, and I am sure that he sees them as an adjunct rather than a threat to his enterprise. I, of course, am in possession of his future. I know what will happen and I cannot stop myself from searching for any signs of premonition. I look back at his red and black letter to me, and I find that he does indeed have some sense of foreboding:

'In my head at the moment there are a number of ideas about what to look at on the way home. I somehow feel I have gone past the stage where I shall allow every experience of a trip in Asia to either destroy or create my philosophy of life. But what I am frightened of is that I shall succumb to twentieth century schizoid man's eternal paranoia: information overload.'

I was troubled by this foresight and my unease was compounded by a story that Roger Hudson told me during our Skype encounter.

'When you told me about what happened on Robin's overland journey across Asia, it caused me to recall the fate of my friend Tom. Both Cheryl and I knew Tom, but not very well. In 1972 we heard that he had set off to travel in Asia but we knew little of his plans and had heard nothing more. Then one day I got a call from the Australian Consulate in Bangkok. They wanted to know whether I would be prepared to come to Bangkok and escort Tom home. He had been found wandering naked in the streets, giving his money away to anyone he met. I assumed he was off his head on drugs of some sort.'

'And did you go?'

'No, in the end they got him back some other way. When we did eventually meet up he was a totally different person. He'd been in Bangkok for just two weeks and now he was completely crazy. He'd not been in our circle of friends but we all knew him as a happy-go-lucky guy. Life and soul of the party. He went downhill from then. I heard that he had been caught breaking and entering a shop that sold incense and ended up in prison'.

'Do you think Robin was aware of Tom and what happened to him?'

'I think it is unlikely but not impossible. I am pretty certain it all happened at about the same time that I was seeing a lot of Robin. But I suspect I did not want to talk about it. It was very distressing and to this day I don't understand how they could have identified me as a potential rescuer'.

Roger is probably right that Robin had not heard about the fate of his friend Tom, but I am haunted by the fact that it was possible that he had. I cannot stop myself from asking: could that story have alerted him to the dangers that lay ahead?

Dear Robin,

*The moving map tells me we are now flying over the
Black Sea. Three more hours. We are running late,
looks like it will be more like an eighteen-hour flight. I
cannot imagine how they have enough juice to keep a
plane up in the air for that long. My seat space is still
compromised on both sides. I have not slept a wink.
I tried to find a film that you might have seen. There
are only a very few from the seventies. It was either Get
Carter or Annie Hall. I chose Annie Hall although it
came out in 1977 and I was not sure whether you went
to the cinema much in those days.*

*I am running out of living witnesses now and
having to rely almost exclusively on your own account
of what happened. There is no chance to triangulate.
All I can do is read between the lines and hope.*

*In your story, you are leaving Perth. You have
settled on a plan. It is ambitious; some may say a little
over-ambitious. But you have so much more courage
than I ever had. You took risks. You appear fearless,
although I know you must have had moments when
you doubted yourself. But you were adopting a policy
that I have used many times. If you are about to do
something brave or possibly foolish, then the way to*

make sure you do not lose your nerve is to broadcast your plans far and wide. That way you shore up your own intentions with the expectations of others. We all knew what you were going to do. You had written to us with detailed plans. All your friends knew. We were cheering you on. We had faith that you were the universal traveller. You had the charm, the empathy and the intelligence to engage with new worlds.

With the benefit of hindsight, I find it hard to sustain the applause. I see you heading into dark waters where there are unseen hazards: deceptive currents, whirlpools and crocodiles lurking with intent.

14. Homeward Bound

If you are wise, you will not look upon the long period of
time thus occupied in actual movement as the mere gulf
dividing you from the end of your journey, but rather
as one of those rare and plastic seasons of your life from
which, perhaps, in after times you may love to date the
moulding of your character – that is, your very identity.

Alexander William Kinglake, Eothan, or Traces of
Travel Brought Home from the East

Roger Hudson recalls that a couple of days before
Robin set off for home on his Suzuki T500 Titan with the
brand-new tyres, he drove Robin an hour up into the
Perth Hills. It was a day off from his final preparations
and a chance to relax and smoke a joint or two with
his good friend. He remembers giving Robin a farewell
gift:

'I gave him a jacket. I'd travelled in Asia the year
before and I knew it would be useful. It was a down
jacket, warm and packed up very small. Easy to fit in a

rucksack. It was red and he really liked it.'

I am taken aback. I can see Robin in his red jacket and, of course, I make the unsettling connection to the moment when I was overwhelmed by Red Shirt, the Rumi poem sent to me by Halimah at the very end of my first visit to Australia in search of Robin.

'Has anyone seen the boy
who used to come here?
Have you heard stories about him?'

That poem made me cry and I find it hard not to cry now. Robin, brave and full of the spirit of adventure, thanks to the generosity of a good friend, will now be visible to me. A red speck on the map: traversing the empty heart of Australia, up past the Barrier Reef, across the sea to Asia and skipping from island to island, hesitating and ruminating then meandering up the Malay peninsular until the red speck hovers over the city of Bangkok. The boy in the red jacket is on his way and I am tracking him. I wish him well, but my heart is full of dread.

'I'd gladly spend years
getting word
of him,
even third or fourth hand.'

* * * * * *

My father was a man of action, not a man of letters. For

Christmas I would give him a collection of the Dear Bill Letters from Private Eye and if he ever bothered to get me a present it would be something practical like a screwdriver set. But he did surprise me in the year before he died. He gave me a second-hand copy of Alexander Kinglake's *Eothan*. 'Best travel book you'll ever read.' This was such an unexpected gift with a fulsome recommendation that I read it soon after. Kinglake writes about his travels in the Middle East in 1834, but as well as being an accessible account of what he sees and who he meets it is as much about the personal and emotional experience of travel and how it changes the traveller. This came to mind as I set about reading Robin's account of his journey home. I like to think that our father, the General, would have seen something of the Kinglake in Robin's description of the sights and sounds as well as his emotional reaction on his travels.

The last we heard of Robin he was setting off for Kalgoorie where he hoped to stay with a friend of Ray Omodei. I have looked long and hard for an account of his trip across Australia but have not found a single mention. There is a disappointing silence. I assumed that some letters might have been lost. The first letter I can find was written from his base in Melbourne. In it I find a reference to a long Christmas phone call. It would appear that he told the story of his journey across Australian rather than wrote it. What we do know is that he arrived safely and the motorbike withstood the rigours of the outback because he had sold it for more than he expected.

The letter dated December 19th 1972 suggests that the journey took less time than he predicted, and far from staying with his good friend Vic Marsh and joining the Alternative Theatre Group, he is living with his first cousins in a rambling home from home and working in a restaurant.

'The clientele are, for the most part, the apotheosis of the Australian middle class. Everything is shoddy but with a nice wrapping so sells well. It's the sort of restaurant where they call one of the starters "paté de chef" when it isn't "de chef" at all but "paté de tin".

He is earning money because he has become fixated on spending much more time in Japan and so he is taking expensive and intensive private Japanese lessons with *'a charming Japanese lady'* Kawahara Mitchiko-san. He outlines his latest plan which is to 'depart on February 4th, going fairly quickly to get to Japan (about 5 or 6 weeks) and then stay there for about three months and then home via Siberia – home about the end of May beginning of June.'

Like me, I feel sure that the parents may have been a little unsettled by the constant changes. It suggests a fragility of purpose. This nagging anxiety will not have been assuaged by the next letter, which comes ten days later.

'Yet another chapter in the strange and wonderful saga of the homeward journey of the Wild Colonial Boy. A review of finances has rendered the Japanese course financially implausible, even with a couple of weeks of extra hard work as a waiter. So once again, the revised plan stands again where it did before that last wild scheme entered my consciousness.'

It would be easy to see chaos and confusion in all this persistent revisionism, but there are signs too that he is thinking things through. I admire his eager aspiration to master a notoriously tricky language and then the good sense to realise that he has taken on more that he can manage. He is researching his journey with the help of a family friend who is well versed in the South-east Asian islands: he is finding out about Bali, Indonesia and Sumatra from where he will cross over to Penang. He has asked his parents for contacts in Singapore and they have clearly come up with the goods so he needs to warn them:

'Depending on my state of mind at that juncture, I can either go down the peninsular and then back up to Bangkok in order to see Singapore or I can go straight up to Bangkok. The point being I may not get to Singapore. I hope that's ok vis à vis your generous arrangements for accommodation in that city.'

I should be pleased that he has half an eye on his *'state of mind.'* He goes on to explain how the anticipation and the rootlessness has already had an impact. He calls it:

'That irritating frame of mind which comes from being half in and half out of a place, of being semi traveller, semi-permanent. The Japanese idea was really only a manifestation of this uncertainty. It will be good to be on the road again.'

On January 13th he writes from *'20 Miles North of Sydney.'* He is indeed on the road again.

'My journey from Melbourne was with an old girlfriend from Perth who wanted someone to travel with. 'The local policeman's daughter,' I call her. She is in fact the progeny of the West Australian Lord Chief Justice Sir Lawrence Jackson. Ah me!'

Her name then was Di Jackson and Marcus had sent me an email address and a photo. In a reply to my inquiry she remembers that trip up to Sydney:

'I last saw Robin in Sydney after we hitchhiked there from Melbourne. I don't think we were really an item, just good friends with 'extras,' very occasionally, for example, on that trip. We stayed at my aunt's on the north shore overlooking the harbour which was a bit of a contrast and spent a lot of time finding her a nice present to compensate for having 'laid on her' the expectation that we could share a room (roundly rejected by the aunt!). We seemed to have time for a lot of things back then!'

He says goodbye to the lovely Di with her *'extras'* and leaves Sydney in the middle of January. He is on his way north, up through New South Wales, then Queensland, the Northern Territories and eventually Darwin. The next we hear from him is a week later on January 27th. It is a cheerful scrawl on a tablemat from the Golden Fleece Restaurant, Tambo, Queensland:

'Hello Everybody,

Rumbling, grumbling, gunning across broad backed, flat and eternal Queensland countryside in a sixteen wheeled 320 hp 4900 lb refrigerated (-20 degrees) truck all the way to Darwin. 2200 miles. Fantastic! With me new mate Bill the long distance truck driver. Good bloke but not much talk: about forty words every ten hours.'

His friend Bill takes him all the way to Darwin. *'Having managed to get such a fantastic lift, I felt really exuberant when I arrived.'* But Darwin fails to respond to his enthusiasm. In a letter written a few days later he recounts a rather dispiriting time:

'Tomorrow I fly out to Dembasa, Bali's main airport, after a rather depressing four days in this sticky town where the heavens open up about fifteen times a day and the sun never shows its face. Very small and claustrophobic, none of the feeling of space I had travelling in the truck. Survival up here is staying sane or not. It seems to be a town without a reason for existing, and one can perceive this absence of life in so many of the faces.'

The couple he stays with are *'fundamentally*

pessimistic obviously in singular contradiction to my own optimistic fantasies':

'Trying to absorb opinions and ideas like their pessimistic view of the world makes travelling such an exhausting, but exhilarating thing. This is definitely a "think letter" rather than a "feel-touch-smell-do" letter. I look forward to magical Bali.'

As I work though the pile of letters from the rest of his journey, I will of course be interested in and enjoy the *'feel-touch-smell-do'* letters, as he does have Kinglake's eye for the telling detail and the revealing anecdote. However, from now on it is the 'think' part of those letters that will become the focus. I am interested in his 'state of mind' because we are entering the critical phase of his emotional journey. We are approaching the endgame and I am on the lookout for any sign that his exuberance and life force might be under threat. Darwin certainly punctured his cheerfulness and may even have dented his *'optimistic fantasies'* about the future. Will Bali restore his joie de vivre?

He finally gets round to writing on 7th February from Kuta Beach in Bali, having procrastinated for several days:

'I have started about four letters in the last few days and each has dribbled to halt as I am again overwhelmed by some new event or new meeting.'

In fact he backtracks to describe his trip from Sydney up to Queensland and I notice that having left

Di and her *'extras'* behind in Sydney, he quickly makes up for the absence. He describes how a *'chance meeting with a young lady provided a delightful interlude of three or four days and then sadly I had to move on.'* Clearly he has not lost his touch and once again I am reminded of a further observation by Di:

'I don't know if this is right, but I have the impression Robin not only attracted women, but also gravitated to them and liked their counsel.'

That would explain a lot! However, I do know that the chance encounter would be the last time on the trip that he refers to the company of a woman and I worry that he will miss the good counsel.

After a further rehash of the Darwin sojourn; *'very sticky and hot, a little depressing,'* he catches up with his location and writes in huge letters:

'BALI?:

The question mark is undoubtedly the significant symbol at this stage. Bali is without doubt a paradise for the exhausted Western consumer. It is cheap, clean, beautiful and exotic but... my hesitation comes from what I can see to be the usurpation of the culture by the grasping naïveté of the average tourist. My own slight depression is an awareness of my own culpability.'

This is his first time outside the white Western world and this unease about his culpability in the cultural impact wrought by tourism and capitalism will increasingly weigh on his sense of wellbeing. I would say he was a little ahead of his time, and my own latent suspicions of the contemporary generation of gap-year hedonists cause me to complain that his prescient awareness of the ambiguous impact of travel and tourism is still not as widely held as it should be.

This unease does not stop him from exploring the island and challenging himself with what he sees. He has set himself the task of trying to make a link between popular graphic forms and the cultures they come from. He is attracted to the beauty of the 'art', but travels inland to visit the factories that produce it. He worries that it is mass-produced. He seeks out a cockfight and whilst lacking Kinglake's Victorian elegance of style, he has a good eye for detail and an inquiring mind.

'A large gathering of the locals with an array of hamburger stalls Bali style. What was most interesting was the uproar that preceded and concluded each bout. I eventually discovered that this chaotic roar was in fact an elaborate betting session. Tight wads of bank notes would be thrown across the arena where they would lie with people, cocks and dogs kicking and stamping on the cash. At the end of the bout, the consignee, who by some magical process knew that he was the winner would scamper out and collect up his winnings from off the blood-stained arena. Everyone knows exactly how much money was kicking around in the dirt.'

Then after another two weeks in this *'paradise'* he sends a *'think'* letter with a markedly different tone:

'The main feeling has been one of complete isolation from my fellow men, both brown and white, due to the large amount of pride that I carry and cannot properly deal with. I have committed so many social crimes, which I only become aware of later, that my spirits are rock bottom and the future uncertain. I feel like a small child learning again how to live with other people and I am a slow learner. But I do have some faith in the power of understanding and compassion and this gives me the energy to keep moving on. Forgive my despondency, but rather like a confession I had to get it off my chest.'

He goes on to worry that so many of his experiences may be *'intellectually interesting but spiritually meaningless due to lack of the language.'* He beats up on himself for his inadequacy in this regard:

I feel this lack most acutely and question my confidence that it would be possible to exist in a country independent of the inhabitants, and other travellers for that matter without even learning the language.

This will be a recurring theme during the rest of his time on the road. He is hard on himself and yet he is also grappling with his feeling of *'complete isolation.'* I know he is sociable and wants to engage, but his pride is holding him back. He is wracked with residual guilt about his crimes against the local culture. I recognise his discomfort because it has had a negative impact on some of my own travels. On the other hand, I have rarely travelled solo and that is because I fear the trials of isolation. Robin found the isolation gave him too much time to brood on what he perceived as his 'many faux pas'. As he progresses, I fear that this insidious cycle could threaten his sanity. And yet so far all his reactions seem predictable. This sort of travelling is hard and I imagine at its worst could send you just a little crazy. Am I getting ahead of myself? I am only a retrospective observer, albeit one who fears for his safety; the journey has only just begun.

'On Monday I will take the boat to Surabaja, a port on the North Coast of Java, then by bus to Djogakarkata and Bandung, then to Djakarta. From there by train to Palambang, bus to Medan and ferry to Penang where I shall arrive (hopefully by the end of the month).'

He seems to know his way. I have checked it out on Google maps and it seems to work, although it is 1375 kilometres from Djakarta to Medan and would take 40 hours by bus!

All goes to plan and the next letter comes from Djogakarkarta where he has met up with a couple of friends from Perth who have agreed to let him travel with them: *'I have given up the idea of the "glamorous lone world traveller". My nervous constitution is not up to the strain.'* There are two letters one after the other. He has been cheered by the company. He writes fulsomely about their visits to the two biggest temples in Indonesia: Borobordur, the largest Buddhist temple in the world, and Prambanan, the massive Hindu shrine. There he learns from a zealous evangelical Christian that *'since the coup of 1968, it is compulsory for all Indonesians to hold a religion.'* And they check out the contemporary cinema scene where they are showing *'The Italian Job, a slick spy thriller starring Michael Caine and Noel Coward. At another The Prodigal Boxer and at a third The Angry Boxer.'*

He is behaving as a traveller should. There are detailed descriptions of the street markets and the Batik factory and the *'small cheap and by our standards, fairly filthy hotel.'* Although he is still frustrated by his failure to communicate:

'I realise I am a slave to my linguistic poverty. Needless to say I am working hard to master even the bare essentials. 'Saya tidakmengerti Indonesian': 'I don't understand Indonesian' is the current favourite, followed closely by 'Bitjara lambat , silakan': 'Please speak slowly.' After that fails I lapse energetically into large gestures, messy drawings and expressive sounds.'

He writes about the sights and sounds of poverty as they walk through the streets at night:

'In the shallow doorways men, young and old lay sleeping on rattan mats covered by frayed sarongs. A beggar woman with her hungry child clutched to her bosom, half walks, half crawls with her hands extending pleading, eyes empty.'

This is all as it should be. He is acting like a

responsible tourist: alive to the rich contrasts and sensitive to the plight of the people. This is normal. He sounds normal. I am relieved. He has banished the loneliness and is fulfilling his aspirations to 'see the world'.

I have no idea how long this merry group of three stayed together. I wanted to know what he made of Bandung and how he got on in Djakarta: even in those days a megalopolis for over four million and surely a daunting proposition for the wandering back-packer. Up until this point, he has managed to write regularly. In the previous months, if the gap between letters was longer than a week, he acknowledged that he was remiss and there were fulsome apologies. But after those two cheerful letters from Djogakarkarta, there is an unprecedented and worrying hiatus.

The next letter I have in my bundle is dated March 26th and it comes from Singapore. It is more than a month later and it begins: *'Hope that the silence of the last couple of weeks or so hasn't worried you too much.'* Well, I suppose there could be a missing letter from *'a couple of weeks ago,'* but as far as I am concerned there has been a five-week silence and as I read this letter I am feeling very worried indeed. I must assume that my parents had felt the same way. He goes on:

'I have been having a rather uprooting set of experiences lately and have not been completely settled enough to put pen to paper in a cogent fashion.'

If you compare this letter with all his previous communications, it is hardly his cogent best. Where he had filled his letters with description and anecdote interspersed with some perceptive introspection, this letter is pale and sparse. Where his handwriting has always been tidy and bold, the writing is hesitant. There is no sign of the graphic flair which added so much to his musings. It is both the form and the content that causes me to read between the lines.

He dispatches the last five weeks in a mere five lines. A ferry to Penang, a night in the Cameron Highlands and then:

'Experiences referred to above have been a three day stay in Berastagi and then a week on the very beautiful North coast of Penang Island, both places, through the people I met, their actions and my reactions forced me to confront myself with a few of my assumptions about life. Only to be expected, though, on the road where there are so many strong personalities.'

I really try not to overreact to those few sentences. After all, he has confessed to being lonely and dispirited during the early stages of the journey. But if this is the best he can do after five weeks' silence, then it is not unreasonable to suppose that something very significant has taken place. If I remove the parental filter of understatement and put this into the context of what I understand is to come in just a few weeks' time, I feel justified in trying to dig beneath these slim pickings and pick at the threads of what seem to me to be genuine distress.

Who are these *'people'* who have caused him to *'confront himself'*? In previous letters he has given us pen portraits of anyone significant. These *'strong personalities'* have closed him down. Later he tells us that he has *'left my Australian friends for the while and may meet up with them in Bangkok.'* So he is travelling solo again and he is low. And then he adds:

'You will by now have the cable. I hope that doesn't cause a lot of inconvenience. Thank you for all your trouble. I feel pretty nervous though about doing that trip alone after the first few weeks away from familiar ground. But something keeps me going and I still consider early June as the ETA, in time to fix up a course for an October start.'

I want to know more about that cable, but as with so much on my journey of discovery, all the witnesses are dead. Once again I beat up on myself for not going through these letters whilst my mother was alive. She would have remembered that cable. I surmise that it will have revealed another change of plan and involved cancelling a rendezvous with friends of my parents in Singapore who, according to a previous letter, had been alerted to his possible arrival. He is in Singapore and yet he does not sound as if he is enjoying hospitality from friends of the General. So, could that cable have said: 'I am on my way to Singapore but will not be meeting up with XX'? It sounds plausible, but I am constructing a narrative in which those *'people'* with their *'strong personalities'* have messed with his head. His *'assumptions about life'* have been so severely challenged that he cannot face reverting to his previous persona: the public-school boy who could make nice to the ex-pat military chums of his parents. And yet, all is not lost, because, although nervous, he plans to travel on for another three months to be back in time to put in applications for those courses. Maybe he still has hopes of making it to New York and Hovey Burgess.

He signs off: *'A little depressed at the moment but figure to take the rough with the smooth.'*

Have I made too much of this letter? Does it merely reflect a wholly understandable low point from which he will bounce back? He has been honest enough to share his lows as well as his highs and provide us with plenty of evidence that he is riding the rough and relishing the smooth. Surely I am over-reacting. But no, I am not. There are too many disturbing intimations of a deeper distress. Every time I read it my heart sinks a little further. And I have to re-read it again and again because this is the last letter he will write on this journey. This is the last testimony I have before a deadening silence. The Sender's address on the aerogramme is *'Poste Restante, Bangkok, Thailand'*. It seems that all roads lead to Bangkok.

* * * * * * *

The next thing we heard was some two weeks later. It was another cable. To my father, asking him to buy a ticket from Bangkok to Heathrow. He was coming home. His journey was over. No more talk of further stages. I do not have the cable nor the exact date, but my father must have obliged because I do know that we were to meet him at Heathrow. I have found the BOAC timetable for 1972 and it looks as if it would have been a VC10 Flight BA 802, stopping off in Teheran, arriving at Heathrow Terminal 3 at 0745. It must have been an early start but we did meet him. Would he be relieved to be home? Something had gone wrong, and as I waited to catch sight of him emerging from the Arrivals channel, I was not optimistic.

Dear Robin,

They are serving breakfast. There is a queue outside the toilets. In anticipation of landing, my fellow travellers are looking to wipe away the grime of a fitful night. In the window I see the dawn, a bright orange smudge across the horizon, easing up into the now dark blue of the retreating night sky. We are on the cusp between darkness and light. The map shows me it is dusk in San Francisco and a bright day in Western Australia. We are chasing the sun.

Another sleepless night has taken its toll on me. My spirits are low. I am thinking of you and your return flight. Unlike me, in my non-stop Dreamliner, you will have stopped off in Tehran: an acceptable option in your day as the Ayatollah was in exile and Iran was still a safe haven for western travellers.

Three hours out from Tehran you would have flown over the Eastern Mediterranean but I cannot conjure up your state of mind. Were you pleased to be getting home? Or were you humiliated? I know you had surrendered. An early return was all that you could do. Were you dreading the thought of meeting up with your parents and explaining yourself? They would be pleased to see you, but I know that there

313

would be a chasm between their expectations and your reality. You were a different person and no amount of remembered ritual will disguise the disjunction.

I am trying to imagine your anguish and despair as you watched the sun rise and listened to the pilot's announcement that there was less than two hours to touchdown. Like me you will not have slept: God knows what fractured scenes were infecting your psyche every time you shut your eyes.

15. A Slow Descent

*What we call 'normal' is a product of repression... The
'normally' alienated person, by reason of the fact that he
acts more or less like everyone else, is taken to be sane.
Other forms of alienation that are out of step with the
prevailing state of alienation are those that are labelled
by the 'normal' majority as bad or mad.*

R.D. Laing, The Politics of Experience /
The Bird of Paradise

I knew that something was wrong as soon as I saw him
emerge from customs at Heathrow. He seemed wild
and restless: in a state of distress. Our mother was too
busy celebrating the return of the prodigal to notice.
But I looked into his eyes, just for a moment, and did
not like what I saw.

He avoided any detail of where he had been, what
he had done, and why he had returned in such a hurry.
He fended off any questions during the journey back
to Hampshire by saying he'd *'run out of steam.'*

I have since collected my own children from the airport on their return from foreign adventures. There is always a dissonance between the traveller, still caught up in the otherness of his or her experience, and the meeters and greeters, welcoming back the person they thought they knew before departure. Both rehearse old rituals and well-worn family scripts. The necessary recalibration has yet to take place. Indeed, a few years earlier, I myself had returned from Canada after four years of different living and I remembered this fog of missed connections, and I was full of empathy for Robin's detachment. And yet I did feel a chill of apprehension.

The next day we went for a walk on our own. I could see that, free from our parents' constraining presence, he was desperate to talk.

'So... what happened?'

'It was bad. Really bad. They were hounding me.'

'Who was?'

'The Man!'

'The man?'

'The Man! I don't know exactly who. But you know, the Man. Maybe the

CIA. They were definitely following me. I could tell. Even though I took evasive action, they were always there. Sometimes they used locals.

Sometimes they were foreigners, like me, but in suits. I was staying in this hostel and they had people staying there. They were watching me, searching my things. They left clues. Deliberately. And they left these signs. Notes. Scraps of paper on the street, where I was walking. Just for me. Reminding me that they had me covered. I collected them. I've got them somewhere. They were trying to get into my head.'

'God, that sounds terrible. Are you sure? Would they do that? I mean, follow you across Asia...?'

'Of course I'm sure. Asia is their territory. Vietnam, Cambodia. The Man is pulling the strings. They'd been following me all along, ever since the demos, the street theatre. They had me marked out. I was a threat to them, and they needed to threaten me.'

However manic the content, his tone was calm, almost reasonable. This all made sense to him, and he expected it to make sense to me. After all, 'the Man' was still napalming Vietnam. 'The Man' was about to bring down Allende in Chile.

I was now firmly embedded in left-wing politics and I wanted so much to agree with him. I knew he had been active in protest, far more active than I had ever been. I didn't want to play the sensible elder brother, spouting establishment rhetoric. I wanted to be on his side. It suited my politics to collude with his belief in the malign covert influence of the CIA in Asia, but that did not blind me to a crazy narrative that had to portend a serious mental instability. I was starting to panic. However lucid he seemed, however in tune with the zeitgeist, this was madness. And I was out of my depth.

Something had happened to my brother. I was no psychologist and at that moment I knew a great deal less about psychosis than I do now. But Robin was detached from reality and I could recognise a serious case of paranoia. I was thrown off balance. I wanted him to be sane and yet on that walk just a day after his return he so clearly was not. As I relive that scene (and unlike so much of my stunted memory, this dialogue comes back to me with startling clarity; heightened emotion once again priming the memory cells) I can feel the acute discomfort and the insidious uncertainty. I ought to have told someone. I should have pressed him, then and there, to see someone. But I didn't then and I didn't ever. I thought it was best to cover up and I know that when we returned to the family home and a carefully prepared dinner of roast pheasant and bread sauce (Robin's favourite) washed down with a decent claret, nothing was said about the Man and covert surveillance. Instead, we reverted to the reassuring family script.

Once I had finished the second brandy, echoed my mother's 'It's so lovely to have you back' and headed off to bed, there was only one question pulsing through my head: what in God's name happened to him in Bangkok?

* * * * * *

I had been in touch with Cheryl, after my first trip to Perth, and I wanted to meet up but I knew she was living in Italy and working in Egypt. She came to London infrequently but there was a visit in the offing and we agreed to meet. In the email exchange I had explained that I wanted to talk about Robin's state of mind and had mentioned that I felt he might have been displaying symptoms of 'paranoid schizophrenia' on his return to England. She was quick to respond:

'When I read your words 'paranoid schizophrenia' – after all these years – many things begin to make sense. I don't know why it never occurred to me that he was ill. In retrospect, as you say, it was fairly clear-cut.'

She went on to talk about how she had met up with him in London:

'In '73, when we first re-connected, he seemed a bit rattled and less confident than he had been in Australia, but on a number of later occasions, and especially at one particular party a couple of years later. I think it was in Acton, a far-flung and alien land for me in those days, and from that night on, I never was able to recognise or connect with the Robin I knew.'

She had information that Robin had told her at that party, which she had kept to herself all these years, and would share it with me when we met.

Some two months later, I was sitting in a café beneath the vaulted ceiling of St Pancras station. The sound of arrivals and departures was loud and full of dissonance. Everyone was in transit but I was waiting for Cheryl. I had no idea what she looked like and was worried that we might repeat the disconnection of waiting in separate corners that had delayed my meeting with Halimah. She, however, recognised me and came straight over: 'I can see the Robin in you,' she said as she settled into the seat opposite.

At first she gave no sign that she had secrets to share. Our initial conversation was a little stilted; she did not appear to accede to my easy assumptions that his relationships from forty-five years ago were rightfully mine to explore. Her account of their time sharing the house on Bulimba Road was circumspect. She confirmed all that she said about Robin in her email. She had mostly good memories of him and his state of mind. I did not press her on the exact state of their relationship. She made it sound as if it had been more one of convenience and pleasure rather than passion. At this point, I still had not found his red and black letter with its description of a rather more fraught relationship in which defences had been lowered and raised in mutual mistrust. But after a second drink I asked her about her impressions of Robin back in London and that party.

'I knew something was wrong the moment I saw

him. Instead of the relaxed, attractive man I had known so well, he seemed shifty and his eyes had none of the warmth that had charmed us all. He was affectionate but guarded. He started to introduce me to the others in the room. I was surprised. They were totally different from the friends we had known. They didn't seem to be Robin's "tribe". There was no evidence of his usual arty, theatrical, eccentric, political people. It surprised me and I was frightened too, that he seemed so strange in himself.

After some desultory talk, Robin put his arm around me and guided me into the bedroom and closed the door. When he took hold of me and hugged me I thought he was making a pass but then he started to cry. We lay on the bed and he held me tight, too tight.

I asked him what was wrong. What had happened? He started to tell me about his time in Bangkok. He said he had never told anyone else. He had got hold of some LSD. It was probably spiked, because he had a really bad trip. Wandering the streets, out of his mind. Then he was picked up by the Thai Police and ended up in a Bangkok prison.

He didn't tell me much more. I didn't find out how long he was kept in jail, but in telling me he was obviously reliving what must have been an appallingly traumatic, life-changing experience. I could barely recognise the man I knew.'

* * * * * *

I am transported to a disreputable hostel in Patpong Soi. I watch in trepidation as he takes a grubby tab of indeterminate origin and waits for the bright lights and incandescence to open up his consciousness. He has been here before. There should be no surprises. But something is wrong, I can see the forces of disruption taking hold; a hopeful smile is replaced by a stunned gasp as he is engulfed in primal fear.

I have visited Bangkok often and it is all too easy to place myself in the scene, just as I did outside the Octagon Theatre when he was the one to envy. Now, in some dystopian flipside, I watch him wandering the streets of Bangkok with his head on fire with tortured hallucinations. Totally lost in his own miasma of dark fears that are tumbling across the wide screen of his psyche. Is this the moment when the paranoia takes hold? Is he seeing undercover servants of the dark state tracking his every move? Is he seeking to escape the demons unleashed by the toxic chemicals that have banished any semblance of stability and coherence? Unlike poor Tom Burns, Roger's friend, he still has his clothes on, but he stands out tall and blonde and he is causing a disturbance, blundering into bemused citizens well-used to deranged hippies, but still angered by the way my brother disrupts their passage and stares with wild eyes devoid of acknowledgement.

Then, from the crowd, a posse of genuine agents of the state. Policemen in olive drabs and armed with truncheons. His instincts for survival struggle into play and he smiles weakly, trying to defuse the threat. But he has no luck. They make no effort to question him, but slam him up against the wall and press his face against the rough concrete, and frisk him with unnecessary ferocity. Now his eyes are wide with nameless terror. The aggression and fear magnified by the screaming synapses. His mind is now detached and floating free. There is a sound of sirens and a battered grey van squeals to halt and he is bundled inside. I am helpless. The handsome face that I have envied so is looking out from the barred window and I have lost a brother.

I am assailed by the thought of my brother, vulnerable and befuddled by the after-shocks of a bad LSD trip stuck in a cell with fifty others. I search for descriptions of what it was like and find that in the seventies remand prisoners would have been sent to Klong Prem Prison, which a relatively recent inmate describes as

'...one of the worst prisons in the world with terrible conditions. Prisoners share cells with about 50 other inmates often having to sleep on their sides as there is not enough room to lie on their backs. There is one toilet.'

And that was in 2008! God only knows what it was like in March 1973. I am there by his side as he thrashes around trying to get back his grip on reality.

Yet, while I am easily engulfed in reconstructions of his nightmare and devastated by the visceral pain he had inflicted on himself, I am also relieved. Cheryl has given me an explanation: something to hold onto. It may not be the whole answer, but it allows me to construct a counter-narrative to the one my mother and the rest of the family have clung onto. Whilst I still need to compute the implications of that last enigmatic aerogramme from Singapore, I now have a fulcrum around which I can pivot his story. Before Bangkok he was everything that we wanted him to be, not flawless and perhaps a little overly introspective, but bursting with creativity and intellectual curiosity. After Bangkok all bets were off. Not totally incapacitated, but badly handicapped by his errant and damaged mind. That fulcrum may, in retrospect, have been somewhat overly simplistic. It diminished the less dramatic indicators of his well-camouflaged fragility. It was a thesis that, whilst offering me some peace of mind, I will need to interrogate. But for the time being it offered a comforting catharsis.

Could one traumatic experience arising from and influenced by a bad LSD trip have tipped the balance of his mind? There is a lot of research about the link between cannabis and psychoses, although the link is far from proven. There is less research on the long-term impact of LSD. I found a team at Imperial College, London, led by Robin Carhart-Harris, looking into the positive impact of hallucinogenics, but they also seemed well placed to help me with the possible negative impact on mental health. It was a speculative email to a busy man but I was rewarded with an almost instant response:

'I'm very sorry to hear of your brother's suicide and its possible to link to LSD use. The circumstances of his experience do indeed sound horribly traumatic. We have good evidence now that the quality of a person's psychedelic experience strongly predicts longer-term changes in mental health outcomes. We also know increasingly well that contextual factors work to determine the quality of one's experience. Tragically, it sounds as though your brother had the worst possible kind of context for his experience, this likely impacted on the kind of experience he had and thus, his subsequent mental health.'

Not conclusive, but certainly suggesting that I was on the right track. To make my case even more convincing I need academic evidence that someone who had taken LSD in the past with no apparent malign effects could be so adversely affected in the long-term by one bad trip combined with a traumatic incident. Such evidence was surprisingly hard to come by, but I intended to keep looking.

The Bangkok experience may have delivered a reassuring explanation, but when many months later I was telling Robin's son Oliver, now a 40 year old corporate lawyer, he challenged me: 'Yes, it makes sense and fits your explanation, but, do we have any other evidence that it actually happened like that?' An excellent question which I was unable to answer. Despite my best efforts, there seemed no way to find the corroborating evidence.

My work had taken me to Bangkok on several occasions and I made some good friends. When I explained my dilemma to Pornchai Tangsunawan, he said that he had a friend in the police department whom he would approach to find out whether there were any records from that time. A month later he reported back:

'In the 70s and well into the 90s, all police records were on paper forms. The standard procedure then was to destroy the records after 10 years. This was because they could not store all the documents and were obliged to destroy them to prevent any exploitation. The practice still continues for records in paper form.

The exception was for the document of significance. It seemed to him that your brother did not commit a major breach in law judging by the short time he served. There is unlikely that the record was still there, even if there was one.'

He suggested that we need to find some clues to be able to further investigate. He believed it was likely to yield nothing if we employ private investigation without important clues.

I had no more clues. I just had some third-hand testimony, and even then a confession imparted whilst entwined on a bed in Acton would not have impressed a Bangkok PI. As a final throw of the dice I contacted the British Embassy in Bangkok. I received a friendly response:

'While we would like to be able to help you, due to data protection the British Embassy does not hold the information you are enquiring about readily available.'

She suggested that I submit a Freedom of Information request and I did. But after an inordinately long wait (it should be twenty days), I receive a reply:

'Following a search, we have not identified any information held by the FCO, including at our embassy in Bangkok, relevant to your request.'

* * * * * * *

Robin never spoke to me again about 'the Man'. He seemed to have found some reconciliation with his troubled psyche. His immediate symptoms improved. He started to make his way in the world. But he was a shadow of the sparkling, charismatic prodigal son who had left our shores so full of promise. Sometimes that early charm would break out and he would laugh and smile and beguile those around him.

As for his future, all that drive and tantalising assortment of ideas for an exciting future had evaporated. There was no sign of the man who had written so passionately about training to be an actor, a teacher or even a circus performer. I recall a few evenings spent in the pub when after a few pints we could have expected to build castles in the air. Instead I retain only a tragic lack of purpose, compounded by his repeated reference to my success. I did not feel particularly successful but I was full of energy and endeavour. I had plunged head first into teaching and was making a decent fist of it in a demanding inner-city comprehensive. I was an active participant in a vibrant coterie of socialist teachers. I had just purchased my own flat and my life was full. I was an affront to his loss of direction and lack of motivation, made more potent by his battered sense of himself. Less than a year ago he was amongst his friends in Perth, Cheryl, Phil Thomson, and working with Ray Omodei. Just as connected and even more engaged than me.

I was sympathetic. I too had suffered on returning home from Canada after four years away: years that had been filled with good friends, creative fulfilment and a degree of self-belief. I had found it hard to start all over again, but because I had retained my confidence and that self-belief, it did not take me long to find my feet. Robin's state of mind had deprived him of the essential energies required to make a new start.

For a while, I caught sight of his potential and capacity. My radical English teacher friends and I were doing our best to put our politics into teaching. We had a progressive vision for education and after organising a successful conference in 1974, had decided to put together a magazine to proselytise our case. In an affront to the education establishment we called it Teaching London Kids. A good friend, Michael Simons, led the way and we gathered in his Battersea mansion flat to lay up the first edition. I have the magazine in front of me and somewhat to my surprise I find that there are two Bethells on the non-hierarchical masthead. So what had Robin done?

Michael is a man of my age and although he has a startling memory for some things, like me, he found it hard to pin down a memory of Robin:

I have tried digging for a more dynamic picture of him but I only seem to get a still image and the feeling of a young man rather lost and disoriented but very gentle and charming.

But he did remember his contribution to the magazine. This was a time well before publishing software and you achieved a professional look by getting your copy typed up on a typesetting machine in long rolls which you then cut up and stuck down. The titles and headings were made up with Letraset, dry transfer lettering in different fonts and sizes:

'I remember having all this typesetting and sheets of Letraset and no clue how to begin. I recall him sitting with me in the kitchen at Overstrand Mansions and

calmly explaining the function of the drawing board and T Square as though he'd been in the print all his life. I'm not sure but maybe he even designed some of the pages.'

Looking at the magazine I do remember that the design was considered original and striking. Despite the almost unreadable graphics of an OZ, radical publications of the time were renowned for their drab and uninviting layout. It still looks pretty good today and Robin's involvement is a source of pride and sadness. He had a shining talent in so many areas, and yet he was never to develop or fulfil his promise.

He had lost all interest in theatre but, as Michael recalls, he had retained his graphic design skills and so my father pulled strings to get him a job in a design studio. It was an opportunity that could have led to a successful career and we had high hopes that he would settle. He was working on the new W.H. Smith logo, the distinctive cube in orange and brown designed by the graphic design guru Richard Guyatt. It was boring work reformulating the logo to fit on letterhead, staff badges and invoices, but it could easily have been a launch pad. Had he stuck with it, his talents would have seen him progress, even without formal training. But Robin's resilience had been shot to pieces and he lasted a few months and then one day failed to show up for work and that was that.

* * * * * * *

I am driving into Totnes in Devon. Its reputation suggests an English Byron Bay, where Robin may have felt at home during his hippy phase. It is where the counter-culture has come to settle down, where alternative lifestyles get cosy. Above all it is a place of healing, of every sort: from 'inner dialogue kinesiology' to 'HOPI ear candle therapies'. And Farhad is a healer too, though rather less exotic. Five years ago he left London and moved to Totnes to practice as a psychotherapist. He has a national reputation as an iconoclast known for his well-researched tilts at the orthodox psychotherapeutic windmills. He is Indian and came to London in 1972 at the age of 18: in every sense an innocent abroad. He was also Robin's closest friend during the lost years. They had a lot in common.

'I was lost, but so was he. We were both detached from what we knew. He was sad and vulnerable but also full of empathy and had a sensitive intelligence. We got on so well, because we supported each other. And we could laugh at the craziness of the world.'

'Where did you meet?'

'We both ended up in a shared house in Clapham. It was a crazy place. The landlord Henry had been given the place by his father and filled it with his public-school friends. I was the brunt of their racist banter. It was such a relief when Robin moved in. We very quickly became close. We smoked a lot of dope together. In fact I was probably stoned most of the time in those first few years in London.'

'Was he disturbed in any way? From what you know now, would you say he was depressive? Psychotic?'

'I didn't think so at the time. We were just two lost souls and respected each other's idiosyncrasies. I stayed friends with him right through to the end, so of course I understood that something was wrong. But I hadn't started my training while I knew him, so it wasn't a professional assessment. I got to know your parents too. I spent Christmas with your family. You were there, I think'

'Yes, I was, but I don't remember the gory details. What did you think of my family?'

'I liked your mum but found your dad pretty difficult. And so did Robin.'

'Difficult? In what way?'

'Robin felt under a lot of pressure from your father. He once told me that he felt bullied by him. Felt he always wanted him to "do the right thing".'

Although Farhad's comments about our father cause me some discomfort, I am not surprised. Robin's relationship with his father was proving problematic. I remember how, in the early months, when his railing against the military-industrial complex was still fresh in my mind, he appeared to move on. He surprised me with a sentimental appraisal of his father and our wider family. He was full of admiration for the General. He wanted to reconnect with aunts and uncles and cousins, which seemed odd as they had all stuck firmly to their class-defined careers and life values. He held forth particularly warmly about our public school, and how if he ever had sons he would send them to Sherborne. Whilst he also liked to see himself as battling against the tyranny of the established order, a deeper part of his psyche seemed to be seeking comfort in his origins. This was jarring. My politics held me in a very uncomfortable space when it came to my parents, my family and their values. My credo was locked in an uneasy truce with my background, and I expected Robin to be firmly on my side of the barricades. Then he surprised me yet again.

About a year after his return, and at time when we were all hoping that Robin was making headway in his struggle to settle down, he found a way to disrupt our fragile optimism. The Todhunters – longstanding family friends – lived up the road from Rose Cottage. Captain Robin Todhunter had been a war hero and a director of ICI. He was a grand figure in our lives and my father was in awe of him. He had always owned a sporty Jaguar XK 50. He was that sort of a man. Robin 'borrowed' it without permission, drove it to the West Country and ended up in a hedge. The damage was minor, but for two days it seemed as though the car had been stolen and Robin had disappeared. This was doubly distressing for my parents – an assault on a deeply valued friendship and a portent of things to come.

I tried to explain to my father that Robin's behaviour was not always rational, that he probably had a mental illness, but it was surprisingly difficult to get the General to buy in to that version of events. This was a man who had been wounded at Dunkirk at the age of nineteen, been captured at Tobruk and escaped from a POW camp. He must have come into contact with PTSD, but when it came to his own son, he seemed incapable of either empathy or comprehension. 'He's just being bloody bolshy.' I assumed then that he simply lacked the necessary emotional intelligence, as was often the case with men of his generation and his station. Of course, after delving into his troubled inheritance I came to understand that the predictable suppression of the turmoil of his father's suicide, the almost certain absence of any counseling or support, and the overwhelming imperative to bury the truth about his father, left my father totally incapacitated when faced with his own son's mental health and eventual suicide.

* * * * * *

The Todhunter Jaguar affair was a portent of things to come over the next five years. There would be periods of apparent calm when, although subdued and underperforming, Robin was holding his own. He had several low-level jobs and in each he was valued if somewhat misunderstood. As with his early departure from the design studio, he would usually terminate the employment himself, often by failing to show up. And just like his jaunt in the Jag, he would disappear for two or three days and then reappear without explanation. Then he would revert to a life of sorts. In this period he was usually alarmingly sane. His sanity could be fiercely articulated with a piercing intelligence that could puncture any suggestions to the contrary. He could be intensely personable with an engaging manner.

As we have seen, my father was a man who needed to solve problems through action. I had removed myself from his sphere of influence. He was not going to be able to intervene in my world. He admired me for being a teacher, that much he could understand, and even that I was somehow 'doing good', but apart from the odd financial bung to help buy a car or a fridge (my first monthly pay cheque from the Inner London Education Authority was £83 45p) I was independent. Robin, on the other hand, was far too dependent. It was not helped by his unlikely allegiance to my father and his kind, which, I now realise, increased his vulnerability to parental pressure.

I am conscious that I have given my father the

critical parental role in Robin's story. I am convinced that his fractured and troubled relationship with the General was an important catalyst in those turbulent years after his return from Bangkok. However, I cannot ignore my mother, although her influence is harder to pin down. As we have seen, and this is not just my sibling resentment, she was more deeply entwined in his psyche than she ever had been with mine. Had he returned from Australia largely unscathed, then he might have been able to effect a partial separation: moved along the trajectory from child to man. None of us fulfils a complete separation, but a normal adult life does require you get halfway there at least. But his vulnerability and distress prevented that. He was, in his turn, inextricably entwined in her psyche. He could be angry with my father but all he could do to protect himself from his mother was to refuse to take her phone calls. As his psychological state deteriorated I have only an opaque image of her torment. Early on in Robin's decline, I realised that I could not stand the heat of my mother's anguish.

My father may have been slow to acknowledge Robin's mental distress, but once he did so, he did try to do something about it. I have to give him credit for that. The Todhunter car was repaired and returned. Apologies were offered and sympathetically received. I was certain that my father had been unmoved by my attempts to assuage his anger, unconvinced by the case for Robin's mental disturbance. But I was wrong. I have recently discovered, from his testimony to the coroner's report on my brother's death, that he had in fact persuaded Robin to attend an appointment with what he would have called a 'trick cyclist': the Chief Army Psychiatrist at the Tidworth Garrison Hospital on Salisbury Plain, near where they lived. It did not go well. He described the outcome: 'The Psychiatrist felt that some treatment might help. The boy was unwilling to accept it.'

I am trying not to be too judgmental, although his use of the word 'boy' speaks volumes. Robin was twenty-four years old, but I fear that throughout these years my father saw him as the 'boy'.

I am not surprised that the 'boy was unwilling to accept any help'. I have no doubt that once faced by the 'enemy' he would have been in a state of intense intellectual acuity; he would have run rings round this version of 'the Man'. If he was even residually still suffering his paranoia about the established forces ranged against him, the Chief Army Psychiatrist was hardly likely to break down his defences.

I was well aware of the strategies he would have deployed to push back on any diagnosis, because he had rehearsed them with me. He was, he had told me, a disciple of R.D. Laing: mental illness was a social construct and he was merely flying in the face of the establishment's compact of subservient normalcy.

It was not him that was ill, it was society. Taking the car of a rich member of the plutocracy was not a sign of madness, but of liberation from the shackles of convention. He was not going to allow 'the formal majority to label him mad' and he was well versed in Laing's anti-psychiatry rhetoric that was much in vogue at the time.

In an article on the anti-psychiatry movement written for World Mental Health Day, Benjamin Noys summarises Laing's thinking:

'For Laing, "schizophrenic" behaviour is "a special strategy that a person invents in order to live in an unliveable situation". In response to the demands of society – demands which are contradictory and maddening, "an infernal dance of false dualities" – the schizophrenic is fragmented, split, depersonalised, and reified (treated as a thing).'

Robin subscribed to this doctrine. He would have been deeply suspicious of any psychiatrist, and since his psychotic behaviour was episodic and in those early days relatively infrequent, I can see exactly how he would have used his formidable intelligence to fend off any therapeutic inquiry.

As time went on and the psychotic incidents started to increase in frequency and intensity, I did my best to encourage him to seek help. By that time, I was in a settled relationship and I had some back-up from my partner Claire. The problem was that both she and I were ideologically inclined to endorse much of Laing's critique. We knew that treatment for mental illness had been medicalised and institutionalised. We had read Sylvia Plath's The Bell Jar with its stark portrayal of electro-shock therapy. One Flew Over the Cuckoo's Nest came out in 1975, two years into Robin's decline. Our assumptions around the treatment of mental illness were informed by the graphic realisation of the worst of 1950s psychiatric practice. Jack Nicholson was a free spirit and Robin would have cheered him along with the rest of us.

We so badly wanted Robin to be right. We were desperate to believe that his aberrations were indeed merely 'a special strategy that he had invented in order to live in an unlivable situation'. We were on Laing's side in the culture wars. And yet we also had our doubts. Darkly held reservations. The theory may have been sound but in practice we were watching on as my beautiful brother began to wrestle with his increasingly insidious demons. Looking back now we both feel very guilty and guileless. How could we have been fooled by Laing and his acolytes? Robin was ill. He needed treatment and we held back. We wanted to respect his self-belief, except that his sense of self had been corrupted. Like far too many others at that time, we colluded in a non-interventionist doctrine that I now believe caused untold damage.

I have since discovered that the drug

chlorpromazine was available then and had success in treating schizophrenia: not eliminating it, but softening the impact. I taunt myself with the thought that I could have put on more pressure and that I could have done more to counter his Laingian arguments. I am haunted by the thought that, had we used our influence to persuade him to seek help, we might have had more success than the General and his Army Psychiatrist. A prescription for chlorpromazine might have saved him.

As his situation deteriorated, this guilt matured into an urgent disquiet. We approached a wise friend, a GP well versed in treating mental illness. He was partially reassuring. He explained that it was a symptom of a certain mental instability that the patient simply will not countenance the thought of treatment. That is true for therapeutic as it is for chemical cures. That advice went some way to assuaging the guilt, but now, in retrospect, it has kicked in with a vengeance. I was in a unique position of influence. I know that Robin respected me. He felt I was on his side. I could have made a difference. Could I have saved him from himself?

The second tenet of Laing's approach, at least in its popularisation, was to blame the family. This went down well with the baby boomers who, in the sixties, had done their very best to throw off the shackles of the restrictive family norms of their parents; parents who had survived the war largely by hanging onto their parents' values. Laing was onto a winner by encouraging us that a malevolent society was crushing the wayward spirit whilst confirming that, if things did go wrong within that paradigm, then we could blame our up-tight parents. In Robin's case you could argue that it was not so much his parenting as his lack of parenting. Boarding school and a distant university certainly kept our parents at arm's length. But then, what of those early days? Did my father's robust approach to child-rearing damage Robin more than it had affected me? Looking back at those troubled 'lost years' after his return from Bangkok I can see that my father did appear to have much more sway over Robin than I would have liked. And yet I am equally sure it was fuelled by love. Where Claire and I had backed off, he did make one more effort to seek help. In that same Coroner's account, he tells PC Alyin-White of the Surrey Constabulary:

'About two years later I persuaded him to accompany me to see the consultant psychiatrist at the Atkinson Morley Hospital, Wimbledon, who again felt that he might be able to help but yet again the boy refused.'

BOUVERIE ROAD, LONDON, ENGLAND.
HEIGHT ABOVE SEA LEVEL: 11METRES.

Dear Robin,

I am back home. You never knew this house. We moved here the year after you died. Thirty-eight years ago. Before that it was the flat in nearby Clapton, and you did stay there. We are not great movers. I suppose it's a reaction against the itinerant Bethell heritage. I wonder whether you too would have stayed in Dorset. In better times I have a feeling it might have suited you. Colvin showed me that you enjoyed the rural life.

I have never been too worried by the physical impact of jetlag. I have found it easy to wrestle my sleep patterns back into line. But as for my spirits, that's a different matter. I have to factor in a week of feeling low. I know it is coming and will end, but that doesn't stop me feeling that the depression will last forever.

The melancholy that has gripped me since my return from Perth is appropriate. It reflects the way our story is nearing its end. There is no more good news. As I have mentioned, even though I was part of the narrative, it has been hard to remember. I have had to piece it together from what others tell me. Everyone has their own angle and their own gaps. I blame myself for my lacuna when it comes to these days, but I think we all find it harder to remember the bad times. We hold

343

on to memories of the good times. It's only natural. But it is not much help when the good times were in such short supply.

16.   Running on Empty

Looking out at the road rushing under my wheels
I don't know how to tell you all just how crazy this life feels
I look around for the friends that I used to turn to
to pull me through
Looking into their eyes I see them running too.

Jackson Brown, Running on Empty

Despite everything, and after a false start, Robin did eventually marry. Carole and Robin had fallen in love on a sailing holiday and ended up living with their two children in a mews cottage in Blandford Forum. She had a lot to put up with in those last few years. She kept much of her trials to herself, but as things got more difficult and his psychotic incidents became more frequent she did get in touch with me. One occasion has haunted me ever since.

It was not the first time that Carole had phoned me in extremis. There had been other occasions when Robin had tested her resilience.

'He's gone. Again. He did not come home last night. No message. Nothing. Andrew, I don't know what to do.'

But I did. I knew exactly what I had to do and where I had to be. Another drive across southern England, this time to Dorset where they lived. They had stretched their very limited finances to buy the cottage. He had a job as a labourer.

'Do you know where he is working?'

'On a building site outside Sixpenny Handley. I don't know exactly.'

'I'll be down in a few hours. I'll go straight there. I'll find him.'

God knows where that certainty came from. I was building on my role of 'he who makes things better'. I combined my father's love of action with my own brand of connivance. I was, after all, on Robin's side. And yet I was just as lost as the rest of them.

I have no trouble in transporting myself back. Some forty years later I am feeling the same helpless despair. Although I barely recognise my determination and feel a distant pride. There is still so much guilt swirling round. I failed in so many ways, and yet on that day I honoured my obligations. At least I tried.

* * * * * *

I have arrived in Sixpenny Handley as the sun is

setting. I find the site: a row of half-built family homes with skeletal roofs and gaping windows. The workforce has left the scene and there is no sign of Robin. I call out. My voice rings hollow, lost in the surrounding trees. A dirt track leads into the woods that back onto the last houses in the row. I follow it and turn a bend and see him; he is sitting on a log outside a dilapidated corrugated shed. He is carving away on a chunk of wood with a Stanley knife.

He shows no surprise that we have met in this woodland glade when I should be up in London tending to my own affairs. Rather an expectation that in a world that made no sense, a brother would come looking. When he does look up, there is no sign of a welcome. Rather a resigned suck of his teeth. He is not pleased to see his brother.

'What are you doing here?' More of an angry grunt than a rational enquiry.

'I was looking for you. You've not been home. We were worried.'

'Typical.' He spits that out as he hacks at his piece of wood. 'I suppose Carole called you.'

'Yes. She did. It's been three days. What do you expect her to do?'

'Of course she called you. You're so bloody wonderful. Andrew to the fucking rescue.'

More hacking away. Harsh crude cuts. Nothing creative, just a release of tension. He is channelling his furies.

'I want to help. You're my brother. I can help.'

That is the wrong thing to say. He rises from his haunches. And starts to move towards me. He brandishes the knife. Waving it at me. Snarling.

'I suppose you're going to tell me how to be a man. Eh. Like you. What the fuck do you know about me? You're so bloody perfect. You have no idea what's happening to me. No bloody idea. So don't try and sweet talk me.'

I hold my ground, opening my arms, turning my palms up. In surrender.

'I am not trying to sweet talk you, I am trying to help. I just want to take you home.'

That gets him going and he lunges at me with the blade.

'I'm not coming anywhere with you. You can fuck off back to Carole and tell her I sent you packing. My big brother! Not so big now, eh?'

And another lunge. I step back. Just in time to avoid a slash to my arm. My instincts cry 'run', but even as I am making up my mind, I see the anger draining from his face. The knife arm drops to his side. He turns away and slumps down onto his log, picks up the chunk of wood and starts to carve away. The rage has dissipated. He is deflated. Depleted. I get the feeling that he barely remembers the assault. He has moved on. Back into himself. The danger has passed. I move to sit next to him on the log. He flinches, but settles again.

There is a long silence. I feel I should react to his fury. But I have been hurt more by the critique than the potential injury. What right do I have to rescue him? Sitting there in the gathering gloom we are not in the realms of normal discourse. I try to mollify, take a more restrained approach

'Are you okay?'

A feeble start. He is so obviously not okay.

'What do you think?'

'No. I don't suppose you are. You don't look great.'

That was an underestimation of epic proportions. He looks gaunt and grubby. He must have slept in the woods. His work clothes seem to hang on him, misfitting and distressed. I had cause to think, 'This is my brother who used to look great in any old gear.'

'I've given up my job. I've had enough.'

'Well, I can understand that.'

'Not just enough of the job. Enough of the whole business. This world is a mess. The whole planet. It's getting worse all the time and no one knows what to do.'

'It's not great. You're right. But it's not all bad. Really.'

God, I am embarrassed at myself. I cannot find a way to hook onto his despair. It floats around the clearing like a demented balloon leaking toxic air and I cannot grab it. Pathetic truisms are not going to touch my brother. He starts to ramble. His tone intensifies. He is warming to his theme and I am lost.

'There's no solution. Just selling, buying and selling. More and more until there's nothing left. They're eating up the planet. Exploiting the planet. It's exploitation. They're exploiting us. Make more money! Buy more things and don't care who gets hurt. And God help you if you are poor, if you can't make ends meet. You're on the scrap heap. You're a failure. You don't exist. I don't exist.'

'You exist. You are here and you have opinions and options. You can protest. Don't let them grind you down.'

That is a little better. Pushing back just a bit. But still he is way ahead of me. He may have swept away the safety net of logic, the coherent link between cause and effect. But there was some coherence too. A residual connection to his days of protest.

'There's no hope. The almighty dollar. Don't you see? There's no more real value, no ideals, nothing to aspire to. It's just profit and loss. It's a game of winners and losers, and don't end up on the losing side. Don't be a victim. It's shit being a victim.'

The diatribe continued for what seemed like hours. Disordered railing at the world. He harangues me with random conspiracies mixed with fragments of half-recalled ideologies. Once in a while I would try to engage in reasoned discourse, but of course it is hopeless. Eventually as darkness descends and we can barely make each other out in the gloaming, he quietens and his eyes lose the fire that has driven him on. His head drops and he begins to scratch patterns in the earth with a broken stick.

'Come on. Let me take you home.'

'No!' A flare of resistant fury. Back to where we started. 'Just leave me alone!'

'What shall I tell Carole? She should know what's going on.'

'I don't care what you tell Carole.' Then a sudden segue into the real world. 'You know she's pregnant.'

'I know. Good news.'

'I'm not sure we can manage.'

'You'll manage. We'll help. Mum and dad will help.'

'I don't want your help. I don't want their help. I just want you all to LEAVE ME ALONE.'

I must say that although I do have a clear memory of that encounter, I feel I can see the clearing and the look of him, I could not remember the attack. It had gone. Deleted. So much for my theory that we remember the moments of high emotional intensity. I needed someone else to tell me what happened. I have reconstructed the scene from someone else's testimony. The only reason I feel justified in resurrecting the scene, even in fictional form, is because Carole, Robin's wife, told me, when we eventually met, what had happened. She could remember me returning from that encounter and telling her about the attempted attack with the knife. Now that she has told me, I can create my own story. It is a fragile construct. It may have little bearing on the truth. But does that matter? It illustrates what is true. When Robin was in the throes of a psychotic episode he was irrational, sometimes violent and always in chaotic isolation from reality.

* * * * * *

The last few years of Robin's story should be easier to come by. He is home and part of the family. I should have a clear recollection of his slow decline. But as I set about reconstructing his last few years of life, I realise that there is even less to hold onto. For those years in Australia I could order his story with his letters. I had a chronological template and better still I had his voice. I could carp that it was mostly parent-ready and devoid of the down and dirty, but those letters have done him proud.

Once back at home, there was no need for letters and his state of mind did not allow for them. That last letter from Singapore was a pale shadow of everything that came before. It was as if the epistolary light was flickering and fading. Once home it was extinguished altogether.

The psychotic incidents were hard to watch at

the time and, perhaps for that reason, hard to record some forty years later. I am snatching at fragmented testimony and trying to put the past in order, and yet it eludes my grasp. My own encounters with him, though more recent in recorded time, seem even hazier than the distant past. I am resisting my own desire to understand. One anecdote collides with another. The dates float around, refusing to fall into an acceptable chronology. The conversations I have with my friends, his friends, anyone who knew him during these years, are far more disruptive than any I had with those Australians. My fragile recollections are disrupted and undermined by the testimony of others. They seem to confirm that I lost him well before he died.

* * * * * *

I had delayed my conversation with Robin's wife Carole, in part because she does not appear until late in this story. That was my excuse, but naturally it is only half the truth. I found it hard and had put off the encounter. I assumed that she would be suspicious of my mission. I was trying to repatriate my brother, when I imagined that she was likely to want to leave his memory behind. Eventually I overcame my own resistance. Of course, she needed to be part of the project. Her testimony was seminal to the last few years: the years that I was finding even more difficult to resurrect. The years when I was part of the story but so absent. As my brother might have said: the time when I was failing to help him survive.

Once I took the plunge, she was far more welcoming than I could have dared hope. Far from wanting to leave his memory behind, she was very open to remind herself of both the good times as well as the bad. We agreed to meet for lunch.

I started with my usual explanation about how my anger had blocked my memories of Robin but that once my mother died I needed to find him again. She was on a different trajectory.

'You know, for me it's the opposite. I don't think I was angry with him at the time, just deeply shocked. Lately I have started to find I blame him. He did abandon us.'

'I am embarrassed to say that I don't even know how you met.'

'I was working as an air hostess for DanAir and a friend and I had rented Laurel Cottage, next door to Rose Cottage.'

That was my parents' cottage, where my mother was living on the day I came to call with news of Robin's death.

'Robin came to visit your parents and we got to know each other. Went to the pub. The usual. He was very attractive and I fell for him, I suppose. Then one of the Todhunter brothers who was rich and owned a yacht in Italy asked Robin to crew for him and look after the yacht over the summer. He was keen and asked me if I'd like to come with him and do the cooking. It seemed like a glamorous opportunity. I quit my job and we both ended up living on the yacht in Portofino harbour.'

That revived some hazy memories. Jonnie Todhunter was the wheeler-dealer son of the Captain whose Jaguar Robin had taken some time before. He had done well for himself importing Australian wool. He lived in Milan and worked in the clothing business. I had no memory, naturally, of my brother and his girlfriend living the dream on the Italian Riviera.

'It sounds wonderful. I had assumed that by then he was a broken man. Clearly not.'

'No, he wasn't broken. Just unusual. I never quite knew what was coming next. Much of the time we lived a blissful life, a fantasy world for me. But there were signs, I suppose. I really felt that he hadn't grown up. He could be very childish. One time, Jonnie came onto the boat for the day with his wife and kids and found a minor thing to complain about. It really wasn't serious, but Robin was furious. We were on our way out of the harbour and he jumped overboard and swam to the shore.

There were other signs too. He would change his mind for no reason. Suddenly and often irrationally.'

I thought back to the abrupt changes in plan

during his journey home.

'But I was in love with him. As you have said, he was a remarkable man and we had some amazing times together. So I stayed with him. We came back to London and moved into a house together. We were happy. I remember coming to visit you and Claire. Robin did some developing in your darkroom.'

Another blank. I had a darkroom in my flat in Clapton, so it made sense, but I have expunged that with so much else.

'I remember that he wouldn't let us have a phone. He said he didn't want his mother ringing him all the time. I wanted a phone and told him he just needed to speak to her about it, but he wouldn't and we didn't get a phone for ages.'

There is something childlike in the way he was both drawn to my parents, while asserting his right to cut them off.

'And the wedding. What happened there? I am assuming that my parents were involved in that decision.'

'No, that came mostly from Robin. I certainly wasn't bothered. I was happy as we were. He pushed for it.'

'Trying to please his parents?' My partner and I had caused much upset with my mother in particular through our refusal to get married. I assumed Robin was trying to claim the moral high ground.

'Well, maybe. But it got much more complicated than that. He persuaded me that he wanted a big wedding. He was very active in the planning. Sent out invitations to all his Australian friends who were living in London. Then, two days before the big day, he disappeared. Later he told me that he had gone to see his parents and had a furious row with your father. Apparently, it ended with your father shouting, "Why don't you grow up and be a man?"'

I was shocked by that story. My father did not shout. We were not a family that had rows. We just used silence as a weapon. This was an extraordinary break with tradition. I saw that the relationship between Robin and my father was even more fraught than I had imagined.

'Robin ran off after that. I remember your father ringing my father and telling him, "The young man has done a bunk." We cancelled the wedding. Then, just four hours before it was to have taken place, Robin appears. Ready to get married! Couldn't see what the fuss was about.'

'You must have been furious. Surely that was the last straw. I know you eventually did get married. I was there. How come?'

'I still loved him.'

'He must have tested that love as time went on.'

'Yes, but it wasn't all bad. Not by any means. For much of the time we were happy. We set up home and had our children. He wanted children. Then later there were times when he withdrew into himself and grew increasingly hard. Sometimes I felt he was just mean. He could be really cruel. But then, I am not sure why, I always thought it was going to be all right.'

'Did he think it was going to be all right?'

'At times he was depressed. He couldn't hold down a job and anyway the jobs were hopeless. In no way matched his education or his brain. They were dead-end. But then he was also full of plans and schemes. They too were all hopeless. He was a Walter Mitty. One time he tried to persuade a friend of ours that we were going to sell up, buy a yacht and sail round the world. Not crazy. If I felt he could pull it off I might have followed him. But there was no way. That friend said to me that Robin was always putting me into the position of having to say no.'

She remembered one other occasion:

'He suddenly tried to persuade me that he was going to move to Wales and there recruit a group of men who he would train to become an army of protest and that they would march to London to re-enact the Peasants' Revolt. It was mad and of course I had to say no.'

Looking to his wife to put barriers up to his flights of fancy, when combined with his unhealthy relationship with my parents, I find it hard to avoid the conclusion that his illness had stopped him from growing up. These were the actions of someone who had not separated from parental control. When they were not there for him to blame, he turned to Carole.

Mentioning the Peasants' Revolt triggered another memory for me. Some six months before the encounter in the woods of Sixpenny Handley, Robin sent me a proposal for a television film. It was about the Peasants' Revolt. He had spotted that the 600th anniversary was coming up in 1981 and he felt that there would be an opening for a film to mark the occasion. It was a good idea but it was ten years before I had any direct experience of the world of television, so I was not able to do anything other than recognise that neither of us had any hope of taking it further. As with so much that he did during those years I had forgotten all about it. But I do still have the proposal itself: ten pages of typed manuscript. Although sparse, it shows evidence of real research: he has mapped out the structure and even written a sample scene. There is nothing mad about the idea; it just was not feasible.

This manuscript is the only piece of writing I have of his from those tormented times. It fills me with remorse. He wrote it when, in every other aspect of his life, he felt a miserable failure. His work as a jobbing labourer was not the satisfying manual work that had liberated him at the sheep station; this was dreary, insecure, mind-sapping toil that diminished him. He was demoralised and depressed. And yet, somewhere in the back of his mind there lingered a vision of himself as someone with creative capacity. He will have motivated himself to research and write this proposal by the prospect that it might turn the tables on his failure and restore him to the man who had relished intellectual challenge and artistic endeavour. It is this faltering aspiration that I find so hard to take. He was battling his torments. He had not given up.

Perhaps his most creative act was not solely of his making. In November 1977, Carole gave birth to their first son, Oliver. She had been pregnant when they finally got married although she did not feel it was a shotgun marriage.

'No, he wanted me to get pregnant. We had been trying for six months.'

'But he was also so worried about his job prospects and his ability to provide for you. It seems strange to have wanted all the extra responsibility.'

'That came later. By the time we had Alun, our second child, two years later, he was much more anxious about the money. And yet he wanted to have children. Much of the time he was a caring father. I clearly remember the day we came back from hospital after the birth of Alun. He was so proud and happy. He immediately invited round all our local friends and spent too much money on drink and food to celebrate. I was exhausted of course, and wasn't quite so up for celebrating, but I still recall his enthusiasm and pride.

He wanted to be the very best father possible, and for much of the time he was. But then as the psychotic incidents started to come more frequently, he would head off without warning, leaving me with the children sometimes for days at a time then return, sometimes as if nothing was wrong and other times in a total state. It was hard to recognise the loving father during those incidents.'

I feel that I was partly aware of the good times and his devotion to the children, but as so often happens, it is the distressing memories that overwhelm the positive recollection. I find it difficult to understand the contradiction between his obvious deep affection for and commitment to his own sons, and then the turmoil he created at other times. Yet I know that he had retained a powerful sense of inheritance. He was unable to separate from his parents. He had an overly sentimental attachment to the idea of our family, whilst simultaneously kicking out at the familial ties that seemed to bind him tighter than he could bear. Perhaps he felt he could succeed as a father where he had failed at everything else. His Alun and Oliver did indeed grow and flourish but I fear that they did so despite him rather than because of him. Like Carole, they built a life without him. A very mixed legacy.

* * * * * *

Back in Totnes, Farhad too is having trouble. He has a better memory of his good friend but is hard on himself.

'I was an emotional coward in those days. And still am, I suppose. I tried to keep up our friendship but it was hard. I have a feeling I could have done so much more.'

'You're not alone,' I assured him. 'This process, finding Robin, was meant to lead to some sort of reconciliation, and yet as we get into those last few years not only is my memory even more fragmented and unreliable, but I have rediscovered and restored my guilt. I admire you. You were loyal. It must have been hard. Did you visit them in the cottage?'

'I did go down there. On several occasions. None of them went particularly well. He was very vulnerable and distracted, and prone to hurtful outbursts. The last trip was the worst. I suppose it was a few months before he died. I remember that I offered him some dope that I had brought and he just exploded and started screaming at me. Accusing me of "flaunting my wealth". Then he threatened me with an axe.'

'God, an axe! Were you frightened?'

'Not really. Actually he was lying down at the time. He seemed to be going through the motions rather than actually wanting to hurt me. He seemed to be acting mad. Anyway, shortly afterwards he stormed out and I didn't see him again. The next thing was a phone call from Carole, on the morning of his death. I think I was one of the first people she rang. I came straight down on the train. I tried to be helpful, but I was out of my depth. I do remember that he had left a very tidy desk. Carol told me that he had seemed very calm. Had a shower and went out to work as usual. She had looked everywhere but there was no note. I thought that was strange, as he was a keen writer.'

* * * * * *

I asked Carole about those last days. She recalls that his suicide came after a period of relative calm. True, he was worried about money and was unhappy in his job but he seemed to be making plans.

'I remember that quite close to the end he was speaking about how he wanted to move back to London. He felt that he would have a better chance of getting a job that suited his intellect. He did have a sense of the future even when he was at his most depressed.

On the day itself I certainly had no idea that anything was wrong. He was calm. I suppose looking back, he was determined to go through with his plan and knew that he had to persuade me that all was normal.'

As for the plan, clearly there was only one person who knew anything about it. And it was not Carole. I imagined that the coroner's report would give me the detailed intelligence to construct a timeline and go at least some way to explaining his motivation.

Like most public services in austerity Britain, the coroner's service has been badly cut, so I was not optimistic when I rang the Bournemouth Coroner's Office and asked if they could dig up a report from 1980. Sure enough, records had not been digitised and were now stored in 'an off-site facility'. It could take a while to retrieve and there was no guarantee that Robin's report would still be there.

I had mixed feelings about the delay and even found myself wondering whether if I could demonstrate that I had made best efforts I might not have to engage with the distressing details of his death. But I had thrown the dice and after several chivvying phone calls, the envelope hit my mat some three months later. Of course, I couldn't open it. I had prudently banished any desire to know the details of his death. I wanted to avoid investigating the sheer cold mechanics of it, although I knew that before journey's end there would no avoiding it. I reassured myself that I would get there, but not quite yet. I would focus on the detective work: reconstructing the last few days of the deceased, and steer clear of the act itself.

I realised that up until this point I had been able to avoid the pain of a final reckoning. I had sustained my investigative momentum by keeping my distance from the facts of his demise. I played on the sympathy of others without ever really feeling the emotions that prompted their sympathy and sadness. I was acting the part of grieving brother. Playing to the crowd, who were generous in their assumptions that I was indeed feeling a real grief. The envelope that sat on my desk, unopened, was threatening me. I knew it would require me to remove the mask and come to terms with some genuine emotion. It took me a while. I am not proud of that. Like Farhad, I was ashamed of my emotional cowardice.

But there was no avoiding it. This was what it had all been about. All the busy detective work, exploring the lines of enquiry and weighing up the evidence. Basking in the empathy of others. All of that was the easy part. The contents of that Coroner's report would do the job that mattered. It would open me up to the reality of Robin's death. Allow me to feel the emotional heft that I had denied myself all those years and denied myself throughout this journey.

I had rather imagined that the report would be a cold document laying out the facts. Short on the detail I craved. But it was extensive, consisting of detailed testimony from all the important players. Voices and testimony from people who I never knew existed and yet had played a critical role in this unexceptional drama. I started by looking for an explanation of his motives. It seemed a safer place to explore before facing the cold facts of his final moments.

Work and bills. The testimony was all about his work and his money, or rather the lack of a satisfactory amount of either. Mundane motivations: hardly worth the trauma of a death. For my father, the General, it all made sense. His testimony to the Surrey constable ends:

'Since the end of 1979 he had found it extraordinarily difficult to obtain any employment save that of a common labourer. Meanwhile expenses of maintaining a mortgaged house, a wife and two children, the problems associated with obtaining any state benefits, having been self-employed, all led to a pressure which he found insurmountable.'

Carole gave her deposition to a Constable 855 Keates from Dorset police.

'Over the last few weeks he has been brighter, not depressed so much as subdued, but still desperately worried about money. He has shown a great deal of concern over me and the children and over the weekend, because he knew we were unable to pay the gas bill, he wrote a letter to the gas board asking time to pay.'

Like the General, Carole wanted to pin the blame on the money.

'I am of the opinion that his worries became much worse from the time we bought the cottage with the mortgage of £97 per month, and that these additional worries added to his already worried state of mind. He

felt he wasn't providing for us. He said he was not good enough for us.'

Then, as an after-thought, Constable Keates asks Carole whether her husband was aware that he was going to lose the job he had. She told him he was but *'he didn't seem bothered about it.'*

Keates asked about the lost job because earlier in the day he had interviewed William Shalders, supervisor in charge of production at the Express Dairies, Milbourne St Andrews. Two weeks before, Robin had applied for a job and Mr Shalders had offered him a temporary post, working on the production line. It was not labouring on a building site, but it was clearly tedious and repetitive. The job was to start on Tuesday 20th May, but Robin didn't show until the following day.

'His work was satisfactory, although he was late the second day. He kept himself to himself and made no friends in the factory. On Wednesday 28th May he walked off the job at 10.30 am, then came back at 11. I tackled him about it and we agreed there had been a misunderstanding. He thought he had lost his job as there was no time card for him. I accepted his explanation and he started work. At about 4pm I saw him leaving the production line again. I spoke to him and he kept saying "I've got to go, I've got to go." I said, "OK Robin we'll see you in the morning." He replied "Oh no I'm not returning," and I was sure that we would not

see him again.'

Surprisingly he did show up for work the next day. Mr Shalders, who was clearly an honourable man, tried to speak to him to establish if there was a problem with the job, but Robin refused to respond.

'He failed to appear at work on Friday 30th May and coupled with a sudden dramatic drop in production demand, it was decided to give him a week's notice along with five other people. As he was not at work, a letter was sent to his home.'

The good Mr Shalders had cut my brother some slack despite the provocation. A hand-written note in the margin makes it clear that, as Supervisor, he was summoned to a meeting with the bosses who had instructed him to lay off eight workers. He had made do with a mere six terminations. Given Robin's erratic behaviour, it was not surprising that he had not made the cut.

For William Shalders, that was not the end of it. The final paragraph of his deposition reads as follows:

'On Monday, 2nd June, I went into the wood, owned by the company, which is adjacent to the south-west side of the factory. There I saw a man hanging from a tree. At about 11.50 am, I formally identified the body to Constable KEETES as Robin Anthony BETHELL.'

Dear Robin,

I am writing this in my studio. It sounds grander than it is. A converted council office, but it suits me. When I am not writing about you, I have been trying to learn how to paint. It is a slow grind but things improved when I started to make art about you and our family. Always better to have a subject that has its roots in lived experience. I have just looked back at how 'Charley' Brown wrote about your time in the art room at school. You both had talent. Martyn is painting still. I was not encouraged to do art. I am still battling a lack of talent.

This is the last chapter. In more ways than one. I have to deal with the cold hard mechanics of how you killed yourself. It feels important. I am not sure why. Does knowing the practicalities of a death make it any easier to comprehend? Probably not. But I have that coroner's report and the details are all there and they have helped me. Nothing I write will surprise you. You were there. It was your plan. You executed it perfectly.

17. The Man in the Yellow Oilskin

They tell us that Suicide is the greatest piece of Cowardice... That Suicide is wrong; when it is quite obvious that there is nothing in this world to which every man has a more unassailable title than to his own life and person.

Arthur Schopenhauer

I am standing in the woods opposite the Express Dairies Foods factory in Milbourne St Andrews. It is 8 a.m. on the morning of Monday 2nd June 1980. It is a grey day. Dull weather. This is the A354. In one direction, to my left, it leads to Dorchester, nine miles away. To my right, it leads to Blandford Forum, another nine miles. Opposite me I can see Raymond and Norman Smith working on the lawn and flowerbeds in front of the factory. They are landscape gardeners and have the contract to maintain the garden that lies between the factory and the main road. Once a month they attend with their tools and keep things tidy. Raymond is mowing the lawn whist Norman is edging the rose beds.

At approximately 8.30, I look up the road towards Blandford and see a figure on a bicycle. He is easy to spot because he is wearing a bright yellow oilskin raincoat. It is not raining. Raymond looks up and sees the cyclist turn off the road, and head towards the woods to the right of the factory. He does not pay much attention, although in his subsequent testimony he does say that the man on the bike looked *'browned off'*. Norman later says that he looked *'exhausted'*.

I cannot see his expression from where I am standing, but I do recognise my brother. I am a helpless observer. Out of time and ephemeral. I watch as he leans his bike up against the hedge that separates the wood from the road. He has no bag, but I notice a bulge in the pocket of his oilskin. He is not carrying a rope. I can see that.

He heads off into the woods. Norman gets back to his edging and Raymond revs up the motor mower and carries on where he left off. They are absorbed in their work. Time passes. They are contracted to spend three hours at the factory. They know the routine. They do not speak much. They have forgotten the man on the bike in the yellow oilskin. I have not forgotten. I am watching with trepidation in my heart. But I am helpless. I would like to dash across the road and into the wood and intervene. But all I can do is wait.

At 10.30 a.m. Raymond is putting his mower back into the van when he looks up. He sees something in the wood. He pauses. The mower is half in and half out of the van. But Raymond is still staring into the wood. He lowers the mower back onto the ground. He starts to walk towards the wood. He is intent. He disappears from my sight. Into the wood. There is a lull. Norman has stopped and is looking towards his brother. Towards where he disappeared into the wood. I am holding my breath. I cannot breath. Breathless in dreadful anticipation.

Then Raymond comes back out of the wood. Not running, but pacing urgently. He says something to Norman, who drops his edging spade, then he starts to run towards the factory. He disappears in through the side door. There is another pause. Norman is transfixed. He stares into the wood. He does not move. A few minutes later he hears the sound of voices. His brother has emerged from the factory with Bill Shalders, the Production Supervisor. Raymond is leading the way. Pointing into the wood. Mr Shalders hesitates. He does not want to proceed but knows he must. Norman stays on the lawn. Bill goes into the wood. There is another pause. Then he comes out, he is running now. He needs to get back to the office to make a call.

I am still watching. I am the silent witness. Useless.

There is another hiatus. But at precisely 11.05 a.m. a Ford Anglia police panda car comes down the A354 from Blandford, and turns into the factory car park. Two police officers get out and are met by Bill Shalders and Raymond. I see Raymond point into the wood. PC William Keates and his partner PC Brian Merchant head off into the woods. I cannot follow them, because I am only there in spirit. In retrospect. After the event. Too late. I am the brother who failed to prevent this modest drama reaching its conclusion. Even if I had been there, I would not have been brave enough to accompany PC Keates into the wood.

Instead I refer to the statement given by PC Keates, who has taken on the lead investigator role. Although there is not a lot to investigate.

'I went with Brian Merchant into the woods to the south west of the Express dairies Food Factory. I there saw the body of a man hanging from the branch of a tree. He was about 300 yards into the wood from the main road and I saw that he had black packing case tape tied around his neck and also tied around a branch of the tree about 11 feet above ground level. The toes of his shoes were about six inches off the ground and his arm was hanging by his side. There was no sign of a pulse. The man was wearing brown shoes, dark blue trousers, a check shirt, a green warmer, a green pullover, an off-white cord jacket and also a bright yellow oilskin mackintosh.

I cut the tape and lowered the man to the ground. There appeared to be no sign of life although the chest and stomach were still warm.'

As I read PC Keates' statement, I find that I have an intense interest in the mechanics of Robin's death. It is the detail that sticks in the mind and causes me to ask questions that will never be answered. How could he possibly have attached a tape to a branch eleven feet above his head? Did he climb the tree, attach the tape, then wrap it round his neck and lower himself? His feet were six inches off the ground. Just like in the movies. But how did they get there?

Then there is the question of all those clothes. It was the start of June. The sun may not have shone, but it was not freezing. A check shirt, a green warmer, a pullover and a cord jacket, as well as the yellow oilskin. Its sounds like his entire wardrobe. On a June day. I know that the homeless often wear all their clothes all the time. Saves carrying them in a bag. But Robin was not homeless. Nor was he weak and vulnerable. He was a 29 years old and physically fit. He should have had the inner warmth required. And yet maybe he was freezing in his heart. He had put on all his clothes to ward off the nameless chill that had taken him over.

PC Keates continues his statement, describing how he searched the pockets of the deceased and found a pay slip and a letter in the name of R Bethel (sic). It was from Express Dairies 'giving notice of his termination of employment at the factory on the 6th June'. That was four days later. I am distressed to find that he turned his back on four more days of gainful employment. Lastly, he found:

'A *copy of the* Bournemouth Evening Echo *newspaper dated 31st May. The newspaper was folded to the situations vacant page and six different situations offered were circled in ink. I took possession of these documents.'*

I have a morbid fascination with the detail. The clothes, the tape, the height of the drop. But it is the copy of the Bournemouth Echo that now grabs my attention. It speaks of someone who saw himself as an applicant for some of the six jobs he circled. He had not drawn a blank. He had spotted jobs that he might apply for. His termination from Express Dairies had not beaten him down completely. He had bought the paper. Read through the ads and found some possibilities. Perhaps he could have relied on the benevolent Bill Shalders to give him some sort of a reference.

He had come to a fork in the path. To the right lay the path to another job. Not satisfying, but employment and some money to pay that gas bill and service the mortgage. To the left lay a path to his own destruction. He chose the left-hand path. He planned it. He bought the gaffer tape. He pedalled all the way to the Express Dairies, some nine miles from home. It seems that he could not separate his work or lack of it from his own demise. He came to work to kill himself. Work was so obviously a canker in his soul. It had failed him and he had failed it.

I have been watching out for these forking paths. Paths not taken. They have taunted me with alternative worlds where Robin succeeds, flourishes and lives. In his short story The Garden of the Forking Paths, Borges writes about:

'...an infinite series of times, in a dizzily growing, ever spreading network of diverging, converging and parallel times. This web of time – the strands of which approach one another, bifurcate, intersect or ignore each other through the centuries – embraces every possibility. We do not exist in most of them. In some you exist and not I, while in others I do, and you do not, and in yet others both of us exist.'

I can apply that infinity of parallel times to Robin and his story. There is a world where the Drapers had sent him to Sydney University rather than Perth and he had taken that cosmopolitan city by storm and be there still looking back at a successful career on the Australian arts scene. Then there is a world where he has turned down that suspect tab of LSD in Bangkok. And what if he had followed up one of those ads in the Bournemouth Echo? Those are just a few of the alternative universes he could have inhabited. He does not exist in most of them, and nor do I. But I do like the idea of that last world: the one where both of us exist.

* * * * * *

I feel comfortable playing an intellectual game. It suits me to use Jorge Luis Borges to impress. It is a classy reference, but I could easily have used the film Sliding Doors to make a similar point. I can hide behind the scholarly quotation. Pretend that I have read the whole piece. It is a sleight of hand just at the moment when I should be engaging with the far more difficult task of somehow capturing my real emotions. And when I look back at most of this story, I realise that much of what I write about this journey has been a similar process of avoidance. I have persuaded myself that I am doing enough in searching out the facts, meeting the witnesses and turning the two into an engaging narrative. I was beguiled by the seductive charms of an active enquiry and failing to notice that at every turn I was avoiding the hard graft of actually understanding how it made me feel.

It has worked, of course. I am not ashamed of the narrative nor of the way I have resurrected my brother's life. It is an achievement and will fulfil several of the objectives I set myself at the outset. But as I put myself into the scene of his last moments, as I watch from across the road from the Express Dairy in Milbourne St Andrews, as I read the plaintive detail of his actual death, I cannot hide behind my literary intent. I have been hit hard by the raw emotional storm those images have unleashed, which in turn causes me to re-evaluate my motives. The brute physicality takes me back to that medicine ball, the one that punched me in the stomach as I heard news of his death in my flat in Clapton. Perhaps for the first time in forty years and maybe ever, I feel the first signs of an authentic grieving. Does that authenticity invalidate all that has come before or is it a merely a logical destination?

I have never been much good at grieving. As well as a brother, I have lost a much-loved uncle in his forties, a father and a mother. The first three deaths were well before their time and caused me great sadness, but I know that I never went through the process of grieving. I cannot identify those much-vaunted five stages. I do not remember denial or anger, and I seemed to move smoothly past bargaining and even depression. In each case I hid behind the role of 'the one who makes things better'. If I did deny anything it was my own grief. I moved smoothly into the process of supporting others. I made phone calls and arrangements. I defended myself against others' grief. Absorbed their denial, their anger and depression. I could make all the right gestures, say all the right things, but rarely did I feel strong emotions. I felt less of a human being, berating myself for not experiencing the powerful feelings that seemed to come to others with so little obstruction. I found that I could survive death of others and I now realise, through the process of this journey and in particular revisiting our school experience, that this failure to grieve was just another aspect of those same survival skills that got me through boarding school. At Sherborne they did not value your feelings, merely your ability to stifle them. I like to feel that I have shaken off some of that dysfunctional legacy, but when it comes to grief, there is no escape.

There have been one or two brief moments when the reality of death broke through my defences. My father died suddenly whilst on holiday in Spain, aged sixty-seven. I received the news of his death on my return from climbing Blencathra in the Lake District. I experienced shock which was almost immediately replaced by action. Train and air tickets: another journey to be by my mother's side. As soon as I arrived, I was making arrangements and absorbing her grief. No time for my own grief and that suited me fine.

Then I was offered the chance to see his body and somewhat reluctantly I agreed. He lay in an open coffin in a cemetery on the outskirts of Calpe in the province of Alicante. I was on my own and suddenly I was overcome. It was raw grief. I cried for my father in a way that now reminds me of sobbing over his letter that first birthday at prep school. For twenty minutes I allowed myself to grieve. I was feeling genuine distress and it was both satisfying and terrifying. And then the aging custodian indicated my time was up and that was it. I got hold of my old self. Back in the car. Back to my mother. Back to coping and putting on a brave face.

When my mother died some twenty years later,

unexpectedly of a heart attack at the age of eighty-six, once again the only son sprang into action. I became the exemplary next of kin asking all the right questions of the hospital administrators. In control. Until, that is, I was asked whether I would like to see my mother's body. My initial reaction was to shy away and hide. Busy myself with anything that was not her dead body. But with the support of my partner who knew better, I agreed and allowed myself to be led down to the viewing room attached to the basement mortuary. Again, for a brief few moments when confronted by the bleak reality of her absence with the haunting physicality of her body, I broke down. I felt grief. The real thing. It was a visceral punch, another medicine ball. But not for long. Once outside the mortuary, I reverted to a phlegmatic acceptance of all that had to be done. I was back in control.

Although I was present at my brother's cremation, I never saw his body and had failed to enquire as to the details of how he died. As I have described, the only really strong emotions that I allowed myself were anger and guilt. This journey has helped me to assuage my anger and put much of that guilt aside. But it did little to help me connect with my grief. The grief that I have put off for forty years. Until, that is, I opened that coroner's report and read that forensic description of my brother's death. Those words and the images they conjured up allowed me to feel that same jolt of sheer grief that hit me in the cemetery in Calpe and the hospital mortuary in Yeovil. What is more, now that time has passed and there is no more need for me to be supporting others, that grief has lingered. I am pleased to say that I am, at last, gently grieving for my brother. I am allowing myself to feel the sadness and the absence. Reliving his last hours has provided me with a peg on which to hang that sense of loss. I know how he died, even if I can never discover why he died. It is a fitting end to this journey of discovery. It has allowed me to achieve the final stage of grieving: acceptance.

Dearest Brother,.

*A few months ago, we went to the theatre. It was a
production of The Death of a Salesman and as you
will remember it is about a man who is ground down
by the pressures of work and family and eventually
commits suicide. As I was reaching the end of my
journey you were on my mind rather more than usual.
When I got around to reading the programme notes
I found that the designer had written about how the
suicide of her father had informed her approach to the
play.*

    *When my father died, I was told by a counsellor
that one of the most important things to know was that
I would never be able to solve it. I would never find an
acceptable answer to why he deliberately left. The best
place for me to get to was to accept and make peace
with the fact.*

    She goes on:

    *I have many and no explanations for why my
father committed suicide. If this has taught me
anything it is the endlessness of human possibility – the
fact that there are no answers, but many questions*

    As you will see that pretty much sums up where

I have got to as well: left with so many questions. However, I do owe it to you and Oliver and Alun, to try and pull together some of the factors that may have had an influence on what happened I have no obvious conclusions. Life is full of contradictions and false trails. That is a bland truism: simple explanations for the vicissitudes of life are for suckers. Instead there is a palimpsest. Layer upon layer of images from our cardboard box of photos each saying something different. Each leading me up a different path. I strive for an analysis of cause and effect that satisfies my logic.

But I will plough on regardless.

I have been trying to decide between two lines of enquiry. The first tells the story of a boy and a man who was indeed a remarkable figure, whose charm, sensitivity, physical prowess and creativity was on track to a golden future. I am sorry if that makes you blush but your letters and the people I met seemed to confirm that you were indeed a man who had exploited all the possibilities of the New Age, lived life to the full, taken risks and shown great determination of purpose. You made an impression on them all that has lasted for forty years. They saw you as a leader and an inspiration to so many. A man with a future. One of the baby boomers who would use the sixties zeitgeist as a launch pad for a triumphant career in the creative arts or education or social purpose. Then, just when the

doors of perception seemed to be safely managed and
your prospects were at their most enticing, you had
the gross misfortunate to take a fatal misstep. It was
fate that let you down. That one malign hit of Lysergic
Acid Diethylamide administered with a cocktail of
accompanying misadventure, fried your brain and
tipped you off the rails that could have led to the Trans-
Siberian Express and a shining future.

The second theory follows an accumulation of
evidence that suggests that perhaps you had always
been sensitive and perhaps vulnerable to mental
disruption despite your outward confidence and
capabilities. There are certainly some potential
indicators that might suggest you had an incipient
proclivity to mental instability, albeit one that could
be triggered by an extreme incident. Remember
your first language was not your mother tongue and
your father's draconian sleep tactics would prove
interesting fodder for a Freudian analyst. Then the
enforced separation from the love of your mother at
the age of seven and the absence of a stable home life
could provide even richer pickings. I could also add
in the potential for a genetic inheritance from our
grandfather whose suicide I am almost certain you
knew nothing about, but may have left some residual
propensity for self-destruction.

On the other hand, this is where I can look to
myself and by measuring the impact on me I think I

can feel confident that you did not end it all because of a break in your attachment to our mother and subsequent isolation from family. Nor do I think the harsh school regime we were subjected to sowed the seeds of a delayed mental disorder. Despite my deep misgivings about that system and my acceptance of the emotional deficit it engendered, I cannot lay the blame for your demise at the foot of our alma mater. It would be too easy.

If I am going to exonerate our beastly education, can I do the same for the adverse longer-term impact of the 'sixties'? You may not have been badly damaged by your fractured upbringing but did it make you susceptible to the perils and pitfalls of the New Age hedonism? You were a big fan of Aldous Huxley, Timothy Leary and Ken Kesey so can I lay the blame on them and their teaching? Whilst I shared your admiration, time has not served them well. I have certainly bumped into enough 'sixties victims' on my journey into your past. Too often the stories I heard from people who knew and admired you forty years ago were tempered with accounts of those who didn't make it. The walking wounded who, in an alarming number of cases, ended up either killing themselves or living out an empty and unhappy life. Of course, there were many survivors, but the Age of Aquarius took its toll of bright minds. You were not alone.

You will of course remember Paul McGillick, the

theatre director who, in your first year in Australia
took you to the Festival of University Drama with your
winning production of Sergeant Musgrave's Dance.
When I asked him what he remembered about you,
he wrote : "even then he seemed to be emotionally
labile, a little delicate". That term has stuck with me.
'Labile' means 'liable to change, easily altered' and
you know that there were numerous occasions when
you switched plans and made impulsive decisions. I
am thinking of your escape to Colvin which seemed to
happen on a whim and had great significance. And
what about how you reacted towards Cy when she
tried for a reconciliation. No one example proves the
thesis but you can see that if you look at the pattern it
does suggest that there is a case to be made that could
undermine my more simplistic first theory.

There is a pattern for sure, but I want to cut you
some slack. I want to argue that we all have the traits
that could, should we be unfortunate enough to
suffer the wrong catalyst, be amplified into a mental
illness. I want to forgive your unpredictability and
vulnerability: put it down to a creative spirit and a
heightened sensitivity. I will call you 'mercurial'. There
are two definitions: 'changing the mind suddenly
and often' and 'intelligent, enthusiastic and quick'. I
believe the two can co-exist in a normal life and there's
nothing wrong with that.

Finally, and I realize I am pushing my luck

because you will be getting pretty fed up with all this
god-like conjecture about your state of mind, I want
to suggest a more noble if mundane version of events.
If you remember one of the things our mother said
when I told her about your suicide was: "It was not
selfish but generous. He thought we would all be better
off without him". As our father said to PC Keetes; "he
found the pressures insurmountable". And Carole
agreed: "He felt he wasn't providing for us. He said he
was not good enough for us".

   And as you can tell from the final lines of the poem
I read at your funeral I offered a similar altruistic
motivation:

   We did not see your final simple step
   All we know is,
   (and this was the purest form of love and bravery)
   It was up not down.

   So, I am going to have to ask you to tolerate my
partial account. What I have tried to do, is to
re-discover, that part of your story that many of us had
forgotten, hidden as it was by the urgent pathos of the
last years of your life. I am going to argue for my first
theory: a one-off fateful conjunction of malign incident
causing a long-term terminal decline. I hope you will
buy that theory although I know you have no option.
So, I want it to be true that had you avoided Bangkok
and headed for Japan and the Russian steppes on your
way home, there would have been a future. A future

*with its set-backs and its disappointments, but one full
of accomplishment and good fellowship. A future that
would mean you would be celebrating your seventieth
birthday this year with your family, my family and
me. Had it not been for a world pandemic (you don't
want to know the details of that future) we would have
held an occasion to delight in another two generations:
your and Carole's sons and my children and their
children, your grandchildren, all of them building on
their inheritance whilst carving out their own futures.*

*I had plans to gather those three generations
together on September 1st 2020, and raise a glass to my
brother in absentia, and say:*

'Here's to the man you were and could have been.
I am happy to say that you have your elder brother
back by your side. I abandoned you and forgot that I
loved you but, on this your significant birthday, I want
you to know that the anger has gone and the love has
returned.'

ROBIN
12.6.80

Your tortured later life
Was a harsh mountain
with no visible peak,
Just eternal false summits to lure you on
And then defeat you.
We waved as you set off
Across the stream and into the pines.
Dark but cool, a very different world,
Where absence put your climb in doubt.
Whilst we the ones you left behind were hazy, beckoning.
(Or was it waving?)
But you went up.
Through intermittent patches
Of dappled light and scary childish shadows.
We saw you next above the tree-line.
Celebrated your reappearance, though the distance
And the shortened field of focus gave us all a false
Perspective.
As the slopes became rocky and your stumbles made us gasp,
We were helpless, taking it in turns to put an eye to the lens.
Your pain was ours,
But glass and its refraction kept us very separate.
When your plans went wrong,
We could see it and felt the implications.
Each glassy overhang and disappearing ledge

Would make us wince
At the pain and the almighty effort.
We recognized your agony because we could predict it.
Close up, we ached to put you right, to add a piton
Or a safe belay to help you over.
But by now you had no time
For the safe technical climbs
On the southern sunny side.
The last few pitches were the worst.
Every handhold gave its reassurance, then
When your weight was living on it,
Crumbled.
By then, even had they reached you,
Our careful cries and urgent pointing
Had no meaning for you,
With your face pressed against the icy cliff,
Shivering and desperately searching for a solid hold.
We did not see your final simple step
All we know is,
(and this was the purest form of love and bravery)
It was up not down.

Written for and read by Andrew at his cremation

ACKNOWLEDGEMENTS

The most fulfilling part of this journey has been meeting up with a host of Robin's friends in Australia. All of them were generous with their time and their testimony and emotional engagement in my quest gave me great comfort. Marcus Collins provided the early catalyst with his devoted investigations on my behalf and the warmest of welcomes to the Perth community. I owe a particular debt to Halimah Russ who from our first meeting has provided me with extraordinary candour, enlightenment and friendship. Vic Marsh helped me connect with Robin's creativity and offered up some of the most uplifting recollections to enrich his story.

Marion Stevenson has been an invaluable source of insight and motivation fuelled by her special friendship with both Robin and myself since our early teens. She showed an early draft to Nick Luxmoore, whose encouragement spurred me, on as did the long conversation I was lucky enough to have with him before his untimely and sudden death.

This book would never have happened without the initial enthusiastic support of Mark Lucas who remembered a conversation about Robin we had in a Moscow hotel some twenty years ago and then encouraged me to write about it.

Others who have been generous with their time their hospitality and their testimony include: my cousin Joanna Holmes, Diana Adams, Roger Hudson, Phil Thomson,

Jenny Hetherington, Paul McCillick, Louise Kennedy, Cheryl Porter, Piers Partridge, Farhad Delal, Jim Singleton, Fiona Cameron, Judith O'Keefe, Jeremy Lefroy, Bronwyn and Stephen Mellor who gave me a bed and considerable kindness during my first trip to Perth and Rachel Hassell the Sherborne School archivist did so much more than just find documents. And Ray Omodei who I was lucky enough to spend time with before his death and whose confused perceptions lifted my spirits.

Dealing with this book has been emotionally disruptive for Carole Collins and her family and especially for Alun and Oliver Bethell. I appreciate their contributions, insights and forbearance. I hope they will forgive me and join me in celebrating a remarkable husband and father.

I have been sustained by the critical wisdom and encouragement from my three children Katherine, Matthew and Ben. Finally, none of this would have happened without the editorial acuity, tolerance, emotional support and love of my partner Claire Widgery.

For access to further related material
including photos, videos and letters please go to
dearestbrother.com